Seeing Ghosts

Seeing Ghosts

EXPERIENCES
OF THE PARANORMAL

HILARY EVANS

JOHN MURRAY
Albemarle Street, London

First published in 2002
by John Murray (Publishers) Ltd
50 Albemarle Street, London W1S 4BD

A catalogue record for this book is available from the British Library

ISBN 0-7195-5492 6

Typeset in 11/13 Palatino by Servis Filmsetting Ltd, Manchester

Printed and bound in Great Britain by Creative Print and Design
(Wales), Ebbw Vale, Gwent

Dedicated to Patrick Huyghe,
researcher *sans pareil*,
who will know why

Contents

Preface

In a notable trial at Tours in 1575, a certain Gilles Bolacre who had rented a house wanted his contract annulled on the grounds that the house was haunted. The landlord's lawyer sought to have his claim rejected on the grounds that ghosts do not exist, citing numerous ancient authorities to that effect. Whereupon the no less erudite advocate for the claimant proceeded to cite authorities who supported the notion of ghosts – naming Origen, Seneca, Livy, Cicero, Plutarch, Athenodorus, Pliny, Suetonius and many more. It seems Gilles's lawyer fielded the better team, for he won his case and the lease was voided.[1]

What this tells us is that the ghost was a subject of both interest and controversy at least as early as the beginning of the first millennium; also that the issues had not been resolved 1,500 years later. This book is not a history of ghosts, but we shall do well to remember that both the phenomenon into which we are inquiring, and the attempts to understand it, go a long way back. 'Thou comest in such a questionable shape,' complains Hamlet to his father's ghost, only a few years after the Bolacre case, and today, after a further 500 years, questionable is what ghosts continue to be.

In embarking on this inquiry, I assume that you are not prepared, on the one hand, to swallow without question the amazing stories you are told, nor on the other to pronounce that since ghosts cannot exist, the ghost experience must be a delusion. I assume you accept the fact that millions continue to report ghost experiences and would like to know what it is they are experiencing. So what I propose we do in this book is to see what we can learn about ghosts by looking at people's experiences of ghosts. I hope that you read it – as I have written it – as a kind of detective story, in which we slowly close in on the entity responsible, guided by the clues contained in each witness's testimony.

But do we *need* to understand? Yes. For one thing, most people who have a ghost experience are troubled by it. Even if they are able to tuck it neatly into their belief system, they often do so without conviction: they would like to be *sure*. Others are anxious in case seeing a ghost means there is something the matter with them: is it a sign of mental unbalance? But most, probably, feel that if they could understand what happened to them, they would know more about themselves and about the universe they inhabit.

By concentrating on what people say actually happened to them, we can keep theorizing to a minimum. Rather than make sweeping generalizations, I have tried to find specific cases to illustrate every aspect of the phenomenon: anything we say about ghosts actually happened to someone, somewhere.

It may be objected that we cannot trust the witnesses: but the ghost experience being what it is, there is no one else we can trust, and I would sooner trust someone who tells me what she experienced, than a commentator who may be trying to make experiences fit a preconceived mould. Ghost-seeing is fundamentally a personal experience, and though some degree of confirmation may be available when two or three people together see an apparition, or when a haunter is seen time and again by independent witnesses, it remains essentially a question of do we or don't we believe people when they tell us what they experienced?

It may further be objected that, even if we can trust the witness, it doesn't follow that we can trust what the witness says. In all sincerity he may tell us of his experience, but we all know how memory can be embellished, tidied, distorted and even fabricated. Couldn't the ghost-seer transform – quite unconsciously – a misty shape into the remembered figure of his Uncle Jack? Indeed, this can happen, and it is something we should be on our guard against. But I have chosen cases where it seems clear that something more than a fugitive impression is involved, and where the likelihood that the percipient was mistaken in her impression is really very small.

The cases are drawn from far and wide, but the two principal sources are the archives of the Society for Psychical Research, which goes to considerable trouble to obtain confirmation; and the popular American magazine *Fate*, which for more than fifty years has published first-hand accounts from readers, uncontaminated by investigation or interpretation. The latter collection suffers from the fact that no attempt is made at verification, but I find it hard to believe that more than a small minority would go to the trouble of inventing a story simply for the thrill of seeing it appear in print.

As far as possible, the case histories are quoted from the experiencer's own words. I have edited the text in the interests of clarity and brevity, but never distorting or changing the narrative.

In favour of this experience-based approach it is tempting to point to the sheer quantity. Can so many people be deluded, one can reasonably ask?

And, yes they can, one can reasonably answer. We can point to the sixteenth/seventeenth century witchcraft mania, or to today's alien abduction mania. In both cases there was or is certainly something going on, but we can be sure that few witches, if any, consorted with the devil at mountaintop sabbats, and that few American housewives, if any, are being taken aboard extra-terrestrial spacecraft. But that does not prevent both these epidemics – and many lesser outbreaks – from being immensely important for what they tell us, on the one hand, about the way people behave, and on the other about the way myths are created. The same considerations apply to the ghost experience. Whatever lies behind the stories people tell, these are interesting stories; and interesting too is the fact that people tell them at all.

I trust this inquiry will be seen as neither unduly sceptical nor unduly credulous, but as a dispassionate attempt to find out what the ghost experience is. We owe it to the witnesses to start from the assumption that they are telling us the truth – at any rate the truth as they see it. At the same time I think we have a responsibility to look their claims in the face and ask whether an alternative explanation may be preferable to the ostensible one.

Terminology

The reader should be warned that, when dealing with a subject as hard to pin down as the ghost, precise terminology is essential, so that everyone understands what is meant. This sometimes means using academic, even technical terms. I have done my best to avoid jargon: wherever possible, words are used as commonly understood. But to avoid misunderstandings, this is what is meant by some terms we shall be using:

Objectively real – something that can be observed by any normal person, and detected by appropriate instruments such as a camera
Subjectively real – something which has reality for the percipient, but not necessarily for anyone else or for recording instruments

Ghosts – in writing about people's experiences it seems best to retain the term they themselves most commonly use. 'Apparitions' and 'hallucinations' are too broad for our purposes.

When we come to specific types of ghost, we find no simple equivalent in English for the French **revenant** – literally, a former inhabitant of Earth, perceived as returning to it. If you see the ghost of your dead Uncle Jack, you are seeing a revenant.

The term **haunter** is used for a type of ghost which manifests persistently, usually in the same place or nearby, over an extended period.

The term **apparent** designates the ostensible identity of a recognized ghost. If the ghost you see appears to be of your Uncle Jack, Uncle Jack is the apparent.

The term **agent** refers to whoever/whatever is responsible. If you see the ghost of your Aunt Jane at a moment when the real-life Aunt Jane is involved in a car accident, she may be the agent who causes you to see her, but it could be that someone or something else is directing your attention to the fact by creating an apparition.

The term **guarantor** designates the authority-figure who guarantees the ghost experience. If the Virgin Mary or a respected teacher appears to you with a warning message, it is likely that they are appearing as guarantors that the warning is genuine and that you need not hesitate to act on it.

The term **psi** is used as a generic term for any form of extrasensory communication or information transfer – telepathy, clairvoyance, precognition, etc. The term is used here neutrally and with no prejudgement as to what process is actually involved, or indeed whether any such faculty exists. The term **super-psi** is discussed in Chapter 8.

The term **extended self** – the secondary self it is widely believed each of us possesses. This seems able to travel independently of the primary self and may even survive after death. It is also known as astral double, etheric body, second self, etc. The **projector** is the person, or her subconscious, who causes the extended self to separate from the physical self, deliberately or spontaneously. Again the term is used with no prejudgement as to whether any such self exists. We examine the concept more fully in Chapter 8.

Measurements have been converted to metric equivalents for the sake of consistency, even though it may sound odd for Victorian gentlemen and American housewives to be using them.

The **SPR** is the Society for Psychical Research, London. *PSPR* refers to its Proceedings, *JSPR* to its Journal. **ASPR,** *PASPR* and *JASPR* refer to the American Society.

Authorities

Certain researchers who have made significant contributions to the ghost debate will be cited on several occasions. Later references will be to surname only:

Broad, C. D. (1887–1971) British, Professor of Philosophy at Cambridge University, President SPR 1935–36, 1958–60

Carington, Whateley (1884–1947) British, psychical researcher, author, SPR councillor

Hart, Hornell (1888–1967) American, Professor of Sociology at Duke University, North Carolina.

Price, Henry Habberley (1899–1984) British, Professor of Logic at Oxford University, President SPR 1939–41

Richet, Charles (1850–1935) French, Professor of Physiology at the Faculty of Medicine, Paris, Nobel prizewinner, President SPR 1905

Rogo, David Scott (1950–1990) American, parapsychologist, investigator and author

Roll, William George (1926—) American, parapsychologist, President of the Parapsychology Association

The SPR-Group refers to the group of senior members of the SPR responsible for producing *Phantasms of the Living* (1886), the *Census of Apparitions* (1894), and related papers. The SPR holds no corporate views, but this group – Edmund Gurney (1847–1888), F. W. H. Myers (1843–1901), Frank Podmore (1856–1910), Eleanor Sidgwick (1845–1936) and their collaborators – did, for our purposes, share a common outlook, so it is convenient to refer to them collectively.

Thouless, Robert Henry (1894–1984) British, psychologist, President SPR 1942–45

Tyrrell, G. N. M. (1879–1952) British, mathematician, SPR councillor

Whatever else a ghost may be, it is probably one of the most complex phenomena in nature.

F. W. H. Myers[2]

I do believe that striving for a unified view of all apparitions has been a handicap.

Karlis Osis[3]

We tend to seek simple answers to very complex questions. There are no simple answers.

Andrew MacKenzie[4]

The stories continue to be told, and our business is with the stories.

Andrew Lang[5]

Chapter 1

THE NATURE OF THE GHOST EXPERIENCE

When someone tells you they have seen a ghost, you have a fair idea what they mean. It is not a scientific term, but there is a shared acceptance of what a ghost experience is like. It could hardly be otherwise with an experience which has been widely reported over a period of some three thousand years, even though all those experiences have failed to answer the question, is there any such thing as a ghost? Simply in order that people can tell others what happened to them, a pragmatic consensus has come into being.

Yet ghost experiences vary greatly. There are many classic ghost stories, but there is no such thing as a typical ghost experience. When someone tells you they have seen a ghost, you know they saw – or believe they saw – an entity which was not a living human being: but the entities that people perceive can range from faceless figures draped in shrouds to apparitions so lifelike as to be mistaken for living persons.

No less varied are the attitudes we adopt towards them. Some of us believe there is a reality, of a sort, to the figure we wake to see standing at the foot of our bed. The more sceptical find it easier to believe that the only reality about it is the subconscious mental process that creates the illusion.

But neither the ghosts-are-real believers nor the ghosts-are-illusion disbelievers have been able to prove their view is the correct one. Nor is this problem confined to ghosts: visitations of the Virgin Mary, abductions by extraterrestrial aliens, rescues by angels and harassments by demons – these, too, challenge the

1

reality-testing skills which are an essential item in every individual's survival kit. In every other department of our lives we rely on experience to help us distinguish the real from the unreal: but our experiences with ghosts defy us by being too real for us to dismiss yet at the same time too unreal to accept.

This figure which several people see gliding over the river at Buntingford, Hertfordshire, England, in January 1931, is, for them, unmistakably a ghost. But it is never identified, and their description suggests a folklore figure rather than the apparition of an individual person

Whether or not ghosts are real, ghost experiences are certainly real. To set the stage for our inquiry, here is a handful of cases, presented without commentary. As our inquiry proceeds, we shall find that each represents a different kind of experience, raises different kinds of difficulties, and may require a different explanation:

1. Miss Barry, Mrs Davis, Rector. New England, c. 1928
The Senior Warden of a small Episcopal Church commits suicide when he finds that some investments in which he had placed church money have turned out badly. The following Sunday he appears in church service, going up with colleagues to the chancel steps after taking up the collection: the Rector staggers back when confronted with the apparition, which is seen also by Miss Barry, the Rector's cousin, in a pew at the far left, and by a Mrs Davis, seated on the extreme right, who utters a shriek when she sees him. All three simultaneously see the figure, which they recognize at once, in true perspective.[6]

2. The Bull and Edwards families. Ramsbury, England, February to April 1932
When Samuel Bull, a chimneysweep, dies, his married daughter Mary Jane Edwards and her family move into his cottage, since his widow Jane is bedridden. Eight months after her husband's death his ghost is seen, dressed in his normal after-work clothes, looking entirely lifelike and solid, walking not gliding, but wearing a very sad expression. He is seen first by Mary Jane and her 21-year-old son Jimmy, and subsequently by her husband and their four younger children, who recognize their grandpa. 'At first everyone was terrified and the children screamed, but later were calmer, but in a state of quiet awe.' The appearances are very frequent. The family sense his presence about half an hour before he is seen, and when he comes he is seen off and on over several hours, for up to half an hour continuously. The widow twice feels his touch (which feels cold) and once hears him speak her name. The apparitions come to an end only because the family move to a council house.[7]

3. James J. Larkin, pilot with the Royal Flying Corps in World War One. Scampton, Lincolnshire, England, 7 December 1918
'David [M'Connell] told me at 11.30 that he was flying a "Camel" to Tadcaster. He said, "I expect to get back in time for tea. Cheero."

3

Between a quarter and half-past three that afternoon I was sitting in front of a fire, writing and reading. I heard someone walking up the passage; the door opened with the usual noise and clatter which David always made: I heard his "Hello boy!" and I turned half round in my chair and saw him standing in the doorway, half in and half out of the room, holding the door knob in his hand. He was dressed in his full flying clothes but wearing his naval cap pushed back on his head. He was smiling, as he always was when he came into the rooms. I remarked, "Hello, back already?" He replied, "Yes. Got there all right, had a good trip." Or words to that effect. Then he said, "Well, cheero!" closed the door noisily and went out. Shortly afterwards Lieut. Garner-Smith came into the room. He said, "I hope Mac [David] gets back early, we are going to Lincoln this evening." I replied, "He *is* back, he was in the room a few minutes ago!" Later that evening I learnt that word had come through that M'Connell had crashed and been killed flying to Tadcaster. Garner-Smith tried to persuade me that I must have been mistaken, that I had not actually seen Mac, but I insisted that I *had*. But there was no disputing the fact that he had been killed, presumably at 3.25 as his watch had stopped at that time.'[8]

4. Mrs Boulton. Scotland, Autumn 1883

For a period of several years, Mrs Boulton has experienced a recurring dream of visiting a house. Where it is located, she has no idea – but she knows the house inside and out and can describe it in detail. In 1883, she and her husband decide to spend the autumn in Scotland. Her husband makes inquiries about renting a suitable house, and decides on one offered by a Lady Beresford. Since their son is in Scotland at the time, they leave it to him to arrange matters. Mr Boulton travels up ahead of his wife, to sign the agreement and get settled in. Lady Beresford tells him she will give him her own bedroom, but thinks it right to warn him that for some time it has been haunted by a 'little lady', though the ghost seems quite harmless. He replies that far from being alarmed, he would be delighted to make the acquaintance of the phantom: however, his night is undisturbed. When his wife arrives, she is astonished to recognize the house of her dreams. Everything corresponds with what she has seen in her sleep, except that in her dream house the sitting-room leads to a suite of rooms which the present house lacks. On inquiry, though, it turns out that the rooms do indeed exist, but following alterations, they are now reached from a different part of the house. Two or three days later, the Boultons pay a courtesy visit to Lady Beresford, whom

Mrs Boulton has not previously met. The moment their landlady sees her, she exclaims, 'Why, you are the lady who haunts my bedroom!'[9]

5. Dr H. C. Britain, place unnamed, 1863
'I was sleeping alone. I woke up suddenly and with all my wits about me, but with a clear feeling that somebody was in the room. There was enough light to make things perceptibly visible, that was all. I saw a tall lady, aged about 40, in a rich black dress, looking steadily at me with a most gentle, meditating gaze. I did not at all recognize the face. There was a far-away look in her eyes, and I felt as if she had been reading me through. She rested the elbow of one hand in the palm of the other, and in the first hand there was a little book. I was entirely calm, eagerly interested, but rather scientifically than imaginatively. I pinched myself to find out if I was really awake. I held my watch to my ear to hear whether it was ticking. I tried my pulse, which was normal. I then said aloud, "This is an optical delusion. I shall now put my hand through this appearance." I did so, and my hand went through as it would through water (only without the slightest sensation), the clothes kept their folds and position. My hand with the white night-shirt sleeve was wholly hid, and when I withdrew it there was no hole left behind any more than when one withdraws one's hand from water. After some 40 or 50 seconds I saw a straight white line crossing the figure: I perceived the apparition was slowly vanishing, and the white line was the top of my towel behind. Bit by bit other objects came into sight, behind what was becoming a faint mist. In about 20 seconds it had completely vanished.'

[Five days later a lady known to Dr C. died, and at the time he connected the two events. However, the apparition did not resemble the lady.][10]

6. Erikson Gorique [pseudonym]. Oslo, Norway, summer 1956
Mr Gorique, a New York importer, comes to Oslo to buy china and glassware: it is his first visit to Norway. When he goes to take a room at a large hotel, the clerk appears to recognize him and has a room ready for him, telling Gorique that he came to the hotel a few months ago to make a reservation. Next day he calls on a wholesaler named Olsen, whom he has never met but who has been recommended to him. Olsen, however, greets Gorique by name, insisting that he visited him a few months earlier, saying he planned to purchase glass and china in the summer. Olsen correctly names Gorique's office and warehouse addresses.[11]

Between them, these six ghost experiences pose most of the major questions that have made the phenomenon so elusive ever since the first ghost was seen. Three people simultaneously see the dead churchwarden, each from his/her correct perspective, and seven see the chimneysweep, sensing his presence beforehand: can they all be sharing an illusion? Larkin cannot be seeing the real M'Connell, whose body is lying dead at the scene of his crash, yet he is seeing *something*: does that 'something' have any substance? Dr H. C. pushes his hand through the apparition. It is insubstantial, yet it obscures the furniture behind it until it starts to fade, when the furniture shows through – but through *what*? How could Lady Beresford see Mrs Boulton, unknown to her and sleeping far away, and how could Mrs Boulton know what the house she has never visited was like before the recent changes?

Who is Dr H. C.'s unrecognized visitor, and is she really delivering a message on some other lady's behalf? Not every accident victim manifests as a ghost: why M'Connell and not others, and in any case, what is the point of his ghostly return? Merchants travelling on business do not usually send a facsimile of themselves to personally book a hotel room and make an appointment, they get their secretary to make the arrangements: so what is this pseudo-Gorique which walks the streets of Oslo on behalf of the real Gorique?

Variations and permutations

Whatever questions they raise, and whatever differences there may be between them, these six experiences have one thing in common: each of the percipients knows, if not at the time then subsequently, that they have seen something that is not objectively real. Most would say, I have seen a ghost. Not because they know what a ghost is and recognize what they saw to be one: rather, it is the impossibility that it could be anything else. They know they saw something they could not, by normal means, see. So they apply the catch-all label: ghost.

Though each of these cases involves the perceiving of a figure who by normal standards is not there, the experiences differ each from the others in many ways. In the first two, the ghosts are of people known to be dead; the third is seen at the time of his death, the fourth is very much alive; in the last two, the events lie in the future. In most of the cases, the apparent is identified: in the M'Connell case the ghost is taken to be the pilot's living self, while the churchwarden and the chimneysweep are well known to all who see them. Gorique's experience is 'explained' by an Oslo professor as an instance of the *vardøgr* – the 'before-goer', a folklore phenomenon traditional in Norway. Only Dr H. C.'s lady remains a total mystery, both at the time and later.

In the course of our inquiry we shall encounter many other differences which may or not be significant. We shall find that some ghost experiences are clearly purposeful, others seemingly pointless. We shall find that some ghosts have close links with the percipient, others are strangers. Some are sacred, others diabolical; some are kindly, others downright mischievous.

We shall also find differences in the way the ghosts behave – whether they are active or static, whether they interact with the percipient or not; and in the way they are perceived – whether sharply defined or fuzzy, whether they cast shadows, or manifest self-illumined in total darkness. Some ghosts reflect in mirrors, others don't. Some make their exit by opening and closing a door, others walk through locked doors without troubling to turn the handle. Moreover, we shall find that the more we try to establish rules of ghostly behaviour, the more likely we are to come across exceptions.

We shall find ourselves asking whether we should regard all ghost experiences as the same phenomenon under different circumstances. Or are they different kinds of phenomena which have little in common beyond the fact that they all involve otherworldly figures? And we shall ask, too, whether encounters with ghosts are an entirely different kind of thing from possession by demons, or visions of the Virgin Mary, or abduction by extraterrestrial aliens.

And above all, we shall want to know whether ghosts are simply figments of our imaginations, or whether some kind of external agency may be involved. Are they a closed system, all in the mind of the percipient, or an open one, an intrusion from another level of reality?

Some of the answers to these questions we may be able to

work out for ourselves, simply by asking the right questions. Humankind has been aware of the ghost experience throughout its history, and always there have been scholars and philosophers who sought to understand it. If ghosts persist in remaining enigmatic, this is largely because the right questions were not asked, because false assumptions were made. Unquestioning belief is the greatest obstacle to understanding, and so long as the intellectual authorities sought to impose their view of ghosts on the rest of society, it was only rare individuals who had the courage to pursue their ideas independently. In Chapter 6 we shall look at some of the efforts that have been made to understand the ghost experience, but it will be helpful if we identify, at the outset of our inquiry, why so many efforts have failed, and continue to fail.

In part, it is because phenomena have been lumped together that should have been kept distinct, and phenomena separated

The appearance of the murdered Caesar's ghost in the tent of his murderer Brutus, on the eve of the battle of Philippi (42 BCE) in which Brutus will be defeated, is a classic instance of a ghost seeking revenge and at the same time predicting an imminent disaster

that should have been considered together. Because the inquirers have come from different directions – priests and policemen, folklorists and behavioural scientists – inquiry has often followed too narrow a path. In arriving at a common linguistic expression to communicate the ghost experience, two assumptions have been implied. First, that *there is a category of experience, the Ghost Experience, which is different from other kinds of experience;* and second, that *Ghost Experiences collectively form a more or less coherent category.* There is a good deal of truth in both these assumptions, but there is also much potential for confusion.

A great many of us, today as in the past, are seeing and even interacting with beings who do not share the same level of reality as ourselves. Christian visionaries have claimed encounters with the saints, with Jesus and his mother Mary, even with God himself:[12] other religions have their own visionary histories. Almost every culture has known encounters with demons. In our own time, the proliferation of claimed encounters with extra-terrestrial aliens has escalated to a remarkable degree. While none of these is strictly a ghost experience, it is evident that these otherworldly encounters have much in common. One of the mistakes of earlier investigators has been to ignore such parallel phenomena, yet they challenge us with the same ambiguity as ghosts do, hovering on the borderline between reality and fantasy.

These parallel experiences, too, have been widely discussed but never satisfactorily explained. At one extreme, they are taken at face value – Mary returns to Earth from Heaven, aliens come from another part of the physical universe, angels and demons come from the Underworld. At the farther extreme, none of these beings exists except as an imagined construct, created by the mind of the percipient. And between the entities-are-real and the entities-are-unreal viewpoints are a variety of other hypotheses, all toying with varying levels of reality.

None of these has proved convincing: each runs into problems. The view officially held by the Catholic Church, that Mary, having ascended in her physical body to a Heaven which must therefore be similarly physical, returns to Earth in her physical body, is challenged by the fact that when she returns she is seen only by those she selects: Bernadette Soubirous sees her, those standing beside her don't. Mary, during her lifetime, couldn't manage that. Is it something she has learnt to do in Heaven? The moment we try to apply everyday common sense to these experiences, they make us ridiculous. And ghosts – well, we shall see that ghosts ring every possible change on absurdity.

A frequently asked question, 'Do ghosts exist when no one is looking at them?' raises issues that take us to the heart of the ghost problem. Apart from a few ambiguous photographs, there is no objective evidence for the existence of ghosts. The only evidence is subjective, the testimony of people who come to believe they have had an experience which, however loosely, can be described as 'seeing a ghost'. In addition, somewhere between objective and subjective are those cases in which animals seem to be experiencing something of the sort. There is no record of an animal having a ghost experience except in the presence of a human percipient: but then, how would we know? At all events it seems that, whatever else may be true about ghosts, they depend, in part or in whole, on the individuals who see them.

Flouting common sense, existing only by grace of whoever sees them – small wonder that serious-minded persons have preferred to banish ghosts into the realm of fantasy. We accept that our dreams are absurd, defying logic and sense, so when we find ghosts displaying a similar defiance, the temptation is to classify them, too, as the flight-of-fancy work of our subconscious minds, subject to no constraining rules as to what can and what can't happen.

Yet the evidence that these beings are something more than imaginary constructs is very strong. For all the ambiguities and inconsistencies of their behaviour, ghosts often display a sense of purpose, a rationality, an access to inaccessible information, which implies not only intelligence but concern. It is all but impossible to account for this without invoking extraordinary mental powers for which there is as little scientific basis as there is for the ghosts themselves. Sophisticated and ingenious all-in-the-mind psychological and even parapsychological explanations are on offer, but they must be stretched to degrees bordering on the unrealistic if they are to account for such well-founded phenomena as crisis apparitions and hauntings.

The nature of the ghost experience

Ghosts: a human phenomenon

If ghosts are 'all in the mind', it is a human mind. If ghosts are spirits, they are spirits of human beings, living or dead. (Animal ghosts present a challenge of a different kind which we shall consider in the next chapter.) Where motivation can be identified, it is human in character. Where intelligence is manifest, we can generally recognize it as human intelligence.

Ghosts may be paranormal, in the sense that we have at present no explanation for them in terms of our normal experience: but there is no reason to think of them as supernatural, standing outside human nature altogether. Ghosts are not monsters. Even when they seem to be malevolent, even when hooded figures appear to menace us in sinister fashion, we do not have to look outside humanity; the most we need do is extend our ideas of human capability.

There is abundant evidence that in exceptional circumstances humans can do exceptional things. The testimony in support of 'miracle' healing, of precognition, of poltergeists and psychokinesis of various kinds, of out-of-body experiences and remote viewing, and many other powers generally regarded as paranormal, is very substantial, even if their erratic and often paradoxical nature has so far resisted all attempts to regularize them on a scientific basis. It is accepted that these are human powers. Ghosts are on a similar footing, whether or not we are prepared to consider the possibility that humanity survives physical death. Whether we see them as emanating from within ourselves, or as projections by humans who are no longer living on our earthly plane, or as artefacts created by unknown forces, those emanations, projections and forces remain human, albeit an extension of what we normally consider to fall within the limits of human experience.

So while it is almost certainly true that in explaining ghosts we shall have to contemplate other levels of reality than the one with which we are familiar, it will nevertheless be a human reality.

But the supreme problem with ghosts is the diversity of the testimony. What the experiencers tell us is ambiguous. There is convergence in some respects, divergence in others. Some ghosts

11

seem to have substance, others do not; some appear purposeful, others do not; some force themselves on our attention, others remain aloof, even unaware. Ghosts come in many forms, and until we know why this is so, we shall not start to understand the ghost experience.

And underlying all our other questions is this: do ghosts come to us from elsewhere, or do we make our own ghosts? There are some who find it easy to answer that question, who are sure that ghosts are spirits of the dead. Others are equally certain they are nothing but creations of our minds. Both, we can be sure, are deluding themselves. If the ghost experience has defied our understanding for three thousand years, it is because there is no easy answer.

Chapter 2

THE DIVERSITY OF THE GHOST EXPERIENCE

The realm of ghosts is a wonderland where the percipient cannot rely on what his senses tell him and the rest of us cannot rely on what the percipient tells us. Revenants seem to be returning from the grave, haunters appear to be haunting, but is that really what they are doing? We have no choice but to start with what ghosts *seem* to be, the subjective reality: but we must always be ready to find that the objective reality may be very different. They may be deceiving us, or we may be deceiving ourselves.

This chapter and the next are intended to lay out the ghost problem in its ghastly complexity. Each kind of experience raises a fresh set of questions: Hopefully, we shall find answers to most if not all of them in later pages.

Ghosts from the past: revenants

7. Lois Alike Kaili. Liberty, New York, 1917
'At high school, one of my friends was Gertrude Miller, a beautiful girl with long red hair. We moved away, then later we moved back and I returned to the high school. On my first day at the old school I was hurrying up a stairway where a group of students stood talking. With them was a red-haired girl who waved to me. I recognized Gertrude. When I reached the head of the stairs she had disappeared. Later I met some mutual friends and mentioned that I had seen Gertie. "Why," one of them said, "Gertie died soon after you left." They told me the circumstances of her death and they all had attended her funeral. At the time I tried to convince myself that I had

seen someone who looked like Gertrude. But I know I didn't. I saw Gertrude.'[13]

This is a typical revenant case, simple and straightforward, and at the same time utterly puzzling. Ostensibly it involves the return to Earth of someone who, formerly alive, is now dead. But is 'return' the right word? Perhaps, in some sense, Gertrude never left, so that her friend Lois was able to, as it were, pick up her image in the familiar setting. Or could it have been simply the

Revenants – friends, lovers or relatives who seem to be returning from the grave – form a large category of ghosts. But their motives are not always friendly, and their visits are not always welcome, as in this illustration to a poem by Christina Rossetti

expectation of seeing her old friend that triggered the illusion? But if so, who did the scene-setting, placing the non-real Gertrude among a group of real students? We shall see many other instances of this cut-and-paste technique: no. 65 is a particularly striking example.

The revenant, returning to right a wrong, to give valuable information to a surviving relative, or otherwise to complete unfinished business, is the most traditional form of ghost and enjoyed something like a monopoly in the early historical period. This was consistent with religious beliefs which taught that souls might be allowed a return visit to Earth if they could show good reason. The classic ghost is a returning spirit with a mission to accomplish.

A closer look, however, shows that revenant cases vary greatly. The return may be spontaneous or forced. It may be manifestly purposeful, or the motive may be hidden or obscure. The apparent is usually known to the percipient, though it may not be recognized at the time. The percipient usually has the sense that she has been specifically targeted: if she is with others, they may not see the revenant. Revenants usually manifest in a natural way even in locations with which the apparent was not familiar while living – for example, standing at the foot of the percipient's bed, leaning on the bed-rail, gazing directly at her. Now, most of these characteristics relate to the percipient, so it is tempting to ascribe revenants, like the imaginary companions we shall consider later, to wish-fulfilment on the part of the percipient, and consequently to deny them any objective reality. Lois's Gertie is perhaps an example. The fact that so many apparents are seen by their partners or offspring soon after bereavement encourages this interpretation, but cases such as this make us think twice:

8. Gertrude Durkop. Columbus, Ohio, November 1952
'I was sleeping in my upstairs apartment. My young brother Ralph, who had been staying with me since the death of our mother fourteen months before, had just come in. As he climbed the stairs he had the feeling there was someone behind him. Reaching the top, he turned and saw a soft blur ascending the stairs. As it came closer, it took on the shape of our mother, until in every sense it was her. He was petrified with fear, but heard her say, "Don't be afraid, Honey. It's just

15

your mother. I just came to see my babies." Ralph lost his fear and followed as she walked into the living room. She embraced him and asked about me. Told I was sleeping, she came to my bedroom, stood looking at me for a few seconds, then gently kissed me on the cheek. She turned to Ralph and said, "I must hurry now, Son. Be good and remember that your mother loves all of you very much." With that, she vanished. A moment later I woke, having dreamed, I thought, that my mother had kissed my cheek. I saw Ralph lying on the floor: he had fainted. He said, "It was no dream, Sis, she was here." I ran to the phone to tell my sister Lockie, who lived 25 kilometres away. She dialed my number at the same time: "Gertie!" she said, "Mother was just here in the house with me!" My elder brother Burnzie, who was home on leave and staying with Lockie, had been drinking and had passed out in his car, parked outside the house. Mother had appeared to him and said, "'Oh Son, Mother wishes you would quit this drinking.'"[14]

To ascribe this to wish-fulfilment, we would have to suppose that four living relatives simultaneously stage a fantasy – not a shared fantasy, but one which adapts to each of them individually. In principle, telepathy could account for this – but if so, it would need to be telepathy of a very intricate kind, between two people awake, one asleep dreaming and one in a drunken stupor! On the other hand, if the apparition is indeed the spirit of their mother paying a return visit, why does she suddenly have an impulse to 'see her babies' on this particular night, fourteen months after her death? Or has it taken that long for her permission to visit to come through from the powers that be?

Often, moreover, the revenant is independently witnessed by people with no vested emotional interest in their 'return':

9. Sis Patterson and others. Newark airport, New Jersey, June 1972
The fatal crash of Eastern Airlines Flight 401, New York to Miami, in the everglades of Florida, killed a hundred crew and passengers, including Captain Bob Loft. Within a month, uncanny events were reported, seemingly from aircraft into which salvaged parts of the crashed aircraft had been incorporated. On one flight, just before take-off, stewardess Sis Patterson finds she has one passenger too many aboard. Checking, she finds the extra passenger is an Eastern Airlines captain in uniform, seated in first class. When she speaks to him, he makes no reply but simply stares straight ahead, though there

is nothing abnormal about his appearance. The flight captain is called: he recognizes the dead man, exclaiming 'My God, it's Bob Loft!' The figure instantly vanishes.[15]

There seems no reason for Loft's reappearance and he seems not to have targeted any individual percipient. Yet here a figure is seen, looking lifelike even if his behaviour is somewhat robot-like, and remaining long enough for the stewardess to fetch the flight captain. Such cases offer a strong argument that some revenants possess objective reality and originate independently of the percipient. But what would Loft's ghost have done if all the seats had been taken?

Ghosts from the past: deathbed and near-death apparitions

Several kinds of ghost experience occur in connection with dying people. The kind that is most frequently reported – thousands of such cases have been collected by researchers – is a vision by the dying one of persons, usually dead relatives, who seem to be welcoming the percipient to the next world. The great majority occur a few minutes before death, they are short-lived, and almost invariably they are of great comfort to the dying person and encourage him to leave this life not simply with resignation but often with eagerness. In a considerable number of cases the percipient also has a glimpse of the next world, which generally takes the form of a stereotypically beautiful garden or landscape, or less frequently a city of dreaming spires and marble halls.

That a person lying on his deathbed, already psychologically halfway out of this world, should see visions of the next world is perhaps only to be expected. That he should see a group of deceased relatives waiting to welcome him is a classic example of wish-fulfilment, especially as they are generally presented symbolically, dressed in flowing robes, smiling a welcome like loved ones in an airport arrivals hall. The previews of the next world are evidently symbolic also: we don't really think that is what the next world is like. It is no more to be taken literally than the Paradise of the Christians or the Golden Age of Greek mythology.

However, there are complications:

17

10. Edith. Near Boston, June 1889

Two girls, Jenny (8) and Edith (9), schoolmates and intimate friends, are both taken ill with diphtheria. Jenny is the first to die, but Edith's parents conceal this from her, fearing the effect of the knowledge on her condition. That they succeed is shown by the fact that one of Edith's last acts is to select some photographs to be sent to Jenny, and to ask her friends to bid her goodbye. Later that evening she talks of dying, and seems unafraid. She appears to see one and another of the friends she knows to be dead, and her grandparents. Then, starting with sudden surprise, Edith turns to her father and exclaims, 'Why, papa, did you not tell me that Jenny had gone? Here is Jenny, come to meet me!' and she reaches out her arms in welcome, 'Oh Jenny, I'm so glad you are here!'[16]

Whereas it might be predicted that an adult might fantasize about being welcomed by people she knows to be dead, it is not what one would expect from a nine-year-old. But even if we allow that Edith may be acting on suggestions from others when she sees persons she knows to be dead, that does not account for the apparition of Jenny, who she supposes to be still living.

If this were the only case of its kind we might attribute it to chance, or to some kind of subliminal signal which Edith unconsciously picked up. But countless cases like this have been recorded.[17] Whether Jenny is indeed manifesting, or whether Edith's subconscious acquires the knowledge of her death in some way not explained, raises questions to which we will return in Chapter 8. But whatever the process involved, it seems clear that deathbed visions are part of the ghost experience.

Another kind of deathbed experience relates to the dying person:

11. Robert C. Henderson. Pecos, Texas, 1962

'[My mother and I were with my father when he died in hospital.] When the doctors pronounced him dead, my mother slumped into my arms as we sat on a settee nearby. Suddenly the nurse said to the doctor, "Do you see it?" We looked up and saw a small figure, above my father's prone body, shining as though wrapped in silver foil. It was in a sitting position, with knees bent and arms outstretched. The two forms were joined by a silver cord. We could see the window through the rising form. All was gone in less than a minute.' [Another nurse also saw it, making five witnesses in all.][18]

18

With so many witnesses, it is hard to believe there was not something objectively present. If so, it seems to have been the father's extended self, or his soul, depending on your interpretation. (The role of the extended self in the ghost experience will be considered in Chapter 8.)

A third kind of deathbed experience is of apparitions seen by others, not the dying person, that seem to be in some way messengers of death. These will be considered in Chapter 5, along with angels.

A fourth kind relates to out-of-body and near-death experiences. Here again there is a wealth of testimony by people who feel themselves on the threshold of the next world but who are turned back and instructed to return to life, with some such words as, 'It is not yet time for you', by a dead relative, an angelic being or even God himself:

> 12. *Unnamed German youth. Switzerland, 1920s*
> 'My situation was so desperate that I could see no way out but suicide. One night I was sitting on a bench out of doors, preoccupied with my intention, when the darkness was suddenly rent asunder and I saw a bright, radiant light, and out of the light there came a wonderful female figure, with her right arm stretched out towards me as if to hold me back, while I heard her say, "Stop – you mustn't – your time has not yet come."'[19]

Angel? Jungian archetype? Folklore entity? Fantasy? Surely no ghost: yet such a case reminds us how unclear are the distinctions between various categories of apparition.

Ghosts from the past: haunters

A haunter is an ongoing ghost. Like the revenant, it is ostensibly the spirit of someone once living but now dead; however, unlike the revenant who rarely pays more than one visit, the haunter manifests repeatedly. The revenant, in leaving this life, seems also to have left this Earth, but the haunter has either never departed, or in departing has left some portion of himself behind.

Such ghosts were familiar even in the fifth century BCE: Socrates, as reported by Plato, speaks of the soul which is dragged down again into the visible world, because she is afraid of the invisible and of the world below – prowling about tombs and sepulchres, near which, as they tell us, are seen certain ghostly apparitions of souls which have not departed pure, but are cloyed with sight and therefore visible . . . these must be the souls, not of the good, but of the evil, which are compelled to wander about such places in payment of the penalty of their former evil way of life.[20]

The prevailing idea about the next world, among those who believe there is any such place, is that when people die, they pass more or less easily into their next phase of existence. But there are exceptions, who for some reason cannot abandon their terrestrial habitat. Typical is the former home-owner who is indignant that strangers are now living in his/her home, like the 'resentful residents' of nos. 108 and 109. But this raises questions. To what extent are they aware that they are dead? Why, if they remember where they lived, do they not also remember that they died? Do they notice that electric lighting and central heating have been added to the old house?

Among the career options they didn't tell me about at my University Appointments Board was that of soul rescuer; yet there are people who set up as such, taking it upon themselves to help these earthbound spirits. One of the best known was Carl Wickland, whose book's title *Thirty Years among the Dead* testifies to his dedication:[21] more recently, Terry O'Sullivan labels himself a 'soul rescuer' and has made this his life's work:

> The skill of the soul rescuer lies in trying to convince the disembodied visitor of three things: first, that they are physically dead; secondly, that they can choose where to go; thirdly, that safe passage can be arranged in their chosen destiny, either to their ancestors or to other realms within the spirit kingdoms.[22]

Clearly, this implies a more specific acquaintance with life in the next world than most of us would lay claim to. Such people are apt to believe they have a better understanding of the relevant 'occult' techniques than you and I, and for all I know they may be right. However, anything we know about conditions in the next world comes to us via communications from people who allegedly are already there. Since they cannot prove that is where they are, or that they are who they claim to be, it is prudent to receive such information with caution. (We shall consider the role of soul rescuers in action in Chapter 6.)

Although tales of haunted houses form the staple fare of ghost story collections, they are in many ways far less interesting than other categories. The behaviour of haunters tends to be repetitive and robot-like: they perform the same actions over and over, they display little if any intelligence, and only rarely show awareness of being observed (the Scott case no. 167 is a notable exception). As for their purpose, it is nearly always obscure, but it seems certain that they are preoccupied with their own concerns rather than with those of the living.

More often than not those who see haunters were not acquainted with the apparent while alive, so fail to identify the ghost. If identification takes place, it is usually later – the house-guest comes down to breakfast, white as a sheet, and learns from her hosts that she has enjoyed the doubtful privilege of meeting the ghost of the Third Marchioness . . . Unlike revenants, haunters do not generally seem to target particular percipients.

Not all haunters walk the corridors of stately homes:

13. Fred H., Miss G. Essex village, 12 October 1927
[Miss G.] 'I was walking up High Street with Fred, about 7.15. There was some moonlight. As we passed the stile opposite Mr W.'s house, I saw a figure seated on the top rail. It looked like an old, white-haired man, very small, as if when standing he could not have been more than four feet. I could not see his face owing to his hat, nor what clothes he was wearing. He held one hand out with a stick in it. I asked Fred who he was. He said he didn't know. On the following Sunday, at Fred's house, I asked if he had found out who that little old man was. His mother asked what little old man I meant. I described him. She said it was supposed to be the ghost of Charlie C. who lived in the house which used to stand near the stile and was burnt down. Fred then said, "I knew all the time who it was, but I wouldn't tell her (meaning me) as I thought she would be frightened".

[Fred] 'I saw the old man on the stile about 7 p.m. when walking to meet Miss G. I saw him again when walking with Miss G. That was the first night I had seen him. Since then I saw him three times.'[23]

The Italian researcher Ernesto Bozzano analysed 374 cases of haunting, and found that in the overwhelming majority (304) there was a strong link between the haunting and a death associated with the location, often a dramatic one. (The figure could be even higher, since often sufficient information was lacking about the remainder.) If these links were recent, it would be tempting to attribute the haunters to the grieving emotions of the living, but many are so remote in time that it seems unlikely that any living person has any emotional attachment to them: besides, the percipient is often a complete stranger. So it seems well nigh certain that it is the haunter rather than the percipient who originates the haunting. This is well illustrated by the following case, which has benefited from the researches of one of England's most experienced investigators, Andrew MacKenzie:

14. Rosina Despard and others. Cheltenham, Gloucestershire, between 1882 and 1889

The figure of a tall woman in black, often holding a handkerchief to her face, is seen by at least seventeen people in various parts of a large town house. Twenty hear footsteps which they cannot attribute to any living person: the ghost is also sensed by animals. The primary witness, 19-year-old medical student Rosina Despard, makes several unsuccessful efforts to 'catch' the entity, to communicate with it or photograph it. The figure passes through strings set across stairs, and is equally oblivious to such obstacles as doors. The ghost is seen both by night and in bright sunlight: on occasion it stands in view for up to half an hour. It is seen in the garden and orchard as well as indoors, not only by family and servants but also by neighbours and strangers. Children make a ring round the figure by joining hands, but it simply passes between two of them and disappears. The ghost is tentatively identified as Imogen Swinhoe, the unhappily married second wife of the house's first owner, who died at age 41 in 1878: people who knew Imogen confirm the likeness.

A typical sighting: [Rosina] 'My sister E. was singing in the back drawing-room. I heard her stop abruptly, come out into the hall and call me. She said she had seen the figure in the drawing-room, close behind her as she sat at the piano. I went back into the room with her, and saw the figure in the bow window in the usual place. I spoke to her several times but had no answer. She stood there for about ten or fifteen minutes, then went across the room to the door, and along the passage, disappearing by the garden door. My sister then came in from the garden, saying she had seen her coming up the kitchen steps outside. We all three then went out into the garden, when Mrs K. called from a window on the first floor that she had just seen her pass across the lawn in front, and along the carriage drive towards the orchard. That evening, then, altogether four people saw her.'[24]

Curiously, the Cheltenham haunting also led to the sighting of a living ghost:

[Miss C. M. Campbell, a friend of Rosina's] 'On the night on which Rosina first spoke to the figure, as stated in her account, I myself saw her telepathically. I was then residing in the North of England, quite 160 kilometres away, preparing for bed, between twelve and half-past, when I seemed suddenly to be standing close to the door of the housemaid's cupboard [in the Cheltenham house], facing the short flight of stairs leading to the top landing. Coming down these stairs, I saw the figure, exactly as described, and about two steps behind

This is how witnesses describe the ghost seen frequently in a Cheltenham house between 1882 and 1889, and occasionally since then: it is tentatively identified as Imogen Swinhoe, the unhappy wife of a former occupant

23

Rosina herself, with a dressing-gown thrown loosely round her, and carrying a candle in her hand.' The details were confirmed by Rosina.[25]

If a haunter can impinge on the sense organs of so many independent percipients, it is hard to resist the implication that it possesses objective reality of some kind. Psi transmission remains an option, as always, but if so, who is doing the transmitting, to a series of unrelated strangers and over so long a period?

At the same time the difficulties with a physical figure are no less puzzling. The earthly physical body no longer exists: it has either been cremated or is rotting underground, in the process of being recycled as component matter of the universe. So is the figure composed of a new kind of body, with one of which we shall each be provided when we pass to the next phase of existence? Formed of what substance, terrestrial or otherwise? If Imogen's ghost is in some way substantial, does she retain that substance between one sighting and the next – that is to say, is she still continuing to inhabit her Earthly body, clothes and all? Or does she re-enter it for the purposes of haunting, returning it to the store-room between times like a dress hired from an agency?

The ghostly image frequently retains details from its living body, as in this curious case:

15. Lucy Gaylord Starnes. Raleigh, North Carolina, 1936
'I came home from my teaching job and sank wearily on the couch facing the front door. The late afternoon sun slanted through the glass portion of the door, and suddenly I saw a mist, the shape and size of a man's head, appear in the soft light. It moved slowly, growing larger as it moved, and assumed the form of a slender man. It walked through the doorway into the dark hall. I watched in terror as the shape passed into the middle bedroom. Walking slowly into the hall, I stared into the bedroom. The shape turned to face me. I saw that it was faceless, with a white blur where features should have been. It moved to the windows, collapsed and vanished. Weeks later I learnt that a young man had come home late one afternoon, went into the middle bedroom and shot himself in the face.'[26]

The ghost is faceless – evidently because the young man shot himself in the face: but Lucy doesn't see a mangled, bloody face, a realistic image. Instead she sees simply a blur, as though to express in sanitized form the manner of his death. But who makes the decision to manifest in such a way? Does her own subconscious censor the image for violence, or is the young man himself anxious to spare Lucy's feelings? Moreover, she sees the ghost just this once: is this its once-in-a-deathtime appearance, or does it appear often, even though there may be no one about to see it? In a way it's easiest to believe that Lucy's subconscious picks up on some latent trace-memory of the suicide, and visualizes the apparition. But does her subconscious also learn about the face, and in which room the shooting took place? Or does the trace-memory create a link with the young man, whose subconscious collaborates in the apparition? And in any case, *why*? It serves no purpose of his, she is in no position to help him, and the information is of no use to her – quite the contrary, indeed.

One of the many difficulties presented by ghosts is that they are inconsistent in their appearance. Some present themselves exactly as they were at the moment of death, some as they were earlier in life, as in no. 57. Some are wearing the clothes they were last seen in, others in clothing which is unfamiliar to the percipient (for instance no. 113). In one autophany (seeing yourself) case (no. 26) the percipient sees herself wearing a garment she owned once but had discarded before the time of her experience. The clothing worn by crisis apparitions, in particular, is often an important aid to identification. But who is the wardrobe mistress?

The whole question of ghosts' clothing is puzzling. If they are truly spirits from another world, there should in principle be no reason for them to wear clothes at all. Whereas clothing is important to us living persons, whether to help us cope with the climate or to conform to social requirements, this would not seem to apply to those who have moved to another world where, to judge by reports, the climate is always equable, and where suits and skirts will have been shed along with the idea that nudity is shocking. Yet naked ghosts such as the following are extremely rare. Ghosts are apparently as mindful of Earthly propriety as are the living, though it will be interesting to see whether, as our society grows more permissive, ghosts also relax their standards:

16. G. Frank Clifton. Mexico City, 1940
'My new young wife and I made a combination honeymoon–business trip to Mexico City. One night I was suddenly wide awake and surprised to see what I took to be my wife kneeling on the foot of the bed with her arms folded across her breasts. She was nude and her long hair fell down her back. My wife wore her hair long and slept in the nude. I sat up and reached to take her by the arm, saying, Why not come back to bed? But she vanished. Then I saw that my wife was asleep beside me. The next morning I told the desk clerk what I had seen. She asked, Was her appearance about two in the morning? When I said yes, she told me others had seen her at about the same time.'[27]

In a fascinating book *The Boy Who Saw True* the narrator, a young boy with second sight, writes: 'I thought I'd ask Grandpa [that is, his grandfather's ghost, who frequently visits him] why he wasn't naked, or why all spirits aren't naked. He said, "Do you think of yourself as going about naked?" So I said, "No, I didn't." Then he said, "Well, neither do we. We look as we think of ourselves. That is why people over here wear such a lot of different sorts of clothes, and why even I wear clothes that aren't the fashion any more with you in your world."'[28]

Why haunt?

In a case similar to the Cheltenham haunting, several members of the W. family see the ghost of a man on several occasions: once, mother and daughter both hear a voice say 'I can't find it'.[29] The suggestion is that the ghost is looking for something, and indeed that is what haunters are often traditionally supposed to be doing. This next haunter, too, seems to be performing a compulsive personal routine:

17. Marion Bradner. Waterloo, New York State, 6 October 1962
'I was driving slowly along a road strange to me, at twilight, when I suddenly spotted a man wearing what appeared to be a faded blue Civil War uniform, walking directly ahead of me on the wrong side of the road. Tooting warningly, I braked to a stop. But when I glanced back, nobody was in sight. Nearby I noticed a lighted farmhouse.

Deciding he must have fled in that direction I drove there, reasoning that he probably was costumed to participate in some local township's centennial celebration. When I inquired, the farmer said, "You must've seen James Johnson's ghost. Folks here says he keeps trying to come home. His Scythe Tree down the road a piece draws him." By daylight I journeyed back to examine the Scythe Tree. There I learned that on 29 October, 1861, 26-year-old Johnson, having joined the Volunteers, stuck his scythe into a then young sapling in the family farmyard, requesting that his family leave it there until he returned. In May 1864 he died of a wound.'[30]

We gather that the ghost is relatively well known in the neighbourhood. Would it have been walking along the road if Marion hadn't come along? Somehow that doesn't seem the right question to ask, just as it doesn't seem helpful to wonder what a Civil War soldier makes of being overtaken by an automobile.

Almost every haunting is firmly located in space. Sightings occur at a specific location or in its immediate vicinity. The Scott sisters (no. 167) always meet their ghost along the same stretch of a country lane, so that one of them can speak of him 'finally fading from view at his usual spot by the hedge to the right'. But this is not invariably the case. Very occasionally the ghost is seen in more than one location:

18. Mrs M. de G. Verall. Brighton/Cambridge, 1887
'As I was washing my hands while staying at Brighton, I heard footsteps, and looking up saw a little old lady coming towards me. I did not see her face, although she was walking towards me. I knew at once that it was a hallucination, but was neither startled nor alarmed . . . During the next two or three weeks, I saw "my old lady" on at least three occasions besides the first, and have an impression that there were others. Though I usually saw her when I was alone, I remember once seeing her when my sister and I were in the dining-room . . . In the end [suggested by a brooch she wore] I called the figure my great-grandmother, but I never saw the face.

I came back to Cambridge, and entirely forgot my hallucination, till one evening I heard footsteps coming along the passage, and saw my old lady coming towards me . . . This was the last time I saw it. The figure always took its place in the surroundings (i.e. hid the things behind it) and was always in movement – coming towards me.'[31]

27

At first sight, this seems a classic haunter, with repeated manifestations in one location. But when we find it seen in a quite different location, the suggestion is that it is Mrs Verall, rather than any house, who is being haunted. If the old lady is indeed a relative, that is something of an explanation, but once again, a seemingly clear line of demarcation turns out to be less than clear. Haunters *can* travel. Or should we classify Mrs Verall's lady not as a haunter at all, but as a revenant of an unusually persistent kind?

Ghosts of the present: crisis apparitions

Although most people, asked to describe their mental image of a ghost, would probably describe a haunter or a revenant from the past, the kinds of ghost we have been considering hitherto are in fact much in the minority: they are far and away outnumbered by ghosts of the living. There have been few attempts to quantify the ghost experience but the SPR-Group in the 1880s found that of the 17,000 who responded to their survey, nine out of ten told of ghosts of the living, and more than half of those were crisis apparitions.

A crisis apparition is a manifestation, generally at a remote location, of an identified individual on the occasion of her death, serious accident or some such critical experience. The percipient is generally, though by no means always, someone closely associated – life partner, business associate and so on.

The crucial factor is the timing: the apparition correlates closely with the critical event. The SPR-Group classify them as living ghosts even though the sighting may take place several hours after the ostensible death of the apparent. They justify this on the grounds that our ignorance of the apparition process is matched by our ignorance regarding the dying process. Deathbed observations and, for what they are worth, post-mortem communications support the notion that death, far from being a simple switching from 'being alive' to 'being dead', may well be a multi-phased process. This being so, crisis apparitions may be produced during one or more different stages of this process.

The SPR-Group can, indeed, be accused of some sleight of hand in this respect. They favoured the hypothesis that apparitions result from telepathy between percipient and apparent. Since telepathy between two living persons is easier to accept than telepathy between the living and the dead, they allowed themselves a fairly generous margin which would allow them to classify the majority of crisis apparitions as occurring while the apparent was still alive. However we, approaching the matter with no such commitment, can see that we have no right to rule out the possibility that crisis apparitions may be initiated as well by the dead as by the living.

Does being in a crisis situation induce an altered state of consciousness in which the mind is able to do things it can't do in its usual state – including spontaneous projection, near-death and out-of-body experiences? Or is it a characteristic of the death process that the dying person, like a criminal suspect under arrest, is allowed one Mayday call to the percipient of his choice?

Perhaps; but crisis apparitions are not limited to death situations, or even to those who feel themselves to be in death-threatening situations. Any sufficiently threatening situation – the menace of rape, for example – may be sufficient to produce one. So what we may be considering is a faculty which is bestowed on people in these special circumstances. By the time we get to Chapter 8, we may have gathered some indications of what form this might take.

The question raised by other kinds of ghost – do they originate with the percipient? – seems at first sight to be superfluous in the case of crisis apparitions. When Aunt Jane's ghost appears to her nephew there may seem little doubt that she is responsible, for it is she, not her nephew, who knows that she is in a critical situation. Often, as in the case of a lone mountain climber who suffers an accident, the apparent is the *only* person who knows that the crisis is taking place.

This view is supported by the fact that crisis apparitions frequently offer information which would not be available to the percipient by normal means – details of the accident, or what Aunt Jane is wearing at the time. Thus a Mrs L. saw an apparition of her husband undergoing an accident while driving a carriage, whereas she believed him to be out driving a dogcart. Later it was found that not only did the accident take place as she had perceived it, but her husband had indeed chosen to drive a different vehicle.[32]

More, some crisis apparitions provide the percipient with information which, if acted upon, could be the means of changing the course of events: when the apparent is seen lying injured, as in no. 176, for example. At first sight it seems there is no way the percipient could be aware of the apparent's predicament unless the apparent informs her. However, we have no right to be dogmatic even about this, for as soon as we state it in those terms we have to recognize that though we do not know of any such process, we cannot exclude the possibility. For example, it is

A crisis apparition may take many forms: at Lowes Water in the English Lake District, in 1889, the Reverend G. M. Tandy sees only the face of his friend Canon Robinson. That same evening he learns that his friend has just died

conceivable that there exists a part of us which is continually scanning the universe like a radar beam, and is thus potentially aware of distant events to a degree to which we have no right to set any limits. In the course of scanning, it may pick up a signal – either a general distress call, or one aimed specifically at us – whereby our subconscious becomes aware that someone known to us is in a crisis situation. It would then present it to us in visual form. (We shall consider this scenario more deeply in Chapter 8.)

Though this super-psi scenario seems at first sight extravagant, there are, in the first place, good grounds for believing that in some circumstances individuals may acquire information to which in principle they should have no access. Countless cases of premonition (unless you prefer to ascribe every one to coincidence or delusion) suggest that some people, if not all of us, possess an intermittent precognitive faculty.

Secondly, the visualization of the event is entirely compatible with what we know of such other mental processes as dreaming and hallucinating, in which elaborate scene-setting and richly detailed storytelling can occur to a degree which goes far beyond our waking, conscious creativity.[33] So, whether or not we think them probable, we must accept that there are ways of accounting for the crisis apparition which do not require it to be initiated, or even contributed to, by the apparent. However, it is extremely difficult to apply this in every instance if only because of cases such as no. 168, where the brother's ghost clearly targets his sister (who doesn't see it) and is indifferent to the fact that it is seen by the nurse.

Most crisis apparitions either simply appear, providing no information whatever, or present the percipient with a more or less factual account of what is happening to the apparent, but this isn't always so. The playwright Ben Jonson, during a plague outbreak, 'saw in a vision his eldest son, then a young child and at London, appear unto him with the mark of a bloody cross on his forehead, as if it had been cut with a sword'. Subsequently, a letter from his wife told him their eldest son had died of the plague. Apart from the mark of the cross, which appears to have been wholly symbolic, 'he appeared to him of a manly shape [i.e. adult] and of that growth he thinks he shall be at the resurrection'.[34]

Some crisis apparitions incorporate messages to the percipient:

19. Mrs J. C. Smith. Durham, England, June 1879
'A friend was near her confinement. She told me she was afraid she
would die, saying "If I go, you will be very kind to my children" who
came to my school. I went into the county of Durham for a holiday.
While there I was roused from sleep by my friend, as I supposed. She
was shaking me, and saying, "I have passed away, but the baby will
live." Then the figure left the room by the door. The second time the
same thing happened: after speaking the figure went as if in a great
hurry. Running after the figure downstairs, I became convinced that
it was a vision. I went to my sister and related the incident. Next day
I received a letter saying that Mrs —— was dead but the baby was
alive.'[35]

Conceivably this could be due to clairvoyance on Mrs Smith's
part – she was, after all, aware of the confinement and the
mother's fears. On the other hand, the timing seems more than
chance, and the survival of the child is unlikely and unpredict-
able. Crisis apparitions that speak intelligently to the percipient
are rare, but here is another:

20. Juliette L. Exline. Los Angeles, CA, 29 August 1954
'My husband and one of his cronies had gone to Nevada on a fishing
trip. On the evening of the fourth day I became strangely apprehen-
sive. I went to bed early but had difficulty falling asleep. I must have
dozed off, however, only to wake in a cold sweat. Larry was calling
me! His voice was faint, as if he were calling from a great distance or
suffering great pain. In utter terror I jumped out of bed, turned on a
night light and stepped into the hallway. At its far end I saw him! He
was clutching at the wall, trying to stand up, and his clothes were
drenched with blood. "Dear God!" I screamed. "What happened?"
"Don't touch me, I have to go back." "Back where? Tell me what happened!" "I can't! No time – got to go back." "I'll call Dr Norris!" I
dashed to the phone but at that instant it rang. It was the sheriff of
Ely, Nevada, to tell me my husband had been killed in a car accident.
I hurried back into the hall – but Larry wasn't there.'[36]

The suggestion that the apparition has only a limited time to get
his message across is a curiously human one. Are we really
expected to believe that someone in such a predicament would be

limited, as if the authorities wish to keep travel expenses to a minimum? Yet crisis apparitions frequently act as though they are in a hurry and can't spare the time to linger. (See no. 120 for another example.) This case is remarkable, too, for the fact that the apparition seems to be as badly injured as the apparent, clutching the wall and trying to stand up. It is as though the victim has been transported in his actual state.

A further complication is that, though generally the apparition is of the person most directly concerned, this is not always the case:

21. Miss W. 1885
'One Sunday, during morning service at church, I looked up from my prayer-book and saw the figure of a man standing in what had been an empty seat opposite me. The appearance was that of an acquaintance, who from his seat in church was much given to staring at me. I had the impulse to say to my brother, "How could Mr —— have got there without our seeing him going across?" but restrained myself. When I looked again it was just not there. Only then did I realize that what I had seen was not real, and it gave me a shock. I heard afterwards that at that exact time he was at the deathbed of his mother, who died at the time I saw her son.'[37]

It seems plausible that the thoughts of the man, at this critical time, would turn to where he would normally be standing at this time, and he may even picture Miss W. whom he is given to staring at.

Here is a 'third-party' apparition of a different kind:

22. Miss S. Money. Redhill, Surrey, England, 27 February 1872
'Between 8 and 9 in the evening I was taking charge of the little daughter of a friend. I left the child sleeping in the bedroom, being absent about three minutes. On returning to the child's room, in the full light of the gas-burner, I distinctly saw, coming from the child's cot, a white figure which turned, looked me full in the face, and passed on down the staircase. I instantly followed, leaned over the banisters in astonishment, and saw the glistening of the white drapery as the figure passed down the staircase, through the lighted hall, and silently through the hall door itself, which was barred, chained and locked. I felt for the moment perfectly staggered, went

back to the bedroom, and found the child peacefully asleep. I related the circumstance to the mother immediately on her return late that night. She said that my description answered to that of an invalid aunt of the child's. Next morning came a telegram to say that this relative, who had greatly wished to see her niece, had died between 8 and 9 the previous evening.'[38]

This is an extremely revealing case, with important implications. The babysitter does not even know of the existence of the aunt, let alone that she is ill and anxious to see her niece: that the incident could originate with her is hardly a serious alternative. If we are desperate to avoid attributing the apparition to the aunt, currently at the point of death, we could hypothesize that the sleeping child provides some kind of telepathic link – but how feeble this is compared to an actual visitation of some kind on the aunt's part.

Ghosts of the present: living ghosts

A very trivial, yet very puzzling case:

23. Clara Giffing. USA, 1909
Clara Giffing, awakened after midnight by a strong wind, looks out of her bedroom window onto the moonlit garden where she sees their maid Lena come out of the house to take down the washing hanging there. Next morning she learns that Lena did nothing of the sort, but that she had lain awake for more than an hour during the night, feeling the washing ought to be brought in.[39]

At first sight this case seems good support for Sir Ernest Bennett who, introducing his 1939 survey of ghost cases, explains that he has included only a handful of living ghosts, since 'this phenomenon is usually explained as the result of telepathy, conscious or unconscious, between the person seen and the seer'.[40] This had been the view of the SPR-Group, who would certainly have proposed that Lena's anxiety somehow communicates itself to Clara, whereupon Clara hallucinates an apparition of Lena. Well, it may be that telepathy is somehow involved, just as a telephone is involved in passing a message: but as an explanation it leaves us standing. Why should Clara pick up this, of all the innumerable thoughts and ideas roaming the airwaves? Why should she make it the basis for a hallucination? We are going to find that while telepathy takes us some of the way towards explaining some kinds of ghosts, it assuredly doesn't take us *all* the way to explaining *all* kinds of ghosts.

It could be argued that we do wrong to make so much of the 'why' of such an event. Perhaps it is mere chance, Clara's subconscious plucks a passing idea at random – Lena's anxiety – and her subconscious playfully works it up into a little playlet . . . Well, maybe so, but here is a similar case with an added complication:

> 24. *Hamilton Boyd. Edinburgh, Scotland, 1891*
> Mr Boyd falls asleep in the smoking room of his club, and has a vivid dream in which he runs home, fearing he is late for dinner: he hurries upstairs, but halfway up the staircase, he looks down and sees his father looking up at him. At this point he wakes, and realizes it is after midnight and he should be getting home. He does so, and is surprised to find the household awake and about. His father, astonished to see him, asks did he not return home earlier, for he saw him rush into the house and hurry upstairs, at one point glancing down at him.[41]

Here again, telepathy may seem to be the vehicle; but that does not explain why this particular dream of all Hamilton's dreams should be communicated to others, and why it should take so powerfully visual a form. In Chapter 8 we shall see that there is an alternative and more plausible explanation.

We do not know if revenants know they are returning, or haunters know they are haunting, but it is certain that most living persons who are seen as ghosts are unaware of the fact until it is revealed by some circumstance which seems, ostensibly, to be no more than chance. We see this most clearly in the 'You are our ghost!' model, in which someone visiting a house is identified by its residents as the apparent whose ghost has visited them on previous occasions. Such cases have been reported sufficiently often to have acquired the status of folklore, but some, such as the Boulton case (no. 4) have good claim to be real experiences.

What makes these cases especially intriguing is that they involve two kinds of paranormal activity. On the one hand, it is ostensibly a ghost of the future, in that Mrs Boulton has foreknowledge of a house she will not visit until a later date; and on the other, she seems to acquire this knowledge not by clairvoyance, but by actually visiting the house in some kind of physical form, solid enough for her to be seen by its inhabitants and subsequently recognized. Then there is the puzzling complication that though Mrs Boulton's ghost is seen contemporaneously by Lady Beresford, her knowledge of the house relates to a time previous to the structural alterations.

The crucial question raised by living ghosts is, of course, How can someone be seen in two places at once? It is surely significant that Mrs Boulton was asleep at the time she obtained knowledge of the house. It would be helpful to know if all ostensible bilocations occur when the apparent is in sleep or some other altered state. It is certainly true of this famous case:

25. Mary Goffe. West Malling/Rochester, England, 4–5 June 1691
Mary, the wife of John Goffe of Rochester, being afflicted with a long illness, removed to her father's house at West Malling, about 14 kilometres distant. There she died. The day before her departure she grew very impatiently desirous to see her two children, whom she had left at home in the care of a nurse. Between one and two o'clock in the morning she fell into a trance: the widow Turner, who watched with her that night, thought her to be in a fit; and doubted whether she were dead or alive. The next morning Mary told her mother that she had been at home with her children. 'That is impossible, for you have been in bed all the while.' 'Yes, but I was with them last night when I was asleep.' The nurse at Rochester affirms, and says she will take her oath on't before a magistrate, that a little before two o'clock that morning she saw the likeness of the said Mary Goffe come out of the next chamber (where the elder child lay on a bed by itself), and stood by her bedside for about a quarter of an hour; the younger child was there lying by her. Her eyes moved and her mouth went; but she said nothing. The nurse, moreover, says that she was perfectly awake; she sate up in her bed and looked stedfastly upon the apparition, and a while after said, 'In the name of the Father, Son, and Holy Ghost,

what art thou?' Thereupon the appearance removed, and went away: she slipp't on her cloaths and followed, but what became on't she cannot tell. She confidently affirmed, 'If ever I saw her in all my life, I saw her this night.'[42]

Ghosts of the present: autophany and bi-location

To see one's own ghost is not so very rare an occurrence: the 'doppelgänger', 'double' or 'fetch' is a favourite literary device and has its counterpart in life. Though 'double' is sometimes used loosely to comprise all living ghosts and bi-location events, it is more useful when applied only to experiences where the percipient is also the apparent. Researchers Celia Green and Charles McCreery draw a further convenient distinction between *autoscopy*, seeing your own physical body while you are in an out-of-body state, and *autophany*, seeing an apparition of yourself while you are in your everyday physical state, which is what we are chiefly concerned with here.[43] This is a striking autophany from their collection:

26. Unnamed lady. Britain, 1951
A woman afflicted with a virus was prescribed a drug which seemed to make her worse rather than better. Lying in bed, 'I suddenly saw myself sitting on my bedside chair, dressed in a frock discarded quite a year before. I did not speak at all but myself in the chair told me that if I wished to recover I should stop taking the tablets at once or they might finish me off. It passed through my mind why bother if they finished me off. However, my chair self said that was a stupid thing to do and finally persuaded me to stop them immediately and tell the doctor, and then she disappeared. I told the doctor I had stopped them and he said "Good Heavens, quite right and I will give you something else!" This he did and I was back at the office in two weeks.'[44]

Doubles frequently manifest at moments of crisis, and generally bring useful information or warnings. But sometimes autophany occurs for no discernible reason:

27. Miss I. B. Britain, nineteenth century
A lady given to hallucinations, 'sometimes several times in a day, sometimes not for months' while a schoolgirl, sees an apparition of

37

herself sitting by her side. This recurs several times, the apparition being always seen on one side of her, and imitating all her movements. It is always accompanied by a sensation of cold and then of extreme weakness.[45]

Autophany is well known to psychologists, who link it to a variety of states: schizophrenia, temporal lobe epilepsy, delirium and depression are all possible conditions, and the *British Medical Journal* reports that of ten people who 'see themselves', six will have a serious psychiatric disorder.[46] This statistic can be questioned since there must be many cases which do not find their way into medical records. In any case, to show a link to certain psychological or pathological states, though interesting up to a point, does not explain why some people in such states have the experience while others don't, nor why they should have that experience and not another. Nor does it account for the content of the experience which, as in the case of the sick lady, involves some kind of self-diagnosis with a suggested course of action. In other words, even though medicine may recognize autophany as being in some cases a symptom of a particular state, all that tells us is that this state is one in which autophany is facilitated.

But what finally prevents us writing off autophany as a purely symptomatic experience is a case such as this:

28. Eva Roe (Mays). Redwood City, California, July 1923
'My husband Howard and I were invited to stay with my uncle Dick. No sooner had we fallen asleep than we heard heavy footsteps walking down the hall towards our room. At our door they ceased. After a short interval they began again at the far end of the hall and approached once more. The third time this happened Howard and I slipped into Dick's room by a connecting door and found him standing with his ear against the door to the hall. After a whispered conference we agreed to fling the door open the next time the footsteps approached. When the steps reached the door we threw it open. Dick flashed his light into the hall and all three of us saw what appeared to be Howard standing there, identical in every detail. As we stared in amazement from the living Howard to the other, the duplicate faded and was gone. Howard expressed bewilderment, even indignation, as if liberties had been taken with his person. Dick said it was most unusual for a man to see his own double. If another man saw it

as well, it meant that the double's counterpart was to die within the year. Moreover if a man saw his own double it meant he was going to die very soon. As Howard was only 23 and in the pink of health this seemed absurd. But one month later he went for a swim and was never seen again.'[47]

To Howard this was an autophany, to Eva and Dick a bi-location: yet all three were participating in the same experience. Whereas in most living-ghost cases the primary self is likely to be sleeping or in trance, Howard here is well aware of seeing himself: it is his normal conscious self which is the percipient, retaining awareness. The double may have been nothing more than a walking simulacrum, with no consciousness of its own, and perhaps the same is true of this case:

29. *Miss A. B. O. Scotland, 1889*
'I was 24 years old, in robust health, and not in anxiety or grief at the time. About 8–9 p.m. it being quite light, out of door, coming down a garden walk, I saw a figure approaching me which, on coming near, I discovered was the double of myself, except that the figure, which wore a white dress, had a charming smile. I also wore a white dress; the figure had black on its hands, gloves or mittens. I had neither. On holding out my hand to it, the figure vanished.'[48]

The difference in the clothing here is curious: and why the 'charming smile'? This next case comes closer than any other autophany to showing us what is going on, yet remains tantalizingly ambiguous:

30. *Boru. France, 22 January 1901*
Boru, an 18-year-old student, is working late one night preparing for a literature exam. Needing to check a reference, he rises from his worktable and goes into the adjoining room. He returns carrying the book in one hand, holding the doorknob in the other. Suddenly he sees himself already sitting at the table, writing the very words that are forming in his mind. Every detail of the scene is clear – the lamp, the table, books and paper. But what strikes him most forcibly is that he is simultaneously aware of standing at the door, feeling the doorknob in his hand, and of sitting at his table, pressing the pen to the paper. Not only can he see the other Boru, but at two or three metres' distance he can read what the 'other' Boru is writing. After a moment,

he moves forward, and as he comes to his chair, the second Boru vanishes. 'Perhaps Boru 1 and Boru 2 became reunited in a single being,' he subsequently speculates.[49]

Concentration on his work may have made Boru more open to this kind of experience, but there is a thought-provoking sidelight on the matter. The subject he was studying concerned a comparison between two characters in two separate plays by Corneille: could this have triggered the experience? If not, it's an intriguing coincidence.

Bi-location, where someone is observed in two places at once, is a staple of hagiographic literature, where it is counted as a sign of grace. Several saints have been credited with the gift, notably Antonio di Padova[50] and Maria d'Agreda.[51] The best-known secular instance is this:

31. Emilie Sagée. Neuwelcke, Latvia, 1845
32-year-old French-born Emilie is a teacher at a girls' school in Latvia, where she is seen on numerous occasions by her pupils in two places at once. Standing at the blackboard, a second Emilie will appear alongside the first, copying her movements precisely. A pupil faints one evening while being helped by Mlle Sagée to do up her dress – for in the mirror she sees two Mlle Sagées attending to her. Once, when the entire school are assembled in one room, working at their embroidery, all forty-two pupils see Emilie outside in the garden, picking flowers. When the teacher watching over them has to leave, her place is taken by Emilie, though they can still see the 'real' Mlle Sagée in the garden. Two bolder girls approach the seated figure and try to touch her; they find they can pass their hands through the apparition, but feel some resistance like soft material. Such incidents seem mostly to happen when Emilie is very earnest or eager in what she is doing. She herself is aware of what is happening, not because she feels any different herself, but because she sees others exchanging looks. She is a good and popular teacher, but eventually parents start to take their children away, and she is asked to leave. 'That makes the nineteenth time!' she exclaims, explaining that this has been happening to her ever since she started teaching at age 16.[52]

A similar case is cited in Chapter 8 (no. 182) when we consider the relevance of such incidents to the ghost experience. Note that in this case, as in no. 27, it is not only the apparent who is duplicated, but sometimes her actions too, whereas in other cases the apparition seems able to act independently.

In a sense *all* ghosts of the living can be described as instances of bi-location, for the alternate self is seen independently of the physical self. Mr Boulton could see his wife in bed while Lady Beresford sees her in her bedroom. Here is a very down-to-earth case:

32. Lavera Harris. Harrow, Ontario, 29 January 1969
'My husband William was confined to bed with bronchial pneumonia. My daughter-in-law and I were watching television, and I went to make coffee. As I entered the kitchen I saw William come out of the bedroom barefoot and in his underwear. He paused by the heater and then slowly went out the back door onto the porch. I was too shocked to say anything to him as I thought he might be sleepwalking. Or perhaps he wanted a cold drink of water from the covered can we kept on the back porch. Helen looked at me in surprise: she had seen he was in his underwear and was a little embarrassed. My foster son Jeff, then six, also saw William. When he did not return after a few minutes, I decided to check on him. He was not on the porch, so I went to get my coat from the bedroom closet to search outside. I was stunned to find him still in bed, and in his pajamas.'[53]

We can pigeonhole the great majority of living ghosts into one or other of these categories, but there can be wide differences between individual cases within those categories. The degree of lifelikeness, for example, varies enormously, so that ghosts may appear as anything from misty shrouded figures to entities so lifelike that the witness describes them as 'more real than real'. Feet may be seen or not seen; the clothing worn by the apparent may be recognized or not, and so on. The sick lady who sees herself in a discarded dress, the sick man seen in his underwear when his physical self is wearing pyjamas – what does this mean?

Do these discrepancies relate to the percipient's ability to visualize? That would argue for the view that ghosts are, in part or even in whole, mental artefacts created by the percipient – but then we have to reckon with those cases where there are additional witnesses. As with revenants and haunters, it is difficult to dismiss the possibility that some living ghosts possess substance of a kind, wherever their point of origin.

41

Ghosts of the future

Ghosts could visit us from the future without our realizing it, for the simple reason that we would not recognize them as ghosts. But some cases of precognition contain figures which are, in a sense, ghosts:

33. Mrs F. C. McAlpine. Castleblaney, Co. Monaghan, Ireland, June 1889
'I went for a walk by the side of a lake . . . I sat down to rest upon a rock, my attention quite taken up with the beauty of the scene. Presently I felt a cold chill creep through me, and a curious stiffness of my limbs, as if I could not move, and as if impelled to stare at the water straight in front of me. Gradually a black cloud seemed to rise, and in the midst of it I saw a tall man, in a suit of tweed, jump into the water and sink. In a moment the darkness was gone, and I again became sensible of the heat and sunshine; but I was awed and felt "eerie". About a week afterwards, a Mr Espie, a bank clerk (unknown to me), committed suicide by drowning in that very spot.'[54]

Here is a case which could well be in the next category – ghosts out of time – but does contain apparent foreknowledge of the future:

34. Wing Commander Victor Goddard. Drem, Scotland, 1935
Goddard, a senior officer in the Royal Air Force, was flying alone in a fighter biplane near Edinburgh when he got caught in a storm: to avoid it he dropped his altitude. As he broke through the cloud deck, he found the countryside beneath him in bright sunlight. Below him was an abandoned World War One airfield which he had visited the previous day. No question, this was Drem – he recognized the layout – but today, instead of the abandoned place he had seen, the scene was bustling with activity. Swooping over the field at an altitude of only 10 metres, he could see open hangar doors, vehicles, aeroplanes of different models, men at work. But he was surprised to see the ground crew wearing blue uniforms instead of brown, and the air-craft – including a monoplane he could not identify – painted yellow rather than silver. He made a second low pass over the field, and was surprised that no one looked up at him. A moment later he found himself in cloud again. Four years later, on the eve of World War Two, Drem reopened, with the buildings Goddard had seen, the ground

crew now in blue uniforms, with training aircraft – including the new Miles Magister monoplane – painted yellow.[55]

In principle, everyone that Goddard saw on the airfield was a ghost from the future. We can only wonder whether the mechanics at Drem ever saw the ghost of an obsolete biplane from the past swooping over them!

Another way in which ghosts relate to the future is as harbingers of misfortune, generally death or severe illness. Often the messenger is a folklore figure:

35. Unnamed nurse. Houston, Texas, 1960s
'Beside the bed [of an old lady] stood this tall figure dressed in a monk's robes with its head covered. He looked up at me when I appeared in the door. His face was a skull with tiny red fires for eyes. His hands, skeletal, were folded over each other inside the dark sleeves. My impression was that he was very patient, waiting.' [56]

36. Elizabeth Henderson. Los Angeles, California, 1932
'Grandpa was in hospital after a stroke. My father returned from the hospital, exhausted, and said he had to lie down. I lay down on the other bed. Suddenly the room felt different. I stared, unbelieving. A robed and hooded figure was standing at the end of the room, indistinct like thick smoke. While I couldn't actually see a face I could feel its eyes upon me. And somehow I sensed the specter's deep sorrow. I found myself dashing to the front door. To my amazement my father too was running toward the door. He had seen the figure just exactly as I had and he too had been aware of the aura of sorrow. The specter had turned and looked at him from beneath that hood . . . Grandfather died during the early hours after this spectral visitation.'[57]

In the next case the messenger is more human-looking, but surely the 'woman in black' can again be seen as a figure from folklore rather than real life:

37. Mrs Meadows. On train to Kansas City, Missouri, 1915
'When my mother was 22 years old, she took her mother by train to have a cancer removed. She was deeply worried, and unable to sleep. She was staring at the door at the end of the coach when a woman, dressed all in black, appeared, walked up to Mother and said quietly,

"I have come with a message for you." Mother had never seen the woman before and wondered what she possibly could have to say. The woman bent slightly toward Mother and said, "I have come for your mother. I will come for you later." Then she turned, walked to the end of the coach and out the door. Mother turned to a woman in the seat behind her and asked, "Did you see the woman who was just talking to me?" The woman had not seen anyone, and another passenger also said she had seen no one. The operation was unsuccessful, and Grandmother passed away a short while later.'[58]

It is noteworthy that in these instances the message is directed not at the person most involved, but at close relatives. So with the next case, but with a fascinating sequel:

38. Mrs Laurent. Sturgeon Bay, Wisconsin, 1918–1919
[Her daughter Harriet writes:] 'About 10 a.m. on 8 July 1918 my mother saw my brother Thomas [then serving in France] walk into the house with a duffle bag in his hand. He smiled at her and said, "Mom, I'm home." She rushed to greet him, but when she reached the spot he was gone. Three days later came a telegram to say he had been killed in action. One year later Father fell ill. Once again Thomas appeared to Mother, carrying the same duffle bag, and said, "Sorry, Mom." That night Father died. Three months later my four-year-old brother had convulsions. Once again Thomas appeared to Mother. She knew then that my little brother would not last the night. He died that evening.'[59]

Thomas, having announced his own death, seems to become a messenger on behalf of others, a kind of family bearer of bad tidings. Did Thomas himself choose to play this role? Or did his mother's subconscious, seeing what a good job he made of announcing his own death, decide to employ him on subsequent occasions?

A favourite form of family legend is a creature which announces a death in the family. Readers of Beerbohm's *Zuleika Dobson* will recall the two black owls who perch on the battlements throughout the night hooting and at dawn fly away none knows whither.[60] But, as Julian Franklyn observes, 'traditional ghosts are in the main rather purposeless, unless the function of presaging the demise of his lordship be considered useful; but the gentleman could surely be relied upon to depart this life without "being called for".'[61] Ghosts warning of impending misfortune are generally seen as kindly spirits breaking the news gently so that those concerned can make appropriate preparations. But we should entertain an alternative view, that this is a premonition on the part of the soon-to-be-afflicted person, or a close associate: the premonition is cast in visual form as a guarantee that the information is sound. In this case, the messenger may correspond to the percipient's own notions of a bringer of bad tidings, and we should not be surprised at such an apparition as this:

39. Nellie O'Brien. Bridgewater, Massachusetts, summer 1944
'My daughter Winifred had a tonsillectomy, then came down with complications. During the night I awoke with a start, hearing my daughter cough and then scream. I was terrified to see a huge black shape hovering over one side of my bed. It had no face, no figure. It was like a huge bat, with wings outstretched, covered with a dark shroud. It seemed to emanate evil. I landed on the rug on the other side of my bed and stood there rigid, willing it to go. Gradually it shrank, faded and disappeared in the shadows. Winifred was moaning with pain: she had an abscess in her lung, requiring months of operations.'[62]

Ghosts out of time

Of all ghost experiences, probably the most fascinating are those which seem to defy the limitations of time. We have already noted one instance of the *vardøgr* (no. 6): here is another, coincidentally from the same year:

40. Mrs McCahen. Grand Canyon, USA, 4 September 1956
'Last year my husband and I went to the Grand Canyon. The first evening I saw a woman walking up to one of the cabins, about 3 to 5 metres ahead, with a man and a boy carrying the luggage. I turned to my husband and said, "There is Mrs Nash, a lady I served jury duty with a year ago. Her husband has one arm. But I will see her in the morning, as she is probably tired." The next day I saw her sitting on the veranda, and I went to talk to her. Our husbands met each other and we had a pleasant chat until I mentioned I had seen her the

evening before. Mr & Mrs Nash both looked astonished and said they had just gotten there with a busload of tourists. He doesn't drive far, because of his arm. We had no idea the Nashes were going to be at the Grand Canyon.'[63]

We can only speculate what Mrs McCahen would have encountered if she had chosen to follow the Nashes to their cabin to renew her acquaintance then and there. Would they have simply vanished?

The best known of all out-of-time cases is this:

41. Annie Moberly and Eleanor Jourdain. Versailles, France, August 1901
Two teachers visit the gardens of the Palais de Versailles, outside Paris. Though they say nothing to each other at the time, later they agree they both felt they had an uncanny experience in the course of their walk. They write down their impressions, which include many details which resist identification with the park as it is: subsequent research seems to confirm their feeling that they travelled back in time to the period in the late 18th century when Marie Antoinette was living there.[64]

While the circumstantial detail, which includes several human figures, buildings, implements and even music that they heard, seems to support some such interpretation, the case remains controversial, and there have been persuasive attempts to explain it away altogether.[65] However, there is one thing that no rationalization can dismiss: the teachers' own conviction that they experienced something unusual during their walk.

The Versailles adventure is by no means unique: investigator Andrew MacKenzie has compiled a collection of time-slip cases which he has researched, which tell of people finding themselves in places not as they are, but seemingly as they once were.[66] Unfortunately, such experiences are difficult to substantiate: the subjective impressions of the percipients are all very well, but everything stands or falls by the details of the scene which the percipient could not reasonably be expected to know – and there is always the chance he may have seen an old photograph and subconsciously remembered it. So long as cryptomnesia (unconscious memory) remains a possibility we cannot conclude that time travel has taken place.

A feature of these time cases is that the ghost comes complete with a full set of stage scenery. Instead of seeing an isolated figure the percipient herself seems to be carried back to an environment of an earlier date:

42. Mrs Coleen Buterbaugh. Wesleyan University, Lincoln, Nebraska, 3 October 1963

Coleen, who works at the university, has to deliver a message to a room she has never previously visited. 'As I first walked into the room everything was quite normal. About four steps in, a strong odor hit me – the kind that simply stops you in your tracks and almost chokes you . . . I felt there was someone in the room with me . . . it was then that I was aware that there were no noises out in the hall. Everything was deathly quiet. I looked up and there she was. She had her back to me, reaching up into one of the shelves, and standing perfectly still. She wasn't at all aware of my presence. She was very tall, with a bushy bouffant hairdo, a long-sleeved white blouse, and a full ankle-length dark skirt. While I was watching her she never moved. She was not transparent and yet I knew she wasn't real. While I was looking at her she just faded away, her whole body all at once. I had the feeling there was a man sitting at a desk to my left: I turned around and saw no one, but I still felt his presence. Then, when I looked out the window, there wasn't one modern thing out there. The street was not even there and neither were the new buildings, just open field. It was not until I was back out in the hall that I again heard the familiar noises. This must have all taken place in a few seconds.' [Later, she saw photographs that enabled her to tentatively recognize the figure as a Clarissa Mills who had worked there from 1912 to 1936 (and who coincidentally had died in an adjoining office at about the same time of day) and a view of the college in 1915 which matched what she had seen.][67]

No question here of anything so simple as a waking dream. Coleen was physically in that building, she went into a room which materially existed in 1963 – except that when she went into it, she seemed to see what she might have seen in 1915. Psychological tests suggested that she might have been predisposed to a psychic experience of this kind, and pointed to associative links that could have helped to determine the nature of the experience. So there may be some 'enabling' factors which made it possible for an experience *of some kind* to occur; but that by no means explains why this particular ghost experience should happen to this particular person on this particular day. It's not as though any traumatic event were replayed: just a woman reaching to a bookshelf, something she doubtless did every day. So why *that* day?

Ghosts out of time: aerial battles and other events

All these time cases present something more elaborate than a straightforward apparition, but some go further still, reproducing complex events:

> 43. *The battle of Edgehill. Warwickshire, England, 24 December 1643 and later*
> The first major battle of the English Civil War took place at Edgehill on 24 October 1642. Two months later, between 12–1 a.m., shepherds and travellers are astonished to see a battle staged in the sky above their heads, including soldiers fighting, the discharge of muskets and cannon, horses neighing: this continues for up to three hours. The spectacle is repeated the following night (Christmas night) and this time it is seen by more educated persons: Samuel Marshall, a minister, and William Wood, a magistrate, are among those who testify. In all, the scene is repeated eight times, the fighting seeming to get fiercer on each occasion. When King Charles I hears of this, he sends three of his officers to investigate. Not only do they confirm the sighting, but they testify under oath to recognizing some of their brother officers, including sir Edmund Varney who was killed in the fighting.[68]

Note that the action changes with successive performances: it isn't a mechanical replay like a television repeat. It is tempting to see this vision as some form of mass delusion, triggered by the battle itself and perhaps coinciding with an unusual atmospheric phenomenon. Aerial signs and portents were dear to early cultures, which interpreted meteors and eclipses as divine signs. A spectacular thunderstorm might trigger a hallucination of an aerial battle – but *eight* thunderstorms? And seen by so many people, night after night? Would the king take time off from waging a war to send two of his officers to look into an old wives' tale? In those days, a testimony under oath carried some weight.

That the pilot of a crashed aeroplane (no. 9) should reappear is difficult enough to believe; the ghost of the aeroplane itself stretches our credulity to the limit, even after Goddard's visionary airfield and the phantom scenery of Versailles. Yet otherworldly coaches, trains, cars, sailing vessels and yes, aircraft have been seen under circumstances which rule out illusion; they too seem to involve a displacement in time:

Battles in the sky such as this 1507 example were quite often reported in the Middle Ages, but few can be related to a particular event: in 1643, however, the battle of Edgehill is so lifelike that individual participants in the battle can be identified

44. Tony Ingle. Derbyshire moors, England, 5 May 1995
A postman sees a World War Two aircraft flying low, but silent. Expecting to see it crash, he hurries to the scene, but finds nothing. Investigation reveals that an American Dakota crashed in that area on 24 July 1945, killing all aboard. Other, similar sightings have been reported from the same area.[69]

Ghosts out of time: archetypal ghosts

45. Lucille Harbour. Anderson, California, 1930
[The household had on several occasions been disturbed by sounds and other phenomena which they blamed on an entity they named 'the Thing.'] 'About daylight I woke up, and started to reach for the alarm clock, this thing was bending over me, with its face not more than 15 cm from mine. I screamed and it floated toward the outside door. It went right through a table and the closed door. It was dressed in black with a sort of hood over its head. Where its face should have been there wasn't anything.'[70]

We have already noted certain types of apparition which appear to have no individual identity, but seem rather to be generalized types. The temptation is to categorize them as fantasies employing folklore stereotypes or Jungian archetypes, such as we shall be considering in Chapter 5; but we shall also see that, like warning ghosts, they sometimes provide specific and generally true information.

The fact that Lucille's apparition occurred at the time of waking encourages the thought that it was a hypnopompic vision (a particular type of dream which occurs at the time of waking from sleep), which in turn could be seen as supporting the archetype explanation, but that still doesn't explain why it took this form. Moreover, not all traditional ghosts of this kind are seen at night or while waking; they are also seen out of doors and in daylight. When four people see such a ghost simultaneously, something more than subjective fantasy is surely involved:

46. Ethel, Freda, Mabel, Elsie Bull. Borley, Essex, England, 28 July 1900
Three daughters of the rector of Borley are returning home through the Rectory grounds when all three simultaneously see a female

figure with a bowed head. She is dressed in black, like a nun, and seems to be telling her beads. The figure is slowly gliding – rather than walking – and looks intensely sad and ill. The girls run to fetch their sister Elsie from the house: as she approaches the figure, it stops and turns towards her. Elsie stands on the lawn terrified, and the figure vanishes. It is seen again the following day, leaning over the garden gate, by Ethel and the cook, and subsequent sightings are claimed from time to time for nearly 30 years. During spiritualist seances in 1937 a spirit purporting to be a nun named Mary Lairre claims to have been strangled there in 1667, but alas, independent confirmation is lacking.[71]

The most puzzling of all ghost photographs seems to belong to the 'cowled monk' category:

47. Reverend and Mrs Hardy. The Queen's House, Greenwich, England, 19 June 1966

The Reverend R. W. Hardy and his wife, of British Columbia, Canada, are visiting England and touring the historic buildings of Greenwich. They wish to photograph the famous Tulip Staircase in the Queen's House (designed by Inigo Jones for Charles I's queen Henrietta Maria). Because visitors are not allowed on the staircase itself, they have to photograph it from below. When the film is developed, a shrouded figure – or perhaps two – seem(s) to be ascending the staircase, clutching the rail. Needless to say, neither saw anything of the sort at the time. Mrs Hardy states, 'I was free to watch for any possible intrusion of anything visible during the exposure time. Actually, a group of people who noticed our preparation apologized and stepped back . . . no person or visible object could have intervened without my noticing.'[72]

No explanation has ever been found for this extraordinary photograph. The film has been professionally examined: the frames before and after, taken during the same visit, are normal. No other visitor or museum staff have ever reported such a figure, and obviously the group who waited for the exposure saw nothing. The possibility that a person so remarkably dressed could have appeared on the roped-off staircase without anyone noticing defies belief.

Photographs of ghosts are rarely convincing, but this is the most enigmatic ever taken. The Reverend R. W. Hardy, of White Rock, British Columbia, Canada, visiting the Queen's House, Greenwich, England, on 19 June 1966, takes a photograph of the Tulip Staircase. When the film is developed, two shadowy figures are to be seen mounting the staircase, though none was seen at the time either by Hardy or his wife, or by two other visitors who waited for the photo to be taken. Previous and subsequent frames on the roll are of other parts of the Maritime Museum: there seems no way in which it could be manipulated. No such figures have ever been seen there before or since, and no plausible explanation has been offered: the photo resists all attempts to show it up as a hoax

Ghosts and poltergeists

It is usually possible to distinguish between ghosts and polter-geists, and it would only complicate our exploration of the ghost enigma to grapple with the poltergeist experience as well. But nothing in the paranormal world is clear-cut, and although today poltergeists are classified as Recurrent Spontaneous Psycho-kinesis (RSPK), and generally seen to be triggered by a disturbed individual – commonly a stressed adolescent – it does sometimes happen that a ghostlike entity is seen along with the physical phenomena. Scott Rogo investigated a case in which 'shadowlike apparitions' were seen in association with poltergeist phenom-ena,[73] and here is a French example:

48. *Sabourault family. Poitiers, Bournand, Loudun, Yzeures, c. 1877–97+*
A builder and his wife and several children are plagued with polter-geist-type phenomena – sounds, movement of furniture, smashing of crockery and ornaments, footsteps, levitation, ejection from bed, etc. – over a period of twenty years and more. Most of the phenomena are auditory or physical, but during the early stages of the persecution the father sees the image of a young woman who slowly crosses the bedroom. She is visible for two or three minutes: young and beauti-ful, wearing a white tunic, with loose hair hanging on her shoulders. Then she simply vanishes. His young daughter Renée one night sees a luminous head at the foot of her bed, which from her description is taken to be a deceased uncle whom she has never met.

An interesting aspect of this case is that the manifestations follow them from home to home, manifesting in four locations: more, if you include similar happenings when Renée – who seems in the latter stages to have taken over the role of focus from her mother, round whom they originally seem to be centred – goes to stay with family friends. Clearly it is the family, not the location, which attracts the manifestations.[74]

The apparitions and the physical phenomena are surely somehow connected: perhaps the same psychological factors which unleashed the poltergeist phenomena also made the Sabourault family unusually suggestible, enabling apparitions to manifest also. Something of the same kind may have occurred in this classic case:

49. Procter family. Willington, Tyneside, Northumberland, 1834–47
Joseph Procter kept a detailed record of the disturbances experienced
by his family on an almost nightly basis in their house which adjoins
a flour mill. The phenomena include several apparitions including a
female figure in a transparent white garment, a priest-like male in a
white surplice who passes to and fro in front of a window for ten
minutes, another man, a disembodied white face, and a monkey-like
figure. More frequent are the noises, including footsteps and a sound
like dragged furniture in empty rooms; disjointed spoken words and
phrases; sounds resembling a clock winding, a bullet hitting wood;
sensations of cold; beds raised and feelings of pressure on people in
bed. There is a tradition that the house is haunted, yet the previous
occupants experienced nothing. After sticking it out for thirteen years
(!) the Procters finally give up and abandon the house: subsequent
occupants see an apparition and hear sounds, and one other family
leaves on account of the disturbances.[75]

Periodically, attempts were made to investigate the phenomena,
and a number of hypotheses were tested, many of them based on
the adjacent mill and a nearby railway. But no satisfactory explanation was ever found.

Ghosts and animals

Ghosts are associated with animals in two ways: ghosts *of*
animals, and ghosts sensed *by* animals. Countless stories of
animal ghosts have been recorded. The vast majority are revenants – that is, favourite pets manifesting after their deaths. Since
most of us jib at the idea of animals choosing to return as ghosts,
which would seem to be an undertaking more purposefully intelligent than anything they did during their lifetime, the conclusion must be that they are fantasies produced by their grieving
owners. But a case like this raises awkward questions:

50. Mary Bagot. Menton, 24 March 1883
Mr Bagot, wife Mary, their two daughters and a cousin, are holi-
daying at the Hôtel des Anglais in Menton. This evening they go
down to dinner. Suddenly Mary sees her dog run across the
dining-room, and without thinking, exclaims aloud, 'Why, there's

Judy!' – only to remember, a moment later, that it can't possibly be Judy, left behind at their Norfolk home. Could she have mistaken another dog for Judy? The waiter tells them there is no dog at all in the hotel, let alone a black-and-tan terrier who could be taken for Judy. Four days later, Mary receives a letter to say that Judy had gone out with the gardener as usual one morning, apparently perfectly well, but at breakfast-time was suddenly taken ill and died within the half-hour. 'My impression is that she had died the day I saw her'.[76]

Only Mary knows the layout of the dining-room; only she could 'stage' the event. But she has no conscious reason to think her dog is ill, no reason to be thinking about Judy, let alone imagine her running across the room in this lifelike fashion. So this is a two-stage operation: first, the obtaining of the news, presumably by psi on Mary's part; and second, the visualization, which seems an unnecessarily complicated way for Mary's subconscious to alert her conscious mind to Judy's fate.

At least in that case the dog is known to the percipient. This next case is stranger still, because the animal is, and remains, unrecognized:

51. Mrs Greiffenberg. Germany, 1884
'We were sitting at dinner at home as usual, in the middle of the day. In the midst of the conversation I noticed my mother suddenly looking down at something beneath the table. "I wonder how that cat can have got into the room?" I was surprised to see a large white Angora cat beside my mother's chair. We both got up, and I opened the door to let the cat out. She marched round the table, went noiselessly out of the door, and when about halfway down the passage turned round and faced us. For a short time she stared at us, then she dissolved away, like a mist, under our eyes.

We had no cat of our own, nor knew of any that would answer to the description, and so this appearance made an unpleasant impression. This impression was greatly enhanced by what happened in the following year, 1885, when we were staying in Leipzig with my sister. We had come home one afternoon from a walk, when, on opening the door of the flat, we were met in the hall by the same white cat. It proceeded down the passage in front of us, and looked at us with the same melancholy gaze. When it got to the door of the cellar (which was locked) it again dissolved into nothing. On this occasion also it was first seen by my mother, and we were both impressed by the uncanny character of the appearance.'[77]

That the same cat is seen in two different locations suggests that it is haunting a person rather than a place, and the fact that the mother sees it first on both occasions suggests that she is that person. Yet the mother does not recognize the animal, and the apparition seems meaningless. For a moment, we are tempted to think in terms of reincarnation: could a relative have been reborn as a cat? Nonsense . . . but what better explanation comes to mind?

During the classic Abbey House haunting, phantom animals were seen by various members of the family on several occasions:

52. *Mrs Lawson's daughter. Abbey House, Cambridge, England, 1908*
'My youngest little girl asked me once about it, as I was putting her to bed. She said: "Sometimes after you go down again at night, Mummy, I see a lot of little brown things walking in at the door and round the room: do you think they is wolfies?" I assured her they couldn't possibly be wolves and suggested it was our brown cat – but she was quite sure it was not and said there were lots and lots of them and all brown. As soon as she was sure that they were not wolves, she was perfectly happy to go on seeing them and never seems the least afraid of going to bed alone.'[78]

Ghosts? We are on the fringes of folklore, poltergeists and imaginary companions here – demonstrating yet again that there are no hard and fast boundaries in the world of apparitions.

Ghosts sensed by animals

The fact that ghosts are frequently sensed by animals is one of the strongest testimonies to their material reality. While we can devise all kinds of theories to show that that ghosts are figments of the human imagination, we have to allow them at least a foothold in the material world if they are detected by animals. Even this *can* be avoided, of course: we could propose that the animals are picking up the percipient's thoughts, so when she sees a ghost on the staircase, the clever creatures know they too must look in that direction.

But in a case like the next, it does seem more plausible that they are sensing something that is actually there:

53. Daniel Amosof. St Petersburg, May 1880
'One evening about 6 p.m., my mother was in the salon with her five children, of whom I, aged 16, was the eldest. An old servant was in the room, talking with my mother. Suddenly our dog Moustache rushed to the stove, barking furiously. We all saw, on the rim of the huge tiled stove, the figure of a boy aged about 5, in a shirt: we recognized André, the son of our milkwoman. The figure left the stove, passed over our heads, and vanished through an open window. All this time – about 15 seconds – the dog barked with all its might, running to follow the movement of the apparition. Subsequently we learnt that André, who had been ill, died at about that time.'[79]

This seems a clear case of an animal which is totally aware of an apparition seen by seven people. Any explanation in terms of telepathy or subjective hallucination communicated to all those present, dog included, is straining the psi theory beyond reasonable limits. Unless we accuse Amosof of concocting a fiction, the conclusion that there was 'something' physically there, and moving across the room, seems beyond any reasonable doubt.

In this chapter we have separated ghosts into a number of broad categories, and we have seen that even within those categories there are all manner of differences – and it would not be difficult to find many, many more.

Even at this early stage of our inquiry it is clear that, though some apparitions can be attributed to the percipient alone, a great many others seem to display some degree of external participation. Even an apparition which on the face of it looks as though we could classify it as folklore or a wish-fulfilling fantasy often offers indications that something more is involved.

Chapter 3

THE PROCESS OF THE GHOST EXPERIENCE

Science recognizes no process that would result in seeing a ghost. Hallucinations, yes: but not a ghost of the kind our witnesses describe. On the other hand, there are known processes which may account for one phase or another of the ghost-perceiving experience. If we piece them together, they may take us some way towards understanding the whole.

Yet we must resist the temptation to impose patterns on ghostly behaviour. The authors of the SPR's 1894 *Census of Hallucinations* noted:

> Most visual hallucinations represent human beings, and most of these resemble human beings of the present day in all respects. Phantoms, both recognized and unrecognized, generally appear in ordinary modern dress. When they move, which happens more often than not, the movement is almost always such as we are accustomed to see. The phantom stands on the ground and appears to walk along the ground, and seems to leave the field of vision as a human being would, by walking out of an open door or passing behind some obstacle.[80]

Yes, this is generally true: but even among the cases cited in this book, exceptions can be found to every one of their assertions. It would be helpful if ghosts would stick to a uniform pattern of behaviour, but they don't. Indeed, the moment we think we have established a rule of ghostly conduct, an exception presents itself. And if we are to account for the ghost experience we must account for the minority of exceptions as well as for the majority who conform to the stereotype.

Do we have to account for *every* sighting, however bizarre? Perhaps not: we can reasonably suppose that *some* of the exceptions have their origin in pure fantasy on the percipient's part, faulty observation or embroidering the facts to make a good story. But we should, by and large, give our percipients the benefit of the doubt; we should start from the premise that they are honestly reporting what they think they experienced. In constructing our model of what could account for those experiences, therefore, we must take note of every detail. Is it significant, for example, that ghosts are sometimes described as trying to speak, but failing, as in the Benton case (no. 96)? Yes, because even that tells us that apparitions can't necessarily do what they would like to do, and that in itself warns us not to take it for granted that every ghostly manifestation turns out as intended. Perhaps the ghost is making his first appearance as a ghost, and is nervous, or has only an imperfect idea how to go about it; or he may know what he should do, but not be able to do it very well. Perhaps it takes practice to succeed as a ghost.

There seems no limit to the things ghosts can do, and we certainly have no right to impose any. So before we start searching for explanations, let us look at some of the things ghosts are reported as doing. Any explanation we offer for ghosts in general must be able to account for the behaviour of ghosts in particular.

At least one specific case is cited in support of each of these behaviours; in many cases, of course, hundreds could have been quoted.

A ghost is generally lifelike in appearance

If you ask a child to draw you a ghost, they will very likely offer you a shrouded figure with a cowled head, but though this popular stereotype (discussed in Chapter 5) occurs quite frequently, it is far from being the norm. The great majority of apparitions are so lifelike in appearance that they are often mistaken for the apparents themselves:

54. Dorothy Spearman. Calcutta, India, 19 March 1917

'I was either sewing or talking to my baby – I cannot quite remember. The baby was on the bed. I had a very strong feeling that I must turn round; on doing so I saw my brother Eldred. Thinking he was alive and had been sent out to India, I was simply delighted to see him, and turned round quickly to put my baby in a safe place on the bed, so that I could go on talking to my brother; then turned again and put my hand out to him, when I found he was not there. I thought he was only joking, so I called him and looked everywhere . . .' [Her brother died in France that day.][81]

Dorothy has no doubt she is seeing her brother in the flesh. She has no impression of the scene of his death or any other circumstance that might make her think his presence unreal. In the following case the appearance is again entirely natural; only the behaviour is unusual:

55. Mountford/Coe: Norfolk, England c. 1845

[The Revd. Mountford was staying with one of two brothers Coe who had married two sisters and lived about 2 kilometres apart.] 'The day was fine and clear. About 4 p.m. I stood at the window, and looking up the road I said, "Here is your brother coming." My host advanced to the window and said, "Oh yes, here he is; and see, Robert has got Dobbin out at last." Dobbin was a horse which, on account of some accident, had not been used for some weeks. His wife also looked out at the window, and said to me, "And I am so glad, too, that my sister is with him. They will be delighted to find you here" . . . Our friends passed at a gentle pace along the front of the window, and then, turning the corner of the house, they could no longer be seen. After a minute my host exclaimed, "What can be the matter? They have gone on without calling, a thing they never did in their lives before." Five minutes afterwards, the parlour door opened, and Mary, the daughter of the other household, entered and exclaimed, "Oh aunt, I have had such a fright. Father and mother have passed me on the road without speaking. I looked up at them as they passed by, but they looked straight on and never stopped nor said a word . . ." Ten minutes later, I, looking through the window, said, "But see, here they are, coming down the road again." My host said "No, that is impossible, because there is no path by which they could get onto this road, so as to be coming down it again. But sure enough, here they are, and with the same horse . . ." [This time they stopped at the house, and insisted they had not driven past ten minutes earlier.][82]

Note that the first sighting is not a preview of the second: the ghosts behave differently from their living counterparts, driving past the house and ignoring the daughter. But what are these ghosts playing at, behaving so utterly out of character? And what are we to make of Dobbin's ghost?

Sometimes the ghost displays an unreal feature. In the following case, the apparent is seen much younger than when last seen:

A lifelike apparition: Kathleen Leigh-Hunt is climbing the stairs of a house in Park Place, London, in July 1884, when a phantom housemaid appears, walking ahead of her: the figure is perfectly lifelike, and despite its uncanny manifestation it might be thought a living person, did it not vanish when it reaches the landing. No one else has ever seen it, so far as is known

56. Maria Beckleman. Santa Barbara, California, March 1930
'My mother had passed away a little more than a year earlier. I was
18 years of age and in bed with pneumonia. I was alone in my room,
feeling terribly low and wondering if I shouldn't just give up the
struggle to live. All of a sudden I felt a peculiar thrill. I looked up and
saw my mother standing at the foot of my bed, her hands resting on
the railing. She looked exactly as I remembered her from my childhood. The gray was gone from her hair and the lines from her face.
She looked much younger than when I'd last seen her.' [The ghost
encourages her to go on living.][83]

Possibly the mother means to add force to her mission by appearing at the age she had been when her daughter accepted whatever she said without question. In the Benoist case (no. 95) Marie
describes Hester as 'younger than I had ever seen', and we noted
in the previous chapter how Ben Jonson sees his son as he might
have grown up to be. Another such case:

57. Unnamed woman. Switzerland, twentieth century
'A very dear village woman had died and I was preparing to go to
her funeral . . . suddenly I felt I was not alone – I turned, and there
this woman stood behind me. She was transparent but perfect in her
glory and beauty. Her hair, grey in her lifetime, was wonderfully fair
and curled halfway down her arms. Her face was clear and white, her
eyes were shining, and her teeth in her smiling mouth were beautiful. Her dress was of an unearthly splendour . . .'[84]

And yet she was recognizable. Even if a ghost looks unreal, the
percipient does not hesitate to accept it: in the Frondorf case (no.
97), the percipient likewise sees that the ghost is transparent but
does not for that reason doubt its reality.

A ghost is usually 'seen' in much the same way as if it was real

In the great majority of cases the act of 'seeing' a ghost is, so far
as the percipient can tell, very much the same as seeing anything
else. It is, ostensibly, a physical action: the percipient has her eyes
open, and sees the figure in what seems to her a more or less
realistic way, even if what she sees is *not* realistic:

58. Captain Colt. 8 September 1855

[A fortnight earlier he had written to his brother Oliver that should anything happen to him while serving in the Crimea, Oliver would somehow manifest in his room]

'That night I awoke suddenly, and saw facing the window, by my bedside, surrounded by a light sort of phosphorescent mist, my brother Oliver kneeling. I tried to speak, but could not. I buried my head in the bedclothes, not at all afraid (because we had all been brought up not to believe in ghosts or apparitions), but simply to collect my ideas, because I had not been thinking or dreaming about him, and, indeed, had forgotten all about what I had written to him a fortnight before. I decided that it must be fancy, and the moonlight playing on a towel, or something out of place. But on looking up, there he was again, looking lovingly, imploringly, and sadly at me. I tried again to speak, but found myself tongue-tied. I sprang out of bed, turned, and still saw poor Oliver. I shut my eyes, walked through it, and reached the door of the room. As I turned the handle, before leaving the room, I looked once more back. The apparition turned round his head slowly and again looked anxiously and lovingly at me, and I saw then for the first time a wound on the right temple with a red stream from it. I left the room and went into a friend's room, and lay on the sofa the rest of the night.' [It was subsequently learnt that Oliver was killed that day.][85]

If the ghost were either a figment of Colt's mind, or an image telepathically transmitted by Oliver, there would be no necessity for it to disappear from Colt's (mental) view when he puts his head under the bedclothes: the fact that he ceases to see it suggests that there is something for him to *not* see! But of course his subconscious, or Oliver's, could deliberately make the image disappear to render the manifestation more lifelike.

Oliver's ghost is firmly located in a particular place – kneeling on the floor. When his brother looks away then back again, there it is, still in the same place: it does not move with Colt's eyes, but remains located as if it is really there. Similarly, an apparition will vanish when a light is put out, and be seen again in the same place when the light is relit:

59. Daniel Amosof. St Petersburg, 1883

Amosof, lying in bed unable to sleep, decides to smoke a cigarette. He lights a match, and is amazed to see the apparition of his dead grandmother sitting on a stool. Alarmed, he throws the match away: the room goes dark, he no longer sees his grandmother. Then, when his first alarm subsides, he strikes another match to light a candle, and there is the apparition again. Having lit his cigarette, he blows its smoke towards the apparition – a curiously disrespectful way to behave towards the ghost of your grandmother! – only to see the smoke divide on reaching the apparition and pass to either side of it.[86]

What would the ghost have done if Amosof had not decided to smoke? Just sat there in the dark, helplessly? Or would it have tried some other means of making its presence known?

But some apparitions don't seem to care about behaving naturally:

60. Mary Mitchell. Martin's Ferry, Ohio, 29 January 1949
Returning from a visit about 10 p.m., she feels she is being followed. When she stops and looks back she sees a sight which almost stops her heart. Hovering 60 centimetres off the ground is the figure of her father, who died five years earlier. He wears a light-colored, almost transparent gown that covers him completely except for his head. His likeness is visible for about 30 seconds, then fades away slowly until it is gone.[87]

It seems that the more the apparition interacts with the percipient, the more lifelike it is, and vice versa.

A ghost may be seen either collectively or selectively

The most impressive ghost experiences are those where two or more people perceive the ghost at the same time. The SPR-Group found that about one in ten of their cases were collective. They inclined to think that actually only one of those present is perceiving the apparition at first hand, as it were: his mind operates on the others, giving them the illusion that they too are seeing it.

But there is no good precedent for a *folie à deux* operating in this way. Granted, a person who sees a shadowy figure might conceivably convince his companions that they see it too; but when the ghost is described in detail this alternative becomes hard to accept. Other impressive collective sightings cited in this book are the Bull case (no. 2), Mr and Mrs P. (no. 114), and the Scott sisters (no. 167).

Sometimes the opposite happens: the ghost is seen by one of those present, but not by others. This is almost always the case with religious visions such as that of Bernadette Soubirous at Lourdes, and not infrequently occurs with ghosts:

61. Tony Cornell. Near Cambridge, England, summer 1967
Cornell, a senior member of the SPR and Cambridge University SPR, is invited to investigate a haunting. He and a colleague go to the house separately. Cornell arrives first, in the early afternoon – full daylight. Mrs M., a widow who lives alone, leaves the front door on the latch for the colleague, and she and Cornell go through the hall to the sitting-room, directly in line with the front door. Mrs M. explains that she is not troubled by the ghost but feels it is time it should move on. It is of a man aged about 60, with reddish hair, who is invariably first seen sitting in a particular chair, wearing a green jacket, holding a pipe which he does not smoke. Often, though not always, he rises and knocks his pipe out in the fire, turns and walks to the french window where he stands looking out into the garden. The entire operation lasts about 40 seconds. He has been identified as the previous owner of the house, who died in 1963. She last saw him three days ago. Leaving Cornell alone, she goes to make tea: on her return, she exclaims, 'Look! There he is in the chair.' Cornell turns but sees nothing. She describes the ghost as it rises and walks to the fireplace, where it turns and looks at Cornell. At this point the colleague appears in the hall, having let himself in by the front door. They walk towards him, but he brushes past, ignoring Mrs M.'s greeting, and asks, 'Where has the man gone?' He explains that a man wearing a green jacket had been standing with Cornell and Mrs M., and had beckoned to him to join them. Then he just seemed to vanish. He describes the figure exactly as Mrs M. did, though at this point he can have no idea how the ghost looks. Mrs M., though watching the ghost, does not see it beckon. She sees the ghost three more times during the next four months: Cornell, though he visits the house on four further occasions, never sees it.[88]

Tony Cornell is known to me personally as a shrewd, hard-headed investigator who would not fail to ask the appropriate questions. If he reports that this is what happened, then I have no doubt it did. Mrs M. sees the ghost, his colleague sees the ghost;

he himself doesn't. Moreover, the colleague sees the ghost do something which Mrs M. has never seen it do, i.e. beckon. That is to say, the ghost behaves naturally in relation to the immediate circumstance of the colleague's arrival. This is straining to the limit any hypothesis that the colleague, though not Cornell, is picking it all up from Mrs M.'s mind by telepathy. 'How P.D. saw something almost exactly as described to me by Mrs M., but also saw it beckon, which was not in the scenario created by Mrs M., remains an interesting mystery to me,' said Cornell.

Clearly, the issue is a crucial one. That some ghost experiences are collective seems to indicate that ghosts have an objectively real presence; that others are selective seems to indicate that they haven't. In this case, the sighting is both collective *and* selective. Though we could argue that the agent chooses that only some of those present shall see the apparition, this doesn't seem to square with the fact that Mrs M. sees the ghost looking at Cornell: apparently it is aware of Cornell's presence, but is perhaps puzzled by his failure to see it. And that failure, surely, must be ascribed to some quality that Mrs M. and the colleague possess but Cornell lacks. (Other selective cases in this book are Dr G. C. H. [no. 74] and Miss C. B. [no. 83]).

Of great importance is the fact that when a ghost is seen collectively, it is seen by each person in correct perspective. The churchwarden case (no. 1) is a fine example of the difficulty, which is well expressed by Tyrrell in his classic study of apparitions: 'It is not merely a feat of multiple *perception* which is performed in [collective] cases: it is a feat of *correlation* in which each percipient sees exactly the aspect of the moving apparition which he would see from his particular standpoint in space if the apparition were material.'[89]

Theoretically, it is possible that three people might be impelled, perhaps by psi operating between them, to simultaneously hallucinate an apparition of a person they are accustomed to see in a particular place. If so, it is reasonable to suppose that their subconscious, or whatever is responsible for creating the illusion, would stage-manage the hallucination to ensure that all see it from the correct perspective. None the less this is a somewhat cumbersome scenario, and though Tyrrell hesitates to proceed to the thought that the apparition may indeed possess objective reality, perhaps we should be more daring. Rather than think that all three who see the churchwarden are simultaneously sharing their own version of a hallucination, let us at least entertain the possibility that there really is a figure there, one possessing sufficient substance for it to be seen by the three percipients.

A ghost may change its appearance during the sighting

Most sightings are very brief, so it is not surprising that the ghost generally remains unchanged throughout. Yet there are exceptions:

62. Miss E. A. 1882
'It was a summer morning, about 4 a.m. I had been awake some time. I saw a figure standing by my bed. It was tall and dressed in something grey, falling in long folds. The face was kind and I was not frightened at first, but it suddenly changed and the whole figure and face, as it were, fell to pieces in the most ghastly manner and vanished.'[90]

63. Mrs L. H. March 1891
'I woke with a start, it then being early morning. On looking round the room, I distinctly saw the head of a skeleton floating in the air, about 30 centimetres from the ceiling. I gazed at it intently (being now quite awake), when I saw it gradually change to my mother's head and face and float away, seemingly through the ceiling.'[91]

Does the ghost change its mind? Or is whoever is creating it unsure what sort of apparition it wants to produce? Or are we being given a rare glimpse of the ghost-making process?

A ghost generally adapts to its surroundings

In almost every case, apparitions walk on the ground, pass round furniture, and adapt to their surroundings as though fully aware of them. A good example is the McKee/Meyer crisis apparition case (no. 169), where Mrs Meyer's ghost comes to a garden which the apparent never visited in her lifetime, and seats itself in a swing-seat which it proceeds to rock – indeed it is the rocking of the seat which alerts Louise to the ghost's presence. There is no normal way that Mrs Meyer could know of the seat's existence, or that Louise would be gardening within sight of it; yet the apparition makes itself at home in the most natural way.

Here is a remarkable instance of such adaptation to surroundings:

> 64. *Lorraine Dudzik's grandmother. Rosebud, Missouri, 14 February 1955*
> 'My grandmother and I usually went to the movies on Saturday nights. On this particular Saturday I heard her gasp, and saw that she had turned pale. But since she said nothing to me and the movie was just beginning I waited until we were on our way out, two hours later, to ask her what the trouble was. She replied, "My Aunt Bel who lives down in Texas has died. I know because I saw her come into the theater and sit down three rows in front of us. She turned her face towards me for a moment. She looked just like she did the last time I saw her. She was visible only for about three seconds, then she disappeared." Later that night a telegram arrived saying that Aunt Bel had died at 4.45 p.m. Grandmother had seen her in the theater at about 7.00 p.m.'[92]

and another which involves even more interaction with the real-life context within which it occurs:

> 65. *Unnamed Swiss woman. Zurich, Switzerland, 14 February 1938*
> 'My friend Trudy and I attended a horticultural college in England [where they became friendly with an English girl, Pat]. Two years later, when I was back in Zurich, I met Trudy at Pfauen Square at midday. As usual at this time, there was a lot of traffic. Suddenly in the crowd I caught sight of Pat. In spite of the warm weather she was wearing her old raincoat and hat. "Trudy, look, there's Pat! I'll call her." I ran across to the tram-stop where Pat was just getting into a No. 5 tram. I saw her take her seat but before I could reach the tram it started off. Trudy had not seen her. Some days later I received a letter from Pat's mother telling me that her daughter had been thrown from her horse and had broken her neck at midday that day.'[93]

What would have happened had the narrator been a faster runner, and managed to board the tram? What if the tram had been full and the conductor had waved Pat off? Was it Pat herself who planned the manifestation, or was some other being master-minding the little drama?

This next ghost seemingly fails to adapt to its environment – and worse, keeps on failing:

66. Eileen Rutherford. Farm near Mount Vernon, Illinois, about 1930
'The "'guest" first called one summer evening, after the family had retired. Suddenly the back door screen, firmly latched, opened and closed with a loud slam. A man's footsteps echoed across the kitchen floor. They continued into the living room where our ghostly visitor clumsily stumbled into the table, setting the table rocking and the china and silver clattering. After a few seconds he continued across the dining room, out the front door screen, which was doubly locked, and into the darkness. During the next two weeks the ghost paid

Lord and Lady V——, touring in Normandie about 1890, have to spend the night in a farmhouse: their night is disturbed by a sinister figure who enters and leaves through the locked door, and passes through furniture

nightly visits. He always made the same tour, never failing to walk into the table and to set the china and silver clattering. We never caught a glimpse of him in all the four years he spent passing through that house. We tried waiting in the adjoining room fully dressed and armed with flashlights, but he would not be heard until we gave up and went to bed. Then within ten minutes he would open the back door . . . his visits would continue for two weeks and then he would leave for ten days . . . He got to be a regular member of the family and even visiting relatives accepted him although he seemed a little shy and seldom walked on the first two or three nights of their visit. Then quite suddenly he left and never paid another visit.'[94]

Although it is never seen, the regular behaviour pattern qualifies this ghost as a haunter. But why doesn't it learn where the table is, and avoid bumping into it? Is that part of its 'act', or are the Rutherford family hearing some kind of pre-recorded loop?

A ghost may appear by forming from a luminous or misty shape

Although most ghosts appear, from the start, in their fully formed manifestation, quite a few make their début as a small luminous sphere, or as a misty or smoky shape which gradually assumes human form:

67. Mrs Gordon Jones. Anerley, England, Autumn, 1881
'A party of young people and myself determined on All Hallows' Eve to play at the childish game of sitting separately in dark rooms, with supper laid for two, with the intention of awaiting the appearance of a future husband or wife. Thinking the whole thing a joke, and not in the least expecting to see anything, I distinctly saw, first, a filmy cloud which rose up at the other end of the room, then the head and shoulders of a man, middle-aged, stout, with iron-grey hair and blue eyes – not in the least the picture which a young girl would *imagine* she saw on such an occasion.' [The man she subsequently married bore no resemblance to this apparition.][95]

Other examples of gradual formation are the Starnes (no. 15), Hooker (no. 102) and De Leon (no. 138) cases. There is an evident similarity to seance-room materializations, discussed in Chapter 5, also to the Schmidt-Falk case (no. 118).

In this interesting case the shape either returns a few days later or maybe never leaves:

> *68. E. Wayne Allen. South Bend, Indiana, 1946*
> 'When my grandmother died, I [aged seven] was sitting beside the bed. Suddenly she sat up in bed, coughed, then lay back down – very still. A puff of white smoke seemed to leave her body, float slowly across the room and out the open window . . . The night of the funeral, I was lying in bed when a light breeze swept over me. I heard someone call my name and when I looked up the puff of white smoke was alongside me. I started crying and calling for Mother, but the voice kept saying, "Don't be afraid, honey. It's me, Nanny." When Mother came to see why I was crying the puff of white smoke disappeared.'[96]

It would be easy to attribute this to imagination – but isn't this a rather sophisticated image for a seven-year-old boy to visualize?

A ghost is generally dressed naturally . . . but sometimes not

The vast majority of ghosts are dressed in a lifelike manner. The SPR *Census* includes four cases in which the phantasm appeared in the clothes in which the dead person was buried, and often the clothing assists recognition. But stereotype clothing, especially ecclesiastical, is also commonly reported. For example:

> *69. T——family. West Brompton, London, 1871*
> 'The figure was very tall, dressed in grey drapery which partially enveloped the head, though allowing the features to be seen. The drapery was shapeless – that is, it had no definite shape, such as that of a dressing gown or a monk's gown . . . the whole figure was shadowy and unsubstantial looking.'[97]

It may be asked, why should revenants wear clothes at all, a question we considered when looking at the honeymooners in no. 16. One percipient, though, sees naked ghosts on two separate occasions:

70. Sadie Pritchett. Shelbyville, Tennessee, 1940s, 1951
'When I was nine years old I saw a man, completely nude except for what appeared to be a loincloth, standing at the window in my sister's house . . . I called to Mother, she watched in amazement until the apparition disappeared . . . many years later as I sat near in my bedroom I suddenly noticed the nude form of a slim young man near an upstairs window in the home of a neighbor across the street. I wondered why on earth any one would be so uncouth as to walk around near a window with no clothes on. The figure seemed to be moving away from the window with outstretched hands, groping as if in a stupor.'[98]

Naked ghosts are extremely rare, but during the 1890s the Fanshawe home, near Montreal, Quebec, is haunted by this thin, naked ghost, which never reveals its identity or its purpose

The apparitions are tentatively identified as her grandfather and a nephew. While to see one nude ghost is rare enough, to see two is exceptional. Is there some quality in Sadie which encourages ghosts to appear to her undressed at windows?

A ghost may be clearly defined . . . or fuzzy

Though most ghosts appear in sharp, natural detail, there are many exceptions:

71. Sister-in-law of J. P. J. Chapman. Bampton, Devon, England, late 1920s
'One evening, after sunset, my wife's sister rode out onto the moor to see if some cattle had strayed. Having seen that all was well she was just about to leave the moor, through the gate which she had left open, when the horse suddenly shied. Nothing would induce it to pass through. After several attempts she decided to dismount and lead the horse through. This time as they reached the gate a curious luminous shape could be seen drifting nearby. It was like an elongated sausage, with baleful eyes: it was a greenish colour, about 25 centimetres across and 1.5 metres high. The whole thing seemed to be pulsating, from dim to bright. It was in a vertical position except for a sideways, wavering movement. To say the least, the girl was frightened but made up her mind to face it. Placing herself between *whatever-it-was* and the horse, she coaxed the animal through. When the horse was half way it broke loose and galloped down the lane for about 50 metres where it stopped and waited. The ghost was seen on several subsequent occasions, always in the same spot, and only when a horse *and* a human were present. It seemed quite harmless.'[99]

Is this an apparition trying to appear but not making it? Surely it wouldn't choose to appear in this obscure form? And what is the connection with horses: is this the ghost of someone who, living, was involved with horses?

A ghost may be seen in whole or in part

Probably a majority of ghosts are seen in full length, but sometimes only part is seen. This is usually the face alone, or the head and shoulders:

72. Mrs B. Ramsgate, Kent, England, 4 August 1837
'I distinctly saw my mother's face upon the wall: it smiled and passed along the wall and faded away. I afterwards heard that my mother died at that time in London.'[100]

But there are some curious exceptions:

73. Gail S. Detroit, 1965
Gail S., lying in bed, sees a 'misty shape' form at the door of her bedroom and then the figure of a man appears. But not all of him: 'I saw him from the waist to the neck: he had on a tie, a white shirt and a dark suit'.[101]

74. Dr G. C. H. Derbyshire, England, autumn 1870
'About 7 p.m. I was crossing Osmaston Park with my brother, and saw distinctly as it were two black legs walking towards us. The legs ended abruptly, absolutely abruptly. I could make out no body. The vision was most vivid. I had time to see them and stop walking, point to them, and say to my brother, "Look! There they are, two legs. Can't you see them?" He failed to see anything, and then they were gone.'[102]

75. Captain and crew of SS Watertown. *Pacific Ocean, 5 December 1924 and later*
While cleaning out the tanks on a fuel cargo ship, two sailors are overcome by fumes and die. Their bodies are buried at sea as the ship heads down the California coast towards the Panama Canal. The following day, the faces of the two dead men are seen in the water following the ship, and are seen almost continually thereafter. They appear about 3 metres apart and about 13 metres astern of the ship; they are seen for about 10 seconds, then vanish, to reappear later. Before the return journey, the captain purchases a camera and is able to photograph the heads.[103]

This is one of the strangest ghost experiences on record, and because it is so strange, we can't be blamed if we hesitate to accept it. None the less, the weight of testimony, and the existence of a photograph – for what that's worth – lend some degree of support.

A ghost's appearance may contain details unknown to the percipient

This is perhaps the most crucial of all attributes of ghosts, for the answer to the question, how could the percipient be aware of such detail without the assistance of some outward agency? leads to the wider question of how *any* of the information implicated in the ghost experience is transmitted (this will be discussed in Chapter 8).

76. Aimée Obalecheff. Odessa, Ukraine, 17 January 1861
'It was 11 p.m. and I was lying on my bed awake. My husband was asleep, and my maidservant, a former serf, was sleeping on the floor. Hearing my month-old son crying, I woke my servant and had her bring the child. She then sat on the floor stretching her legs beneath an armchair. I was breast-feeding my son, when I saw my sister's husband Nicolai come slowly through the door, dressed in slippers and a dressing-gown which I had not previously seen. He stepped

Two sailors on the American steamship Watertown, *Courtney and Meehan, die from fumes in the hold in December 1924, and are buried at sea. Soon after, their faces are seen in the ship's wake, and Captain Tracy is able to photograph the ghostly manifestation*

over the servant's legs and slowly sat in the chair. I said to the servant "Claudine, do you see?" and she answered, trembling with fright, "I see Nicolai Nilovitch". At these words, he slowly rose, stepped over Claudine's legs and left through the door. I woke my husband, and asked him to take a candle and follow the apparition into the salon. He went but found no one there. I said surely this meant that Nicolai had died at Tver, and had come to say goodbye. This turned out to be the case: he died at just that time. Subsequently we learnt that the dressing-gown we saw him wearing, and which he was wearing when he died, had been made only a week earlier.'[104]

A single tell-tale detail distinguishes this classic case:

77. Mr F. G. of Boston. St Joseph, Missouri, 1876
'In 1867 my only sister Annie, 18 years old, died suddenly of cholera in St Louis. My attachment for her was very strong, and the blow a severe one. [He subsequently became a commercial traveller.] I had 'drummed' the city of St Joseph, and had gone to my room at the Pacific House to send in my orders, which were unusually large, so that I was in a very happy frame of mind. I had not been thinking of my late sister, or in any manner reflecting on the past. The hour was high noon, and the sun was shining cheerfully into my room. While busily smoking a cigar, and writing out my orders, I suddenly became conscious that some one was sitting on my left, with one arm resting on the table. Quick as a flash I turned and distinctly saw the form of my dead sister, and for a brief second or so I looked her squarely in the face; I sprang forward in delight, calling her by name, and as I did so the apparition instantly vanished. I was near enough to touch her, had it been a physical possibility, and noted her features, expression, and details of dress &c. She appeared as if alive.

This visitation so impressed me that I took the next train home and related what had occurred. My father was inclined to ridicule me, but was amazed when I told them of a bright red line or scratch on the right-hand side of my sister's face, which I distinctly had seen. My mother rose trembling to her feet and nearly fainted: then with tears streaming down her face she exclaimed that I had indeed seen my sister, as no living mortal but herself was aware of that scratch, which she had accidentally made while doing some little act of kindness after my sister's death. She said she well remembered how pained she was to think she should have, unintentionally, marred the features of her dead daughter, and that unknown to all, she had carefully obliterated all traces of the scratch with the aid of powder, and that she had never mentioned it to a human being from that day to this. Yet *I saw the scratch as bright as if just made.'*[105]

The case was investigated by the noted researcher Richard Hodgson, who obtained affidavits from everyone concerned. The facts are hardly in dispute, but how we explain them is another matter. The primary question is: who is the agent? If Annie herself, why should her apparition suddenly appear on this once-only occasion nine years after her death? If it is the mother, the only living person who knows of the scratch, does the memory of the accidental happening suddenly come into her mind, and does the son somehow pick up on that recollection and use it as the basis for a fabricated apparition? And is it just coincidence that the mother dies a few weeks later? Has Annie appeared to announce her mother's shortly-to-happen death, whose early stages may be just commencing?

A ghost may be opaque or transparent, may reflect or not, cast a shadow or not

Are ghosts substantial? The majority occlude objects behind them, just like a living person, but transparent phantoms form a substantial minority – we have noted two or three already. Dr H. C.'s mysterious visitor (no. 5), which has blocked the view throughout the sighting, gradually fades so that the furniture behind becomes more and more visible. The SPR-Group account for this paradox as a partial failure of the process of hallucination, which they consider as a purely subjective process; yet they do not explain why, if the ghost is subjective, it should go through the material process of fading.[106] Perhaps the agents responsible for hallucinations do sometimes fail in their intentions, as might be the case when a ghost tries to speak but fails, but it is rather feeble to fall back on this as an explanation for something we don't understand.

Mirrors present us with a similar problem:

78. Louisa Du Cane and sisters. Britain, 1 November 1889, late evening
Four sisters go upstairs to their bedroom. Louisa suddenly sees the figure of a young man, wearing a peaked cap, gliding noiselessly

towards her from the next room. He continues to glide towards her sisters, two of whom first see the figure reflected in a mirror, before it appears in their line of vision; they exclaim at the same moment that Louisa sees it. The fourth sister Mary does not see it because she is looking the other way, but feels a cold air as it passes. (The figure does not call to mind anyone any of them has ever seen; it never appears again; is never accounted for.)[107]

Mrs Sidgwick, who investigated the case for the SPR, comments: 'It seems to me to have been a genuine and interesting case of collective visual hallucination.' She suggests that Louisa 'may have produced the hallucination in the others by suggestion' but admits there is no evidence that the sisters were unusually suggestible. She does not seem to find it of particular interest that Louisa's sisters see the ghost in a mirror, and makes no comment on it: yet if Louisa initiates the sighting, the suggestion she imposes on her sisters must include the fact that it is located where they cannot see it directly, only reflected in a mirror. This is carrying the telepathy–suggestion hypothesis to its limits.

But the ability to reflect certainly makes the apparition more lifelike:

79. Mrs E. Britain, June 1847
Mrs E. is alone in her house (which has the reputation of being haunted) sitting on the piazza which opens off the drawing-room, into which she has an uninterrupted view. Suddenly a female figure appears, and strides across the room, but always keeping its face turned away. The outline is clearly delineated, the dress so distinct that she remembers it forty years later. Casting her eyes on the mirror on the drawing-room wall, she sees the side or profile of the figure reflected there. So exceedingly real does this latter circumstance make it, that Mrs E., certain there is a strange woman in her drawing-room, rises and rushes into the room, saying 'I wonder how you got in, indeed!' only to find nothing there.[108]

So some ghosts reflect. Ah, but others don't . . .:

80. Mr W. G. D. Britain, 1893
Since January 1893, Mr W.G.D., four members of his family and a servant have all seen the figure of a tall, slight woman, unknown to

them, in various parts of the house; they get so accustomed to seeing it that on the whole they cease to give it much thought, except that four of its appearances coincide with a death in the family, suggesting that it is acting as a kind of messenger. One evening: 'I saw the door of my father's room was open, the gas full up, and standing before the dressing-table, resting her hands on it and gazing into the mirror, was the apparition. I stood still for a second, then moved to try to see past the figure into the mirror in order to get a view of her face . . . by moving a little to one side I could see very well into the glass, when what was my surprise to see there was no reflection.'[109]

We may wonder whether the apparition sees its own reflection. Here, to complicate matters yet further, is a ghost seen *only* in a mirror:

> *81. Anita Johnson. Elmira, New York, December 1961*
> 'My mother-in-law moved into an old home and found a dressing-table left behind. She said she didn't want someone else's junk and gave it to me. Three days later, while I was combing my hair before the newly acquired mirror, a young lady about 22 years old came up behind me. She was looking right at me in the mirror. Her dress was green silk, cut in the style of another era. I quickly turned to face her but there was no one there. Turning again to the mirror I saw her looking out at me. For an instant I was so afraid I could not move. Then I ran . . .'[110]

Another kind of reflection case is where the percipient is looking at her own face in a mirror, which gradually changes into someone else's: see nos. 133 and 188.

As the ghost of Mr P.'s father (no. 114) 'passed the lamp, a deep shadow fell upon the room as of a material person shutting out the light from us by his intervening body'.[111] So with this living ghost:

> *82. Miss A.S. Albemarle County, Virginia, before 1889*
> 'At about 11 p.m. at my grandmother's house, I sat leaning on the sofa-arm in the parlour. The shadow of a human form fell on the moonlit floor. Half turning my head I saw a tall woman dressed in white, her back to me. By the contour and the gleam of the plaits round her head I recognized my cousin, with whom I had just been talking, and deemed she had doffed her black dress to try a white one.

I addressed an ordinary remark to her. She did not reply and I turned right round upon her. Then she went out of the door, and as she disappeared I wondered I had heard nothing of a step or the rustle of her dress. I found my cousin with my grandmother, wearing her black dress. She said "I've been with grandmother since I left you."'[112]

On the other hand, some ghosts are specifically observed *not* to cast a shadow:

83. Miss C. B. Norwich, Norfolk, England, 31 December 1879?
'At 10 p.m. my sister and myself were walking home from a quiet evening with relatives. Quietly out of a passage came an old woman about 1.5 metres in height, wearing a large black shawl and a small poke bonnet. She walked before us some yards, exciting my wonder by her noiselessness upon the gravel path, and finally by the fact that she cast no shadow [despite plenty of gaslights]. Putting my hand upon my sister's arm I said "What a funny old woman," but with the movement of my hand she disappeared. My sister saw nothing.'[113]

Ghosts think nothing of passing through material objects. Rosina Despard, at Cheltenham (no. 14) places strings across the stairs, but the ghost walks through them without displacing them. The ghost of Mr P.'s father (no. 114) is seen by both percipients to leave their bedroom through the wall, yet despite that the husband insists on searching the house: in no. 160 both figures walk through the bed before disappearing through the wall. (Other cases are nos. 22 and 45.) But if ghosts can walk through furniture, why does the ghost in the Rutherford case (no. 66) bump into the furniture night after night?

A ghost may or may not be seen by its own luminosity

Whether haunters or revenants, some ghosts are seen in pitch darkness:

84. H. family. West Brompton, London, nineteenth century
'[The haunter] was never seen save in the dark, and would appear, therefore, to have been faintly luminous, for it was seen in all parts of the house, and sometimes in rooms almost entirely dark.' [114]

85. Unnamed woman. Switzerland, 24 December, early twentieth century
'When I was nine I lost my father . . . One Christmas Eve, many years later, I was overcome by stomach colic and had to stay in bed . . . my beloved father came towards me, shining and lovely as gold, and transparent as mist. He looked just as he did in life. I could recognize his features quite distinctly, then he stopped beside my bed and looked at me lovingly . . .'[115]

86. Miss H. Wilson. 'A long time ago' , before 1887
'I was lying asleep, or nearly so, when I felt a hand laid gently on my shoulder . . . I opened my eyes. No candle or lamp was in the room, it was quite dark; but close to my bedside stood, enveloped in light, a figure like my sister Alice . . . It stood for a few moments, then vanished, and the room was all darkness again.'[116]

Other ghosts need light to be seen, as in the Amosof case (no. 59); or they may vanish when the light is switched on, as in the Frondorf case (no. 97), or this:

87. Miss F. D. 1879
'I had been asleep, but awoke in fright. I saw two figures dressed in brown, monkish habits, with cowls over their heads, and long grey beards. They appeared to come out of a cupboard in my room and walk to the bedside. Opposite the bed was a recess in the wall, not deep, which was illuminated by a phosphorescent light. The apparition continued for some minutes, until I had time to light a candle, when it disappeared.'[117]

Ghosts can make sounds

'Phantom footsteps' are a standard ingredient of the ghost experience, and clothing may be heard to rustle if the apparition moves:

88. Mrs Polson. Probably 1850
'As I reached the top of the stairs a lady passed me who had some time left us. She was in black silk with a muslin "cloud" over her head and shoulders, but her silk rustled . . .'[118]

89. W. M. Ellwood, of Leominster. 1889
'I suddenly heard the door open, and saw a short figure in a night-shirt walk in and stand looking at me by the side of the bed. I distinctly heard a sound of breathing or rustling of the nightshirt . . .'[119]

Here the sound is directly associated with the ghost. Sometimes footsteps and other poltergeist-type noises are heard without any ostensible connection with the apparition:

90. The H. family. London, c. 1880
The house has the reputation of being haunted and the figure of 'a pale woman, in black, with an evil face' is seen by many in the household. Noises as of footsteps are heard not infrequently in the dusk and at night along one of the rooms in the building; these noises appear to pass quite close to the servant who hears them, but nothing is ever seen. Other strange noises, as if someone is digging, are constantly heard in a parlour on the ground floor. These noises are heard by two or three persons at a time, either at night or in the daytime. No natural origin can be assigned for them.[120]

A ghost may perform a physical action . . . but if so, the action is trivial

This is the most provocative thing a ghost can do to establish its objective reality, for if, as most theories hold, ghosts have no material substance, it is inconceivable that they should perform material actions. But this ghost seems to have had a dislike for fresh air:

91. Ralph Hastings and the B—— family. Brook House, England, 1873
In a seaside town in southeast England, the B—— family are subject to many strange experiences, as reported by their friend Ralph. He witnesses many incidents, including several phantoms, one of them recognized as Rhoda, a daughter who has been dead twelve years. On several occasions a ghost is seen to close a window which the inhabitants had opened, sometimes turning the hasp which secures it. The hands are actually seen in the act of closing the window, at a time when investigation shows there is no one in the house.[121]

In the Benoist case (no. 95) the ghost is reported as eating and drinking: in the Bruce case (no. 140) the apparition leaves a written message. The mind boggles at the thought that a material effect can have anything less than a material cause, but by the time we reach Chapter 8 we shall find that the accumulation of testimony will compel us to ask, Should we revise our notions of what constitutes 'material'?

A ghost may be touched and felt . . . but lack material substance

Most ghosts are seen in circumstances where touch is out of the question, but sometimes it happens:

92. Agnes McCaskill. Cassel, Germany, August 1891
'I was paying a visit to some cousins, and I shared a room with them. We had stopped talking, and I was lying with my face to the wall, when I was startled by a scream from my cousin, and, turning round, saw a tall white figure standing in the room, near L.'s bed. I did not at the time feel frightened; my one idea was to find out what strange thing it was. It turned and came towards my bed, and I distinctly remember noticing that it made no sound on the polished wood floor. Its eyes were green and glistening, but the rest of the face seemed muffled up. As soon as it was close to my bed, I seized it, and seemed to take hold of something soft, like flimsy drapery, but whatever it was seemed dragged from me by some invisible power, and the thing literally sank into the floor by my bedside.'[122]

93. Gail S. Detroit, 1965
The family report seeing the figures of a man and woman on the hallway wall. Investigator John Buta does not see them, but does see a 'misty shape' about a metre above the floor, and some 15 by 20 centimetres in size. Having no particular fear of the thing, he moves his hand back and forward across the area, and notes that the hairs on his hand stand up as if affected by static electricity.[123]

Other touch cases in this book are Malleson (no. 174), Dodson (no. 125), and Driesen (no. 134). By contrast the percipient may come, inadvertently or deliberately, into what would be contact with the ghost, only to find there is nothing there to make contact with. Captain Colt (no. 58) passes through the figure of his brother as easily as if it were a holographic image.

A ghost may respond to the percipient or act as though s/he isn't there

In the Mr and Mrs P. case (no. 114) there is no doubt that the apparition is there to confront the percipients, and it addresses them directly; in the Colt case (no. 58) the ghost of the percipient's brother is described as 'looking lovingly, imploringly, and sadly at me', and as the captain passes from one part of the room to another, the ghost turns its head accordingly. On the other hand there are innumerable cases where the ghost neither looks, speaks or gives any sign of being observed, and occasionally where it actually seems to 'cut' the percipient:

> *94. Unnamed adjutant. Switzerland, c. 1950s?*
> 'My husband was walking to his club when he saw his Colonel hurrying towards him. As his adjutant my husband was much attached to him, and was always very pleased when their paths happened to cross in civilian life. My husband lifted his hand to raise his hat. But the Colonel looked at him with a fixed stare and suddenly turned off to the right. My husband returned home tormented with the idea that his Colonel had not wanted to recognize him and had deliberately avoided him . . . Next morning the newspaper said that the Colonel had died two nights earlier.'[124]

Suppose this apparition originating with the adjutant: it is surely most unlikely that he would picture his colonel cutting him. If it originated with the colonel, why should he seek to avoid his colleague? The apparition seems to be behaving intelligently, yet unreasonably.

Ghosts who speak are not uncommon. Often, the percipient is too frightened or astonished to reply, uttering at most a simple 'Who are you?' or 'What do you want?' But occasionally quite detailed exchanges are reported:

95. Marie Benoist. Washington, DC, June 1951

'During World War Two, I worked in the Treasury Department, where I met Hester Marshall. She was considerably older, but we became close friends. After work we often went to Huyler's Candy Store and had a light dinner. She was a Christian Scientist and I was a Catholic, but when my fiancé was killed in the Battle of the Bulge, I thought of giving up the Catholic faith. We often talked about death: I told Hester whichever of us goes first should communicate with the other if possible. However, neither of us took this seriously. After the war she went home to Detroit. For a while we corresponded, then her letters stopped. About a year later, I went into Huyler's to have a soda and saw Hester, dressed in black, sitting at a table waiting for me. She looked younger than I had ever seen her. Strangely, she was not wearing any of her jewelry. I sat down and ate with her. She drank a coffee and ate a sandwich. She said she had come to Washington especially to see me. She told me I must stay with my Catholic faith. I asked her what had happened to all her jewelry, and she said, "Marie, where I am now I don't need jewelry". She walked to the streetcar with me, and when I invited her to come home she declined. She said she and I would meet again some day and I would understand everything then. When I called the Treasury Office where she had worked, they told me she had died three months before.'[125]

In this exceptional case, apparent and percipient seem to have a long and entirely normal conversation. What's more, the apparent eats a sandwich and drinks a cup of coffee. What would the other customers of the café have seen? It would be nice to have the bill. It is tempting to think that Marie is fantazising the whole episode, but such details as the fact that Hester looks younger than Marie has ever seen her support the alternative: that Hester herself is in some sense really there.

But such lengthy exchanges are very rare. Ghosts are usually very limited in their conversation, and sometimes they say nothing even though they would evidently like to:

96. Willa Benton. United States, c. 1945

'During the latter part of World War Two I met and married Jake Westorlin; almost at once he was called for Paratroop Training. Then one night I had a vision: Jake came into my room. He wore a large bandage over his head and most of his face. I saw his lips move, as if he were trying to tell me something. Then he faded into the darkness. The next morning I had a telegram to say he had been killed.'[126]

Jake's ghost seems to be trying to speak, but failing. Or is it Willa who is unable to 'hear' him? We shall take up this matter of 'apparent failure' in Chapter 8.

A ghost generally makes a once-only visit . . . but sometimes returns

Most ghosts are seen only for a very brief period, often seconds rather than minutes. But some stay longer: both the Cheltenham ghost (no. 14) and the dead father's ghost in the Bull case (no. 2) remain for half an hour.

Haunters apart, most ghosts appear just once, though if they have a warning to deliver they may keep coming back until the percipient acts on the warning. This next case is also remarkable as a rare instance of more than one ghost appearing at a time:

97. Margaret Frondorf. Walla Walla, Washington and Pendleton, Oregon, 1945–1947

'I was 18 the night I woke in terror and blinked unbelievingly at the two men who stood beside my bed gazing down at me. I was aware they had been calling my name for some moments. Both were vaporish and I could see through them: nevertheless they seemed real. They stretched their hands toward me, imploring me. "Don't be afraid; we aren't going to hurt you. Come: it is time. We're your grandfathers and we've come for you." I lunged across the bed and turned on the light. They disappeared. Several months passed before they came again. It took me a little longer to turn on the lamp but again they disappeared with the light. However when I snapped off the light they were standing as before. Within a year I married. A couple of months later they woke me again. This time they did not leave when the light came on. "We're not here to hurt you, Margaret. We're here to spare you troubles and heartaches you never dreamed possible . . . We're not sure you will be strong enough to go through what you are going to face if you remain here. You cannot avoid it unless you come with us now. We can't tell you more. This is the last time we will be allowed to come for a long time." "I can't. Not now!

I have to stay," I replied shakily. "Then we'll tell you this much, though we're not supposed to. Hold onto your mind. And if you can make it through the times ahead you will find happiness and reward. The next time we come you will have to go with us, but you won't be afraid." When I told my mother about it, she questioned me closely about the two men. Then she told me they must be my grandfathers, one of whom I'd never seen. She said that I had described them as she had seen them last.'[127]

This intriguing case, rich in puzzles and implications, will be discussed in Chapter 9.

A ghost may appear in two places simultaneously, or within an impossibly short space of time

98. Unnamed brother and sister. Zurich, 18 October 1940
[Brother:] 'I took my usual way back to work after lunch, suddenly I saw my father. Strange, I thought, he's been away for the last fortnight, why has he come back so unexpectedly? I hastened my steps and called out, Hello, father! The words were hardly out of my mouth when he disappeared. I looked around on all sides, my father was nowhere to be seen. Deeply perplexed and absorbed in thought, I went on to my work. No sooner had I arrived than I had a phone call from a relative, telling me that my father had died of a stroke in the night. I immediately rang up my sister to give her the bad news, and told her about my eerie experience. What did she tell me? At that very time, Father had appeared to her in the Bahnhofstrasse, and had suddenly disappeared again. Then I understood. Our father, who loved us so much, had wanted to show himself to us once more as he was when still alive. It was his farewell.'[128]

It seems clear that the father appears to his son and daughter almost simultaneously. Untypically, this crisis apparition occurs some hours after the father's death. Why the delay? Does the ghost have to wait until the percipients are in a receptive mood, not occupied with other matters? Does it prefer to manifest outdoors where they are alone, rather than seek them out in their offices where they may be with colleagues? The manifestation of a ghost during a business conference might be inconvenient.

A ghost may depart naturally, or vanish abruptly, or simply fade away

Whenever possible, indoor ghosts leave by the door – even though that door may be locked. That is to say, even though it seems that neither presents a barrier, a ghost will choose to exit by the door rather than through a wall. Light affects ghosts: in the Frondorf case the apparitions twice leave when the lamp is switched on (though the third time they stick it out, and on one occasion they are still there when the percipient switches the lamp off again). There are countless examples of ghosts vanishing suddenly:

99. Mr G. Q. Melbourne, Australia, November 1979
'As I was walking up Collins-Street, about 4 p.m., I was amazed to see, amongst a number of people on the other side of the street, a very intimate friend who I believed to be in New Zealand. I ran across to speak to him: as I neared the kerb-stone, it seemed that a hand was passed momentarily before my eyes, its direction being downwards. In that instant my chum was gone: though I could distinguish others I had seen before the curious darkness, I never saw him again. About three weeks after, I learned that he had died that very day and hour.'[129]

. . . and a more bizarre disappearance:

100. Pearl Ullrich. Bellingham, Washington State, 3 July 1944
'A neighbor boy enlisted to the Marines, and was serving in the Pacific. His parents heard nothing for about six weeks, his mother was wild with anxiety. One morning I stood looking across our yard toward our neighbor's mailbox thinking "If only Bob's mother could get a letter". As if in answer to my prayer, there stood Bob, right near the mailbox, in his Marine uniform. He and his uniform appeared pale in color and fuzzy in outline. He neither moved nor spoke. Yet his mind spoke to me as clearly as though he had spoken the words aloud – that he wanted his mother to get the letters he had already written because he could not write any more. After Bob stood there for a minute or two impressing his thought on my mind, his "body" started to rise. It stretched out longer and thinner – not straight into the sky, but at an angle of perhaps 30 degrees from the vertical. When the head and shoulders were perhaps 3 metres above

where they had been at first they suddenly turned into (or went into) a bright shaft of light, like a very bright electrical bolt. The balance of the figure followed the head and shoulders into the light and disappeared. The bolt appeared about a metre long and 12 centimetres in diameter. The queer thing was the sparks of blue and green light that appeared to radiate from the lower edge of the bolt, and the yellow and red sparks that came from the upper end . . . Bob's last two letters came that day, and in September came a "missing in action" telegram.'[130]

For a ghost choosing a 'normal' exit see Driesen (no. 134), and Husbands (no. 104): for sudden vanishing cases, Greiffenberg (no. 51).

A ghost never leaves any souvenir, memento or trace

It is said to be a sign of the perfect guest that

> She left no little things behind
> Excepting loving thoughts and kind . . .[131]

but it would settle the matter of their reality status for good and all if the Virgin Mary or extraterrestrial aliens would leave us some tangible evidence of their visit. But they don't, and neither do ghosts. Just occasionally, though, they come close:

101. Alice M. Huhtala. Chicago, Illinois, March 1950
'I was living in a one-room apartment in a private home. At 6.55 one morning I was awakened by a knock on the outside door. There stood my Uncle Frank leaning on his crutches and smiling at me. Although half asleep I opened the door and asked him to wait a minute while I put my robe on. He nodded. It had snowed heavily during the night and when I opened the door again I found nothing outside except a pair of footprints and crutch tip marks in the snow. I ran to the sidewalk and looked up and down but there was no one to be seen.' [Soon after, she learnt that her uncle had died in hospital that morning. She showed her father the crutch marks but he remained sceptical.][132]

A ghost may be seen by the 'wrong' person

In the Ullrich case above (no. 100) the ghost is seen not by the apparent's mother, but by a neighbour. Here is another case where the apparition manifests to someone other than the individual most directly concerned:

102. Dorothea Willard Hooker. Georgia, USA, November 1922
'I was married to a widower twenty years my senior. He had two sons, the elder of whom I had never met. One day, very disturbed, he showed me a letter, advising him that this elder son, a soldier and the apple of his eye, had left Camp without permission and was listed as a deserter. The shock nearly killed my husband. He made every possible effort to find him, employing detectives, but there was still no news. One night I found myself unable to sleep, and was lying in bed awake as the clock struck three. Suddenly I noticed a pale light moving toward the bed from the direction of the bedroom door, which was closed. I followed this strange glow with my eyes until it reached the foot of the bed, where it disappeared. In its place stood a man. He wore a rumpled gray flannel suit, a soft brown felt hat. His features were plainly visible, although the room was quite dark. At first I felt no fear at all, then I had a sudden panicky feeling that the man was a burglar. I roused my husband, who turned on the lamp. We saw no one, though my husband searched the house. Next morning, at breakfast, the telephone rang. It was my husband's son, calling from a hotel in town. We jumped into the car and drove rapidly to Columbus. As we entered the lobby, I saw the same man I had seen at 3.30 a.m. He had arrived on the seven o'clock train.'[133]

Why should the apparition manifest to his stepmother, who never met him, rather than his own father who is so worried about him? Another very suggestive 'wrong witness' case is the Clerke case (no. 168).

Of all categories where we might think the ghost would appear to the 'right' person, a pre-arranged compact would be the surest. Yet not always:

103. Arthur Bellamy. Bristol, England, 1874
'When at school my wife made an agreement with a fellow pupil, Miss W., that the one who died first should, if Divinely permitted,

appear after her decease to the survivor. In 1874 my wife, who had not seen or heard anything of her school-friend for some years, casually heard of her death. The news reminded her of her agreement, and then, becoming nervous, she told me of it. I knew of my wife's compact, but I had never seen a photograph of her friend, or heard any description of her. A night or two afterwards, as I was sleeping with my wife, a fire brightly burning in the room and a candle alight, I suddenly awoke, and saw a lady sitting by the side of the bed where my wife was sleeping soundly. At once I sat up in the bed and gazed so intently that I can still remember form and features. I was much struck with the careful arrangement of her coiffure, every single hair being most carefully brushed down. How long I sat and gazed I cannot say, but directly the apparition ceased to be, I got out of bed to see if any of my wife's garments had by any means optically deluded me. I found nothing. Hallucination I rejected as out of the question, and I doubted not that I had really seen an apparition. I lay till my wife some hours later awoke and then I gave her an account of her friend's appearance, all of which exactly tallied. "But was there any special point to strike one in her appearance?" "Yes," my wife promptly replied, "we girls used to tease her at school for devoting so much time to the arrangement of her hair". This was the very thing which so much struck me.'[134]

Commenting on the case, Gurney of the SPR-Group considered a telepathic explanation more probable than that 'a direct influence (so to speak) missed its mark, and was exercised on Mr Bellamy by a stranger who cared nothing about him'. But if Mr Bellamy rather than his wife sees the apparition, the reason could simply be that he is somehow more 'receptive', or that the ghost encountered some resistance on his wife's part.

A ghost frequently fails to establish its identity

There are countless instances where the percipient sees an apparition which he knows very well is not a living person, but does not recognize the apparent until later – if ever. This occurs most frequently in respect of hauntings, of course, but here is a revenant whose identity is not at first known:

104. John E. Husbands. Madeira, January 1885

'I was sleeping in a hotel. It was a bright moonlight night. I felt some one was in my room. On opening my eyes, I saw a young fellow about 25, dressed in flannels, standing at the side of my bed and pointing with the first finger of his right hand to the place where I was lying. I lay for some seconds to convince myself of some one being really there. I then sat up and looked at him. I asked him what he wanted: he did not speak, but his eyes and hand seemed to tell me I was in his place. As he did not answer, I struck out at him with my fist, but did not reach him, and as I was going to spring out of bed he slowly vanished through the door, which was shut, keeping his eye upon me all the time. Upon inquiry I found that the young fellow died in that room I was occupying. I saw his features so plainly that I recognized them in a photograph which was shown me some days after.'[135]

There is no plausible explanation that would make Mr Husbands responsible for this apparition, unless we suppose some quite remarkable psychic perception which would enable him not only to learn that the young man died in his room, but to conjure him up so vividly that he can later identify his photo. Moreover, the action of the apparition, seeming to accuse Husbands of being in his bed, is hardly something he would invent.

Ghosts are frequently sensed

Percipients quite often tell us they have a feeling of something strange before they actually see their ghost: this is notably true of the Cheltenham hauntings (no. 14) and the Mitchell sighting (no. 60). This could be explained as a psychical presentiment, but when it affects an entire family, as in the Bull case (no. 2), it suggests something more objectively real, and this is confirmed by the frequently reported circumstance where an animal – usually a dog – seems to detect an uncanny presence even if the humans present see or sense nothing. At one point during the Cheltenham case, Rosina Despard notes, 'I felt a cold icy shiver' when the ghost bends over her while she is playing the piano. On another occasion five of the witnesses feel 'a cold wind, though their candles were not blown about'.[136] Whether or not this is a subjective impression, it is reported sufficiently often for us to wonder whether actual cold is involved, or something that is mistaken for it. Other cases of the kind are I.B. (no. 27), McAlpine (no. 33) and Du Cane (no. 78), and here are two more:

105. Miss K. M. Kensington, London, c. 1869
'We were all sitting in the drawing-room with the door open, it being a very warm evening. Suddenly I experienced a cold shudder, and on looking through the door I saw a figure of a little old lady glide down the stairs and disappear . . .'[137]

106. Mrs F. R. 5 May 1879
'While my father was lying on what proved to be his deathbed, I was obliged to go to the dentist. While waiting in the ante-room, I seemed to feel a shudder and to see a white cloud before me and heard my father call me by name. I immediately left and found my father insensible and he died a few hours after.'[138]

Interestingly enough, a similar effect is frequently noted in spirit seances. If this is indeed real, one possibility may be that ghosts and spirits require energy to materialize, and they draw this from the air, causing an apparent – or even a real – drop in the ambient temperature. Investigators of haunted houses have claimed to register a temperature drop on their instruments, which they relate either to a manifestation or to a traditional 'cold spot' on the premises.

This sensation of presence is also reported in countless non-visual cases. It could be said that something so subjective cannot be accepted as evidence, were it not for the fact that people who are visited in this way are not only certain in their own minds that they have been visited, but derive a very real comfort and reassurance from the incident. We could of course put this, too, down to a psychological process: the subconscious has arranged the visit to bring comfort to a person who is unhappy or worried. If so, we may look on the 'presence' as a milder form of ghost experience.

Ghosts do a lot of other things besides those mentioned here, but these are sufficient to illustrate their paradoxical nature: on the one hand they challenge our explanations, but on the other they provide us with clues.

Not every ghost displays all these features, and we must be on our guard in thinking that ghosts are all of a kind and behave in the same way. Researcher Hornell Hart points out, for example, that no 'fully conscious' apparitions form or lose their shape gradually; they are not transparent, or self-luminous.[139] We must be prepared to find that living ghosts on the one hand, and revenants and haunters on the other, may be of a different nature, or come about in a different way.

A provisional assessment

In detective stories there is often a point where the sleuth sets out the evidence he has collected so far, and makes a tentative evaluation of the findings. Let us do the same.

For the SPR-Group, as for Tyrrell and other successors, it seemed as though there are, fundamentally, only two approaches to explaining the ghost experience. We can take the physical, material, 'ghosts are real' approach, or we can take the psychological, 'all in the mind' approach.

Each of these approaches has its attractions, but neither meets all the requirements. To be fair, this was recognized at the time even by those who proposed them. Some researchers tried to get round this by dismissing some of the evidence, or by interpreting it differently, but the fact is that no all-physical theory and no all-psychological theory, however much we bend and shape it, can be stretched to explain *every* one of the features we have looked at in this chapter. Tyrrell makes the bravest attempt, with a complex theory which takes the major step of recognizing that, in some cases at least, *both* parties to the transaction – the agent *and* the percipient – must play an active part, implying that there may be an agent external to the percipient, and further implying that this agent could be a person who is no longer alive. But his speculations on how this might be done are cumbersome and not very convincing.

It would be possible to account for a large proportion of ghost experiences by some purely subjective psychological process which we could formulate somewhat like this:

- given that all ghosts are hallucinations
- given that the subconscious is capable of hallucinating apparitions in the same way that it creates dreams
- then the subconscious may of its own volition, responding
either to a perceived need, fear, anxiety or wish of the individual, or to a message received in the form of a suggestion from
an external source, hallucinate an image which it projects as an
externalized figure or scene, which the conscious mind perceives either via the senses or by some internal visualizing
process.

Such a process saves us having to go beyond accepted psychological behaviours, and is perhaps the absolute minimum require-
ment for the ghost experience. Conceivably it might account for
revenants, and could be stretched to include crisis apparitions.
But it is not adequate for the entire spectrum of the ghost experience, if only because information is frequently obtained by the
percipient which could not have been gained by any conventional means. There are strong indications that only an external
agent could provide, or some component of the percipient
capable of accessing the agent could obtain, that information. If
we shrink from the option of an external agent, we must suppose
that the subconscious is employing super-psi not only to obtain
that information, but also to recognize that the information exists
at all, and that it is worth obtaining.

Three other types of ghost experience, while they do not absolutely rule out the psychological model, certainly make it
extremely unwieldy:

- collective cases, particularly when the apparition is seen
simultaneously, acting naturally, from different perspectives;
- projections where the projector is aware, and later has memories, of being at a remote location, and where she is observed
behaving as she subsequently remembers behaving;
- haunters, which are virtually impossible to accommodate
within such a percipient-centred psychological framework.

So at this stage of our inquiry it is fair to say that, like it or not,
we must accept that there are forceful indications that the ghost
experience is *not* exclusively subjective. We must be open to the

possibility that we shall not find the explanation for the ghost experience either in commonly accepted notions of reality or in currently accepted psychological processes. To find it, we must be prepared to go farther than the SPR-Group or even Tyrrell were prepared to go: we must let the experience dictate the limits of explanation, rather than seek to impose our own limitations. We must allow it to extend our conception of what is possible and be prepared, if necessary, to embrace a new way of thinking about reality.

96

Chapter 4

THE PURPOSE OF THE GHOST EXPERIENCE

Why should anyone want to see a ghost? Why should anyone want to *be* a ghost? The question of motive – *cui bono? who gains?* – is as crucial to our inquiry as to a murder mystery. If, on the one hand, we find there is every reason why we on Earth should want to see ghosts, but no reason why they should want to be seen, we could reasonably suppose that the ghost experience arises from wish, fear or expectation on the part of the percipient, and can probably be accounted for in psychological terms. In this case we might conclude that no such thing as a ghost exists outside the human imagination.

On the other hand, if we find there is every reason why ghosts might wish to manifest, while their human percipients are reluctant, scared or downright hostile, we might reasonably conclude that the responsibility for their appearance is entirely theirs: which would be the best of reasons for thinking that some ghosts, at least, exist in their own right and are able to act autonomously, intelligently and purposefully.

So, as we ask *why* ghosts appear, let us be aware of how much hangs on the answers.

Why do ghosts look like people?

The answer to this seemingly simple question provides an important clue to the purpose of the ghost experience. The bodies we have here on Earth are, on the whole, superbly adapted to Earthly conditions: but that is what they are, machines to live on Earth with. There is no reason to suppose that when we move to the next world we shall find ourselves lumbered with the same kind of machine, and every hope that we shall be freed from its limitations. If out-of-body experiences offer any kind of preview, that will be the case. Yet with the exception of a relatively small number of monsters and shapeless forms, the vast majority of apparitions are so lifelike that they are frequently mistaken for living people.

Throughout the history of mankind, otherworldly beings have been pictured in more or less human shape. Angels are beautiful androgynous beings, some winged, others wingless: their fallen cousins, demons, are also often winged (though bat-like rather than bird-like) and liable to be hoofed and tailed, but basically they too are humanoid. Folklore entities are no exception: from fairy-folk to mer-folk, from vampires to Valkyries, most have human shape with the occasional fin, wing or claw to distinguish them from you and me. God the Father is as like us as Father Christmas. Even extraterrestrial aliens are bipedal, two-eyed creatures who breathe our air and sustain our gravity without difficulty.

Clearly, if ghosts are lifelike, it is because, whatever their origin, they choose to appear so. And the most probable reasons must be that if they appear in this form they will be recognized; they will not unduly alarm the percipient and they will carry some degree of credibility.

The motivation of haunters

Most if not all haunting seems pointless. To wander about the place where you once lived, over periods of time that can extend into centuries, is something it makes no sense to do. Some – Cheltenham's Imogen Swinhoe (no. 14) is an example – seem to be bewailing their earthly fate, but we need no grief counsellor to tell us it is overdoing things to stay in mourning for fifty years.

On the other hand, none of us has any first-hand experience of what it is like to be dead, and it may be that to become a haunter is one of the accidents that may befall us when we move from this world to the next. Here is a remarkable – perhaps unique – case:

107. Three unnamed women. Switzerland, early twentieth century
[A young girl recalls:] 'One day I was coming home from school when I met my mother and grandmother on the stairs, deep in conversation about our coal-merchant who hanged himself. Suddenly both women looked down the stairs staring as if petrified, and then all three of us screamed in utter horror, for up the stairs came our former coal-merchant with a heavy sack on his back, his face congested and blue, his tongue hanging out. He said that he had to carry coal till the moment when his life would have reached its natural end. Then, suddenly, he vanished.'[140]

It's a pity we don't have a complete transcript of the conversation. Did the horror-struck ladies interrogate the suicidal coalman, or did he volunteer the information? Whose idea was it that he should, as it were, 'serve his time'? Was it a self-inflicted penance?

One sub-category of haunters is that of 'resentful residents' – the ghosts of people who formerly lived in a particular house, and seem less than pleased that strangers now occupy it:

108. Anthony M. Giacobbe. North Brunswick, New Jersey, 1972
'I bought an old lot on Church Lane, and had to tear down an old house on the property. I was backing up my bulldozer when out of the corner of my eye I saw an elderly woman dressed in a "granny" dress and bonnet and carrying a stick in her hands. She was yelling, "What are you doing to my house?" This scared the daylights out of me. Anyone standing in that position could be run over by the tracks of the bulldozer. I stopped immediately, but when I turned around to say something to the woman, there was no one there! I asked my partner if he had seen anyone behind me and he said no. When I checked with the neighbors, I learned that an elderly woman matching that description had lived in the house for many years. She had died about fifteen years earlier.'[141]

109. Gertrude Mummert. York, Pennsylvania, 1937
'A few nights after moving in to a rented house, I felt something heavy on my chest while in bed. This occurred for several nights and kept me from sleep. One day when I was alone in the house I was impelled to look at the stairway. I saw a man standing there and watching me. I never had seen him before. I noted that his left arm had been amputated. As I stared at him I was amazed to see him

99

disappear before my very eyes. A neighbour said my description fitted that of a Mr Wineholt, who had killed himself with gas in that house. A short time later I was alone in the house again, when I felt impelled to look up. There stood Mr Wineholt. I was determined to find out what he wanted, so I spoke his name and questioned him. I heard him say, "What are you doing in my house?" I explained, "We rented it. You do not live here any more. You are dead." "No, I am not. Get out of my house. You sleep in my bed. It's my bed and this is my home." I pointed out that he had committed suicide in the kitchen by taking gas. It seemed he did not remember, and was somewhat surprised by the information. I told him I would pray for him and in this way help him to find his way to higher spirit planes. This apparently released him from his earthly bonds, for that was the last I ever saw of him.'[142]

A thorough account of such a haunt is given by poltergeist victim and healer Matthew Manning, who discovered that his family home was still haunted by one or more of its former occupants, members of the Webbe family, who lived there in the seventeenth and eighteenth centuries.[143] 'It was becoming clear that as far as Robert Webbe was concerned, the house belonged to him, and not us. We were strangers . . . [but in time] we all began to regard Webbe more as a "friend" or person than a ghost.' Matthew was 16 when he first saw him, standing on the staircase: he seemed as solid as a human being, and 'spoke in a perfectly ordinary human voice'. Matthew made a sketch of him then and there, asking Webbe to wait while he fetched paper and pencil, which he graciously did. Thereafter he was able to communicate with him via automatic writing, and a great deal of information was obtained direct, so it seemed, from the horse's mouth. Webbe appeared glad to converse with Matthew, who seemed to be supplying the energy that made communication, and Webbe's activities, possible. Subsequent research suggested that at least two members of the Webbe family were communicating.

It is an intriguing but frustrating story, heavy with unanswered questions. Though the many and various poltergeist-type phenomena in the house were observed by other members of the household and by visitors, the Webbes were shy of everyone except Matthew himself. Some might think the whole affair was subjective, a fantasy devised by Matthew's subconscious. Since the age of 11 he had been associated with phenomena which became so upsetting that he had to be taken from school, and he had other behavioural characteristics which are vaguely termed 'psychic'. We could surmise that in the context of this sensitivity, his interest in his house and its history could have resulted in the apparition, the physical phenomena including noises and graffiti, and all.

That the Webbes permitted themselves to be seen by no one else is ambiguous. It could simply mean that Matthew was the only one they felt a rapport with; equally, that they had no existence except insofar as Matthew's subconscious gave them life. The Robert Webbe who was Matthew's principal communicator was well aware that he was dead, even specifying what he died from (gout), so puzzlement rather than resentment seems a more accurate term to describe his feelings.

Driven by resentment, grief or whatever, haunters are preoccupied with their own predicament. If they were living persons, we would say they need help; and indeed we shall see in Chapter 6 how some people have thoughtfully extended the social services to care for these unfortunates marooned on our planet like involuntary asylum seekers. We might think, though, that such help would be better provided by rescuers from the next world, whose first-hand experience of dying would surely qualify them as fitter guides through the process of resettlement, and better informed as to the emergency procedures available for those who find themselves stuck on the wrong side of the great divide.

Possible support for the 'failure to adjust' theory comes from comparison with the reincarnation experience. Dr Ian Stevenson, who has devoted the greater part of his career to investigating reincarnation, has noted: 'A violent death figures so prominently in the cases we have been able to study that it is difficult to avoid concluding that such a death plays an important part in the occurrence of imaged memories'. He suggests that violent death acts as a 'concentrator of attention, fixing the memory of it and making that memory somehow more transmissible to a later-born person'.[144] There could be a parallel here with haunters: could it be that the same factors which cause some victims of violent deaths to reincarnate (or to give the appearance of doing so, for Stevenson is the first to admit that his studies by no means establish that reincarnation is taking place) may cause others to become haunters? Haunting and reincarnation may be alternative strategies available to the victim who cannot come to terms with being untimely hustled from one life to another.

The motivation of spontaneous ghosts

In 1938 Zoe Richmond, a prominent member of the SPR, collected a selection of those cases reported to the Society which seemed the best evidence that ghost experiences are *purposeful*. We may be surprised that she should feel the need to do so. Throughout history, it has been assumed that ghosts manifest, not because they choose to, but because they *need* to. Medieval commentators took it for granted that ghosts are spirits returning to Earth because they have left something undone in their lifetime, which they had obtained permission from the powers that be to set right. To Daniel Defoe in the early eighteenth century there is no question but that apparitions manifest for sound reasons, be they ghosts of the living or the dead:

110. Unnamed prisoner. Britain, seventeenth century?
A murderer is brought to trial 'on suspicion of murder, which however he knew it was not in the power of human knowledge to detect'. He pleads not guilty, and is on the point of being acquitted when 'he saw the murdered person standing upon the step as a witness, ready to be examined against him, and ready to shew his throat which was cut by the prisoner, and who stood staring full upon him with a frightful countenance' whereupon the prisoner breaks down and confesses.[145]

111. Unnamed young lady. Britain, seventeenth century?
A young lady is on her way to an illicit rendezvous when she is halted by the apparition of the minister of the town, who is seen also by the maid accompanying her. He speaks to her: – Come, come, young lady, you can't conceal your wicked purposes: you have made Mr —— an appointment, and you have now deck'd yourself up with your ornaments to meet him, and prostitute your virtue and your honour to his corrupt vicious appetite, My advice to you is to go back and break your vicious promise . . .' which, alarmed at such a meeting, she does.[146]

By far the biggest single category of ghosts is of relatives or friends who come to announce their own death. This may be done in many symbolic ways – a sound associated with the individual is heard, his picture falls off the wall, a clock stops at the moment of death (my mother's did this), and so on. Countless apparitions are of relatives whose purpose, evident to the percipient, is to warn of their just-happened or just-about-to-happen death. Many, of course, fall into the category of crisis apparitions, but in most cases there is no suggestion of a call for help, and the purpose seems simply that the dying person doesn't want to leave home without saying goodbye.

Two eighteenth century cases narrated by Daniel Defoe (writing as Andrew Moreton). A man on trial for murder, confronted by the ghost of his victim, breaks down and confesses. A girl on her way to an immoral rendezvous meets the ghost of the minister, who dissuades her: yet the minister himself is unaware that his double is acting independently of him

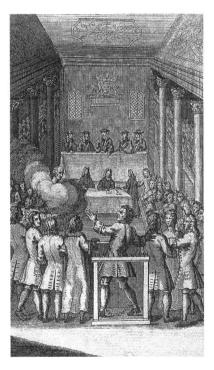 

Apparitions leading to disclosure of information of potential use

Augustine of Hippo, writing in the fifth century, tells of a young man assailed by creditors who insist that his father, recently dead, owed them money. Fortunately Papa appears in ghost form to tell him the money was paid and where to find the receipt.[147] This is so classic a ghost experience that it has passed into folklore; however the SPR *Proceedings* contain several real cases in which information, apparently unknown to anyone living, is brought to light by a ghostly visitation.

The famous Chaffin Will case, because legal issues were involved, is fully documented with affidavits from everyone concerned, so the facts are not in dispute:

> *112. James Pinkney Chaffin. Davie County, North Carolina, 1925*
> In 1905 James L. Chaffin, a farmer in North Carolina, makes a will bequeathing his farm and entire estate to his third son Marshall, leaving his wife and other children unprovided for. When he dies in an accident in 1921, the will is carried out since no one has any reason to question it despite its unfairness. But in 1925 the second brother, James, has a series of vivid dreams in which his dead father appears, wearing a black overcoat. His father indicates that he will find a revised will in the coat pocket. The coat is found, and the pocket, which has been sewn up, is opened. Inside is found, not a will, but a message in the father's writing: 'Read the 27th chapter of Genesis in my daddy's old bible'. Inside the bible they find a will dated 1919, in which the estate is shared among his family.[148]

The younger James first said he was awake but later admits he might have been in a 'doze'. The lawyer who interviewed him said, 'I believe he does not know himself'. But waking or dreaming, it seems as though a purposeful revenant is involved. Our options are limited:

- cryptomnesia (memories of which we are not consciously aware) – the dreaming James subconsciously recalls something his father said or did; or
- psi of some kind – his dreaming mind paranormally becomes aware of the whereabouts of the will and presents the information to him in the form of a dream; or

- a visitation by the father's spirit – which of course is what those concerned believe it to be.

Ostensibly the most motivated person is the younger James, deprived of an inheritance he might reasonably think he deserved: but four years have elapsed since his father's death. There is a strong emotional motivation for the father, who evidently revised his will under considerable emotional stress: the new will has been elaborately inserted in the family bible at the episode in Genesis where Jacob cheats Esau of his inheritance, and specifically states that it was made after reading that chapter. We can hardly imagine his son going through this elaborate charade, though we can't rule it out. Probably the farmer intended to reveal the new will on his deathbed, but his unexpected accidental death prevented this – which could account for his return to put matters right, if we accept that those in the next world retain some concern about the shortcomings of their lifetime.

Apparitions offering comfort, counsel, help

This next case must be one of the least scary ghost stories ever recounted, but it is also one of the clearest cases where an apparition manifests solely for the purpose of reassuring the percipient:

113. Canon J. B. Phillips. Place unnamed, November 1963
'The late C. S. Lewis, whom I did not know very well, and had only seen in the flesh once, but with whom I had corresponded a fair amount, gave me an unusual experience. A few days after his death, while I was watching television one evening in full daylight (my wife was in an adjoining room preparing supper), he "appeared" sitting in a chair less than two metres away, and spoke a few words – "It's not as difficult as you think, you know," – which were particularly relevant to the difficult circumstances through which I was passing. He was ruddier in complexion than ever, grinning all over his face and positively glowing with health. He was dressed in rather rough, well-worn brown tweeds: I realized later that I had never seen him in ordinary clothes – on the one occasion I saw him in the flesh he was

wearing a black cassock. (Later, I learnt that it was his habit to wear tweeds that would be comfortable rather than smart, but I did not know this at the time.) I had not been thinking about him at all. I was neither alarmed nor surprised: he was just *there* – "large as life and twice as natural"! A week later, this time when I was in bed reading before going to sleep, he appeared again, even more rosily radiant than before, and repeated the same message, which was very important to me. It seemed obvious that he wanted to speak to me.'[149]

Here the need felt by Canon Phillips is evident, whereas Lewis's ghost has no reason to appear other than to meet that need. So we may well be tempted to think that the sighting has been set up entirely by Phillips's subconscious to reassure him, conscripting the figure of Lewis as a guarantor. But if so, the fact that the ghost appeared in everyday clothes, rather than in the cassock which is how Phillips remembers him, is rather odd. And was it Phillips's subconscious that prepared the reassuring message and, as it were, fed it to his own conscious mind? And what about Phillips's insistence that it is Lewis who wants to speak to him?

Here, by contrast, is a case where it is well nigh impossible to suppose that the percipient has created the apparition, since the wife knows neither the apparent nor any reason why he might appear:

114. Mr and Mrs P. Britain, 1869
Mr and Mrs P. are just going to bed: '. . . when to my great astonishment I [Mrs P.] saw a gentleman standing at the foot of the bed, dressed as a naval officer, leaning on the footrail of the bedstead. Instantly touching my husband's shoulder (whose face was turned from me) I said "Willie, who is this?" My husband turned, and for a second or two lay looking in intense astonishment at the intruder; then lifting himself a little he shouted "What on earth are you doing here, sir?" Meanwhile the form, slowly drawing himself into an upright position, now said in a commanding yet reproachful voice, "Willie! Willie!"'[150]

The figure then moves away and leaves through the wall. Mr P. springs out of bed and insists on searching the house. Returning, he explains to his wife that it is his father, a naval officer who died fourteen years before; Mrs P. never saw her father-in-law. Her husband reveals that he is in financial difficulties and was on the point of taking some dangerous advice. Clearly the apparition of the father is intended to prevent this.

It would be possible to explain this as a mental artefact emanating from Mr P.'s subconscious. Under the stress of his financial worries, he wonders what his dead father would have thought of his proposed action. His subconscious takes over, visualizes the father and projects the image, wearing naval uniform to reinforce his identity and to assert his authority. His wife picks up the image, perhaps because some kind of thought-field is created (we shall consider such fields in Chapter 8), and – perhaps because she is the more suggestible of the couple – she is the first to see the apparition.

This elaborate scenario offers a possible alternative for those reluctant to believe in ghosts of the surviving dead: but a manifestation by the father seems a simpler explanation, especially as the apparition seems to know its way round a bedroom which the apparent doubtless never visited during his lifetime.

Sometimes it is quite easy to suppose that the subconscious is responsible, without any external intervention:

115. Florence Ague. Tice, Florida, 19 July 1963
'A little more than a month after my daughter Mildred died, I was settling down to sleep when I felt someone sit down on my bed. I turned to see if it was my sick husband wanting something – and I saw Mildred sitting there on the edge of my bed! She said, "Mom, go to the doctor." I told her, "Honey, I am all right, I don't need a doctor." Mildred left but she came again the next night. Again, I told her that I didn't need the doctor. The third night she reappeared saying, "Mom, please see Doctor Bill before it is too late!" I promised my daughter I would see our family doctor in the morning. He sent me right to the hospital for emergency treatment for diabetes. He said that if I had delayed seeing him one more week it would have been too late to do anything but make me comfortable 'til the end.'[151]

A sceptical reading would be that Florence's subconscious is aware of her sickness and stages these fantasy visits as a way of forcing her to go to the doctor. Similarly with the following, more elaborate case:

116. Joshua Slocum. Atlantic Ocean, 1895

During his round-the-world solo voyage under sail, crossing the Atlantic eastwards, Slocum is seized with stomach cramps so severe that he goes below, even though his sloop has run into squalls and needs his attention. He throws himself on the cabin floor in agony. When he wakes, he is amazed to see a figure at the helm, steering the

American circumnavigator Joshua Slocum is crossing the Atlantic single-handed when, on 26 July 1895, he falls sick and has to go below. He wakes to find that his boat is being steered by the pilot of the Pinta, one of Columbus's ships

ship. He seems like a rough foreign sailor, and identifies himself as one of Columbus's companions, the pilot of the *Pinta*, who has taken it on himself to guide the *Spray*. He tells Slocum that his cramps were due to mixing cheese with plums. The boat is still sailing correctly – 'Columbus himself could not have held her more exactly on her course'. The next night he receives a second visit from the pilot, but this time only in a dream.[152]

It is hard to doubt that this is a fantasy created by Slocum's subconscious. He is of course familiar with the accounts of Columbus's voyage, and the pilot of the *Pinta* would be a likely choice to play the leading part in this imaginary drama. Certainly it is hard to suppose that the fifteenth-century sailor is the agent. Still, we must wonder how Slocum's boat is kept so skilfully on its course: is this, too, the work of his subconscious? Dare we speculate that the figure might be his 'guardian angel', protecting him while disguised in this reassuring way?

The same could apply to the three following cases, where in each instance the percipient's life seems quite clearly to have been saved by timely intervention:

117. Walker Anderson. Queensland, Australia, January 1885
Crossing a river on horseback, he is carried downstream by the current which is too strong for his horse to cross. He gives himself up for lost, when he sees his aunt [who died many years before] standing on a floating tree: he takes it as an indication that he should abandon the horse and seize hold of the tree, which he does, and is carried safe to the bank.[153]

Again, this could be Anderson's subconscious giving him practical instructions, but casting them in the somewhat indirect form of a crisis apparition in reverse.

118. Elsa Schmidt-Falk. Bavarian Alps, 1950s
Frau Schmidt-Falk is climbing alone, when she happens to miss her way: 'You will understand that this is rather a heavy mountain tour, but there is a good way as well up as down, but one must not miss it as I did. Having started a little late for the return, and light beginning to fade, all of a sudden I found myself in a really dangerous position. As a matter of fact one year later a young girl fell to death exactly on

the spot where I realized myself to be in an almost hopeless position. All of a sudden I noticed a sort of a big ball of light, and this condensed to the shape of a tall, rather Chinese looking gentleman. Extraordinarily I was not a bit frightened, and also not astonished, it all seemed then quite natural to me. The gentleman bowed, spoke a few words, led me a small path to the tourists' way, and disappeared as a ball of light.'[154]

Frau Elsa is well aware of her predicament, and again we may think her experience is entirely subjective, that her subconscious creates the apparition as a guarantor to reassure her conscious mind that the information is reliable (she is of a Theosophical cast of mind, and the 'Chinese-looking gentleman' could be a bodhisattva, a divine being in which Theosophists incline to believe). But how do we explain how she is able to show herself the proper way down the mountain?

And sometimes the percipient is *not* at the time aware that she is in any danger, and this is not nearly so easy to explain on a subjective basis:

119. Eva Roe. Pacific Palisades, California, January 1940
'A friend and I were driving home late one night. We were proceeding down the narrow pass at Castellemore when I asked him to stop because I wanted to get out. He wheeled up to the shoulder of the road and asked me to hurry because it was late. I put my hand on the door handle and looked up in surprise because there, in that lonely spot, a man and a woman loomed up beside the car door, very friendly and chatty, but apparently determined to linger and deter me. I gave up getting out of the car and let them talk. They seemed to know me very well and were full of jolly anecdotes and laughed a great deal. My friend finally roused himself and said, "Who are you talking to?" I looked around and they were gone. Then Casey got out and went round to the rear of the car. In a moment he got back in, very sober-faced and pale. He backed the car out slowly and carefully and then parked it again. "'If they hadn't stopped you, you would have stepped out into space. It is a drop down to the rocky beach of about 300 metres . . . They had no place to stand. They could not stand in the empty air, could they?" Whether they could or not, they did. They held the car door and talked until Casey got out, refusing to move away until then. I had never seen either of them, and did not know them, but they seemed like ordinary people in ordinary clothes.'[155]

The apparitions are total strangers, and Eva has no reason to suppose she is in any danger. Do the ghost couple, whoever they are, realize her danger, and hurry to save her? Or are they invented for the purpose by her subconscious, which is somehow aware of the situation? Suppose the latter to be the case: we have to imagine that, the moment the car stops, Eva's subconscious instantly realizes – but how? – the danger, and takes immediate steps to prevent her leaving the car, creating in an instant the entire scenario – strangers, jolly anecdotes and all. And indeed, why all the talk? Why can't the chatty couple simply say 'Don't get out because there's a sheer drop here'?

This next case is interesting on three counts: the percipient learns from her husband's ghost of his death; she sees him 'symbolically' with wings; and it embodies the traditional belief that the dead may be given time to revisit Earth:

120. Dorothy Bullock. Chicago, Illinois, October 1935
'I entered hospital for an operation; my husband, Nathan, was with me until it was over. He returned home, promising to visit me the following afternoon. He never came. A week passed and I heard nothing from him or anyone else. One afternoon during visiting hours I heard my name being called as if from a distance. I saw a grayish figure, floating midway between the ceiling and the floor, come through the door. I saw a head and shoulders and on the shoulders were wings like those shown on angels. The rest of the figure seemed covered by veils. It floated up to my bed, still suspended in the air. I now saw that it was my husband. He said, "Dorothy, I've been granted a little time to visit you and to tell you that I died in an accident. I also want to warn you that my folks are going to try to take the children away from you. Don't ever let that happen. My folks will tell you about the accident. My time is up and I must go back. Goodbye and good luck." He floated through the door and vanished. My mother-in-law refused to believe my story and said I must have been dreaming. I insisted I had been wide awake. My children had been placed in foster homes, however, I managed to regain possession of them. I often wonder what I would have done if my husband had not visited me after his death.'[156]

Wings? No, even if Nathan has gone to Heaven, these are fancy-dress wings! Either his apparition is wearing them to emphasize to Dorothy that he is dead, or her subconscious has dressed him, with a similar intention. As for 'my time is up', the idea that the dead are permitted only a very little time to return to Earth seems an all too human arrangement, reminiscent of prison visits; and yet ghosts use it as a pretext for cutting short their stay. Of course it provides a convenient explanation why they are not more forth-coming with details about their own present state, but that hardly seems sufficient reason to be so brusque. This next ghost is only marginally more communicative:

121. Mr Jim and Kathy H. Flint, Michigan, October 1923
'In May 1923 my wife and I lost our one-year-old firstborn in an acci-dent which also took the life of my mother. My wife mourned our baby until it became an obsession, so to get away from familiar sights we took a house in the country. One evening we were sitting listen-ing to records when the wind blew the front door open. I closed the door and sat down: immediately the door blew open again and a gust of wind blew out the only lamp. My wife said, "Look, Jim, over there by the door!" There was a white shadowy outline which seemed to be moving towards us. Needless to say we were frightened. All at once there was a flash of light and there stood Mother with our baby in her arms. "Oh! Mother!" My wife collapsed in my arms. "Jim," the vision spoke. "Tell Kathy not to worry about little Jimmy. I will take care of him. We are very happy in our heavenly home. Goodbye, my son." The light slowly faded and the vision went with it, leaving us in complete darkness. The vision cured my wife's grief.'[157]

The need here is clearly on the parents' part, particularly the wife, and it is tempting to dismiss it as a wish-inspired fantasy. Yet *both* parents saw the apparition and clearly identified it, leaving the case open to the explanation that there was an objectively real figure there, whether created by Kathy or by Jim's mother.

The next case is interesting because of the roundabout way the help was provided:

122. Louise Savage Mapp. Onley, Virginia, October 1941
'When my Daddy died our assets were frozen pending settlement of the estate, and I found myself, a young widow with a son to raise, reduced to small change five days before pay day at my job. That night I tossed uneasily until 2 a.m., when I became miraculously calm

and slept. Next morning, the doorbell rang. Mr Wilson, who Daddy had trained, was standing there, pale, disheveled, shaking. "How are you, Sally Lou?" he asked. "Fine," I replied. "No, you are not." Breathlessly the words tumbled out. "Your father stood by my bed at 2:00 o'clock this morning and told me you needed help desperately for a few days." Placing an envelope on the table he hurried away before I could speak. It contained a 20 dollar bill.'[158]

The need is Louise's, so the simplest explanation is that her subconscious creates the apparition of her father and sends it to the home of the most likely benefactor, Mr Wilson, to encourage him to help her. Or, if we think that unlikely, we may suppose that Mr Wilson somehow becomes aware of his former employer's daughter's cash flow problem and invents the ghostly visitation to force himself to take action. Or, in the last resort, we may think that Louise's father, sensing his daughter's predicament, thinks to himself, Now, which of my acquaintance can I best ask to help her?

On some occasions, a solid, physical action seems to be involved:

123. *Marlene Brenner. Rye Beach, New York, 4 July 1938*
'My friend Mildred decided to swim out to a breakwater more than 1.5 kilometres distant. Although only a mediocre swimmer, I bravely followed. Halfway to the breakwater I suffered a cramp and went under, gulping water. Terrified, I gulped more water and went under a second time. As I surfaced, I prayed, "Oh God, don't let me die." A second later I heard the voice of a fair-haired, blue-eyed young man. He was in a rowboat. "Hang on," he said, "I'll pull you over." Gratefully I grasped the stern of the boat. We reached the breakwater, and with a word of thanks I scrambled up the rocks. "If that man had not rescued me, I would have drowned," I told Mildred. "What man?" she asked. I scanned the horizon to point to my rescuer. In that short time he could not have traveled more than 30 metres, but the waters around us were empty. He had disappeared. Years later I found an old photograph album. Abruptly I stopped before the smiling portrait of my father's brother, who had died before I was born. He was my rescuer.'[159]

Not only a ghost, but a phantom boat, oars and all! Where does reality stop and hallucination take over? Is Marlene actually swimming and only imagining that she is holding on to the boat?

What would Mildred have seen if she had been looking in the right direction? Or was she indeed looking, but saw nothing out of the ordinary?

Apparitions requesting comfort, counsel, help

By contrast, sometimes it is the ghost who needs help. The Burke case (no. 163) is one example, and here is another:

124. Miss M. C. Herefordshire, England, 1866
'When I was 39, I had a situation as governess in Herefordshire. One Sunday I was suffering greatly from headache. Mrs M. placed me on the sofa, and said she would take charge of the children, in the hope that perfect quiet would do me good. Shortly after, she came to me and touched me on the shoulder, saying, as I thought, "Take care of the children." Knowing she was in delicate health, I immediately followed her out of the room, seeing her until I reached the hall, when I supposed she passed through one of the doors leading out of the hall. I then went to look for the children, and to my surprise found the mother reading to them. She asked why I had disturbed myself: my reply was, "You called me." She laughed, and said, "You have been dreaming". Though I knew I had not slept, still I should have fancied I had done so, if I had not followed her across the room into the hall. Mrs M. died in less than a fortnight from that time.'[160]

The 'need' in this case is far stronger from the mother's point of view than from that of the governess: the living ghost seems to be foreseeing her own imminent death. In the next case it is the dead apparent who has foreknowledge of her daughter's death:

125. Lucy Dodson. London, England, 5 June 1887
'When I was 49, between 11 and 12 at night, being awake, my name was called three times. I answered twice, thinking it was my uncle, but the third time I recognized the voice as that of my mother, who had been dead sixteen years. I said "Mamma!" She then came round a screen near my bedside with two children in her arms, and placed them in my arms and put the bedclothes over them and said, "Lucy, promise me to take care of them, for their mother is just dead." I said, "Yes, mamma," and I added, "Oh mamma, stay and speak to me, I am so wretched." She replied, "Not yet, my child," then she seemed

to go round the screen again, and I remained, feeling the children still in my arms, and fell asleep. Two days later I received the news of my sister-in-law's death at Bruges, Belgium. She had given birth to a second child three weeks before, which I did not know about until after her death.'[161]

Lucy had never met her brother's wife, and certainly had no anxiety about her, particularly since she did not even know of the

Some ghosts are motivated by remorse, and their return is to remedy errors or misdeeds committed in their lifetime. This seems to have been the reason for the ghost seen in the 1890s by Bertram Armand of Winnipeg, Canada, which he takes to be his father's murderess

second child. There seems no reason to think the sister-in-law would appeal to her for help: the agent seems most likely to have been the mother.

The need for help or reassurance can sometimes seem too trivial to provide a motive – but who are we to say what concerns may preoccupy the revenant?

126. The R. family. Philadelphia, March 1846
Mrs R. and her two daughters (aged 19 and 17) are sitting at their needlework, when the two who face the door see a female figure enter the room: the second daughter, seeing their interest, turns and also sees the figure, though only briefly. It seems to them totally real. The figure advances into the room, then stops, gazing for about half a minute at a portrait of Dr R., husband/father of the ladies. Then it turns towards the door, where it vanishes. The figure is at once identified as Dr R.'s mother, the girls' grandmother, dead ten years before. The ladies had been neither thinking or talking of the grandmother, but later that day Dr R. comes home and announces that that afternoon, unexpectedly, he has finalized the purchase of a house. Discussion reveals that this must have been about the time the figure was seen. Dr R.'s mother had been very keen that he should buy a house in this district, and it seems logical to suppose that the coincidence in time was significant, for it was just then that the old lady's hopes were realized.[162]

It would be carrying scepticism rather far to suggest that the synchronicity here is due to chance, yet the successful purchase of a house hardly seems to justify a ghostly visitation. But three people, none of whom is aware of the transaction, see the ghost and – comparing notes afterwards – agree not only on the figure's behaviour but also on details of clothing, bag and so on. The apparent had never actually been in the house, yet she knows where to find her son's portrait. Would she have come even if the ladies had not been in the room, or was her visit for their benefit?

Apparitions warning of danger

The message brought by the ghost is, more often than not, a warning: there are several examples in this book. But frequently the ghost goes to all the trouble of paying a visit, yet expresses its message in such vague terms that the percipient is unable to avert the catastrophe:

127. Henrietta W. Oakville, Iowa, 17 July 1965
Henrietta is awakened by a loud clashing sound from another room. Then she hears footsteps outside her bedroom. Recognizing them, she gets up and opens her door. Her dead husband stands there. He says, 'Get the hell out of this house.' Then he disappears. Frightened, not knowing what to do, she goes back to bed just before a heavy bolt of lightning strikes the house near her bed. She recovers consciousness only when her nightclothes catch fire and she manages to stumble out of the house just in time.[163]

Even if we discount the husband's apparition as no more than a guarantor, preferring to think that Henrietta's own subconscious is voicing its foreknowledge of the catastrophe, we are faced with the same question: what is the use of a warning if it's too vague to act upon? Fortunately, there are many warnings which achieve their ostensible purpose:

128. Hy Cohen. Normandie, France, June 1944
'Our family ghost story is laid at the scene of the Normandy invasion, after my brother-in-law Hy landed with the American forces. Our men met strong resistance, and he found himself hiding with a few other soldiers in a freshly-constructed dugout. Suddenly a silent figure appeared before Hy. Uttering not a word the apparition pointed to the dugout's opening. My brother-in-law stared in amazement. He had recognized the apparition as his dead father. Soundlessly the spirit reappeared several times, always pointing at the aperture of the dugout. Eventually Hy realized his father was warning him to leave the dugout. He said to the other soldiers, "Hey, fellows, I'm leaving. Come with me?" No one chose to follow him and a few minutes later the dugout received a direct hit: everyone inside was killed.'[164]

Hy's father would have got his message across more effectively if he had spoken. And he could have saved the other men if he had appeared to all, not only to his son. Still, Hy could be grateful that he both understood and followed the warning apparition. Jeanie Gwynne Bettany's mother (no. 176) must have been equally grateful that her daughter acted sensibly on seeing the vision of her lying on the floor. But the warning in the following case is presented as obscurely as an utterance by the oracle of Delphi:

129. Paul B. Lee. Elkhart, Indiana, 23 February 1958
'After attending an evangelist meeting, my wife and I left about 11 o'clock and walked to where our car was parked. The nearest street light was over a block away so I was using a flashlight to pick out our black Ford which looks like many others in the dark. A little old lady was sitting in our car, on the right-hand side of the driver's seat. I checked to make sure it was our car, then went to the driver's side and opened the door. Before I had a chance to say anything, she said, "I'm sure you don't mind giving me a ride back to town, it's too far to walk." I told her that was all right, but asked how she was able to get into the car, which I always lock securely because my work involves expensive equipment. "Oh no," she said, "all the doors are open, as you can see." They were all unlocked. The old lady got out of the car while we stood there and said she would rather ride in the back. Though the night was chilly and damp, with patches of snow, the only wrap she had was an old-fashioned shawl. Neither my wife nor I had ever seen her before. When I asked for her address, she said, "Just let me off downtown." Those were the only words she spoke all the way back to town, in spite of my wife's efforts to draw her into a conversation. When we got near the business district she asked us to stop. She got out on my side of the car and spoke to me through the window. "Since you were kind enough to bring me here, I will do you a kindness. Listen carefully. Don't ever cross a street where five streets come together and where one of them comes up a hill with a stop light on top of it. If you do something terrible will happen to you." I figured she must be some sort of a crack-pot, so I assured her I would be careful. She said, "I'll be all right. I can see the house from here. I live at 6328 Eggleston." With that she hurried off. Her parting statement left my wife and me speechless. It was the address of an apartment house where we had lived some ten years before, in Chicago, at least 100 miles away! Last Monday I started across the intersection at Second and Harrison Street. I was almost halfway across when it suddenly dawned on me that here are *five streets that meet, one of them does run up a hill, and it does have a stop light.* I instinctively went back to the curb I had just left. As I did so there was a muffled boom and a manhole cover blew seven metres or more into the air and landed across the street some twenty metres away. No one was hurt, but if I had taken two more

118

steps forward, instead of stepping backwards, I would have been right on top of the manhole cover when it blew up. This story is true. I have no explanation for it.'[165]

This is something like the 'phantom hitchhiker' cases we shall look at with folklore apparitions in Chapter 5. There seems no reason why a ghost should need a car to take it back to its home, or indeed need a home at all. The apparent seems to have been a complete stranger, though her reference to the couple's previous address may signify that their paths crossed there but that the couple fail to remember her. The idea of giving them a warning by way of a 'thank you' for her ride seems more like a fairy's thank-you gift than a purposeful message, but the fairy-tale character is countered by the very material reality of the accident. Here is another under-worded warning:

130. Bruce Kaplan. Glencoe, Illinois, 17 August 1960
'My parents and I had been invited to a party. The night before, about 11 o'clock, my mother and I looked up from our books to see my aunt Barbara, who had died three months earlier, aged 61, standing before us. She said, "I have a message for you. Don't go to the party. Now I can rest." Then she was gone. We decided not to go to the party, and we stayed at home that night. At about 10.30 we smelled smoke. Our television set had burst into flames and the walls of the room were already on fire. We managed to put the fire out before it did too much damage. If we had gone to the party, as we certainly would have done if Aunt Barbara had not warned us, our house would probably have burned down.'[166]

Who did the warning come from – dead Aunt Barbara, or the subconscious of one of the Kaplans? And why, if they knew what was going to happen, didn't the message say 'Don't go the party because your TV set is going to burst into flames?' or even ' If I were you, I'd unplug that TV set *now*, before it bursts into flames'? Instead, the event occurs, but its consequences are diminished. Puzzling, too, is the 'Now I can rest' statement, which implies real concern. But how, we wonder, do ghosts rest?

Even with the simplest of cases, alternative explanations offer themselves:

131. Mrs Norah Gridley. Chicago, Illinois, September 1889
Norah Gridley and her 16-year-old daughter Queena are living in
lodgings when both awake one night around midnight and are aware
that a figure is in the room, dressed in white but transparent (she
could see the furniture through it), which the mother and daughter
identify as son/ brother. Both hear him say 'Mother, you must go
away from here.' Next day Norah insists they move to another apartment, though Queena tells her she is crazy. Later they learn that the
night after they left, a man who had a grudge against her broke into
the room: finding a new occupant there, he said 'I don't want anything of you' and left.[167]

Myers considers this experience wholly subjective: in his view,
Mrs Gridley and her daughter share a premonition of danger and
both simultaneously hallucinate their relative as an outward projection of their apprehension. That both waken at the same time,
see the same apparition and hear identical words can be explained
on a telepathy basis only if we suppose that Norah hallucinates
the apparition so intensely that she compels her daughter to
share it in a kind of *folie à deux*. Can we really prefer the psychological explanation – that their subconsciouses are collaborating
in a shared illusion – to the ostensible visitation from the
son/brother?

A further reason for thinking that, despite appearances, these
warning apparitions are creations of the percipient's subconscious is the fact that not all warnings come via apparitions:

132. Unnamed Swiss woman. Switzerland, 1950s?
'One morning when I woke up, I had an uncomfortable feeling. I
couldn't get any peace, no matter what I did. I lay down on the sofa.
A picture was hanging on the wall. I had been resting for about a
quarter of an hour when I heard the voice of my inmost self, it cried,
"Get up!" and again "Get up!" I jumped up and looked around, but
there was nothing to be seen. Full of uneasiness I went into the
kitchen to make some tea. I had hardly been out there two minutes
when I heard a bang . . . the picture had fallen from the wall straight
onto the sofa. If I had still been lying there the glass might have cut
my face to pieces.'[168]

Whereas most such warnings seem to come from outside the percipient, and are often credited to a guardian angel or other pro-

tecting entity, here the percipient credits her 'inmost self' . This is the clearest possible indication that it is her own subconscious which receives a premonition of the impending danger, and takes steps to avoid it. In this instance, the subconscious evidently feels that no guarantor is needed: in other circumstances, it might have conjured up an apparition to convey the warning. But is the entire episode, initial uncomfortable feeling and all, created simply to make her aware that the picture is inadequately secured? For after all, if she hadn't had the uncomfortable feeling, she would-n't have lain down on the sofa, and the picture would have fallen with no one beneath. Unless we are going to wonder whether the picture fell *because* she was lying there . . . but no, stop! that way paranoia lies . . .

Tempting as it is to speculate that *all* paranormal warnings originate with the percipient's subconscious, cases such as those in this next category point in the contrary direction.

Apparitions seeking to complete 'unfinished business'

It seems that some of us carry into the next world quite trivial worries which prey on our minds:

133. Carrie Exell. Pittsburgh, Pennsylvania, 1927
'My father, city marshall of Edenburgh, Texas, tried always to keep his given word. After his death, one night I stood before the dresser brushing my hair and, as I looked into the mirror, my face changed. I was looking into the face of my father. A voice seemed to say, "Daughter, give my pearl-handled .45 to Jack." Then the face was gone. A week later I gave the pistol to Jack Baylor. With tears in his eyes he said, "This gun saved my life one time. Dan promised me he would give it me if anything happened to him."'[169]

But usually a revenant has something more serious on its mind:

134. Baron von Driesen. Russia, 29–30 November 1860
'My father-in-law, M. Ponomareff, died in the country after a long illness, obliging my wife and myself to be with him: I had not been on good terms with him, but he died after giving his blessing to all his family, including myself. A liturgy for the rest of his soul was to be

121

celebrated on the ninth day. The night before, after reading the Gospel for a while, I went to bed. I had just put out the candle when I heard footsteps in the adjacent room. I called out, "Who is there?" and re-lit the candle. I saw my father-in-law standing before the closed door, in his dressing-gown . . . "What do you want?" He made two steps forward, stopped before my bed, and said "Basil Feodorovitch, I have acted wrongly towards you. Forgive me! Without this I do not feel at rest." I seized his hand, which was long and cold, shook it and answered, "Nicolai Ivanovitch, God is my witness that I have never had anything against you." My father-in-law bowed, moved away, and disappeared. Next morning, the liturgy was celebrated by our confessor, Father Basil. When all was over, he led me aside and said to me, "This night at three o'clock Nicolai Ivanovitch appeared to me and begged of me to reconcile him to you".'[170]

Had the apparition appeared only to the Baron, we might suppose it was he who imagined the manifestation, born from the

Revenants are often driven by thoughts of revenge. In Japan, the ghost of Yoichi appears to his friend Ichibei and asks him to avenge his honour on his misbehaving widow and her new husband

ill-feeling between him and his father-in-law. But the independent appearance to the priest encourages us to think it may have originated with the dead man, suffering posthumous remorse. The second witness adds strength to the case for a substantial ghost, as of course does the fact that son and father-in-law shake hands – a rare, possibly unique event in ghostly literature.

Ghost experiences following agreements with friends or relatives that whichever dies first will try to appear to the survivor are a frequent occurrence: we have already noted the Colt (no. 58) and Bellamy (no. 103) cases, and the classic instance is that of Lord Brougham, the nineteenth-century statesman. Here is a simple example:

135. *Miss J. E. L. London, 14 June 1885*
'I left home in May, and on saying goodbye to my friend, she asked me, should she die while I was away, might she come to me in spirit and tell me so? I said "Yes", hardly realizing what was meant. On June 14th, while awake, I suddenly saw the figure of my friend at the door. She looked very ill, came to me, and bent down and kissed me. The next day I received news that she had died at that hour.'[171]

Miss L. knew her friend was likely to die, but the precise timing suggests that it was the compact which drew her friend back for a farewell visit.

Apparitions manifesting malevolence

People are in general frightened of ghosts, but this is because they are unexpected or uncanny, not because we feel any particular reason to feel at risk from them. However, cases occur in which seemingly purposeless malevolence is displayed:

136. *Gertrude A. Poulsworth. Unnamed American city, early twentieth century*
'When I was 10 years old, we had to move to a large city, and my mother took the first partially furnished house she could find. The first night, she put us all to sleep in one bedroom. An old mattress which had been left in one of the other bedrooms was especially dirty and stained, and Mother was going to dispose of it. I had not been

asleep for long that night when I was awakened by something pulling at my throat and choking me. I was frightened to see the horrible face of an old man above me. His hands were clutching my throat. His head, arms, and shoulders seemed to come right out of a corner of a dirty, stained mattress. I screamed and screamed as I tried to pry his fingers from my throat. My mother and father came running, to find me at the top of the stairs. Seeing that I was in a trance, they shook me to find out what had happened. The drawstrings of my nightgown were tied tightly round my neck. I was near death. Beside me was the dirty old mattress which had been in

Though a ghost's motives are usually self-evident, some seem to be driven by sheer malevolence. In the 1890s a Mr Hoonigan, of New York, is alarmed by a glowing male spectre, whose identity and intentions are never revealed: fortunately his menace is confined to his appearance

124

another room before I went to sleep. The next day my mother asked our neighbour about our home's former tenants. She told us that an old man and his granddaughter had once lived here. One day, the man went insane and choked his granddaughter to death. He then cut his own throat and died on the mattress which seemed to be the source of my horrible experience.'[172]

Our immediate thought is that the too-tightly drawn strings of her nightie induced a nightmare in which Gertrude fantasized about the filthy mattress: which would be a neat way of explaining the experience away, except that it doesn't explain how she knew about the tragic events that had taken place before they arrived. The idea that objects, such as the mattress, can 'carry' memories of a former owner is supported by the phenomenon of psychometry, whereby certain gifted people seem, by holding an object, to enter into rapport with its owner, past or present. Perhaps the same process can lead to an apparition? But no such explanation can hold good for this next case, which forcibly suggests a haunter with the most evil intentions:

137. Margaret Mortimore. Wareham–Poole, Dorset, England, July 1947
'At dusk one evening, I was alone in a railway carriage travelling from Wareham to Poole, a journey of 15 kilometres. The carriage was dimly illuminated by one light bulb. After some minutes, I became aware of a presence. At the far corner of the carriage was a woman seated with her back to the engine, facing directly towards me. Fighting against panic, I tried in vain to explain what I saw. As I watched, the woman rose and walked past me. She was enveloped from head to foot in black flowing robes, like the apparel of a nun, wrapped over her head in a cowl and stretching to the floor. She had a dead-white face and terrible, staring eyes that were fixed on me with an expression of burning malice. She stood with a white hand on the door handle. She moved the other hand in a beckoning gesture, motioning me towards the door. I realized, with a sense of cold horror and fascination, that she wanted me to step out of the speeding train. I was frozen to my seat but I felt something drawing me toward the door. There seemed to be a dark, urgent and magnetic force in the woman's gesture, which I had to fight with all my strength to resist. I solemnly believe that in another few moments I would have obeyed the summons, but then I felt the train slowing. I did not actually see the woman go, but she was not on the platform and the ticket collector had not seen her.'[173]

Margaret speculated, 'Was she the ghost of someone who had jumped from a train, and who returned to lure travellers to death?' and this certainly seems a rational explanation in the best ghost-story tradition. Despite her black nun-like robes, she is more of an individual than a folklore entity.

Apparitions as messengers of doom

Paranormal sightings are frequently interpreted along the lines of 'a death is about to occur in the family' and folklore is rich in pre-monitory animals and other happenings. It is tempting to read into these the fears of the superstitious primitive mind for which eclipses, comets and black cats are portents of something nasty

Ghosts often act as messengers, warning of events to come. At Dalbeattie, Scotland, about 1825, a girl is walking home when she finds she is being accompanied by a misty white figure. Three days later her brother is drowned at sea, and in retrospect she thinks the wraith was warning her what was to come. But why couldn't it have been more explicit?

about to happen. However, there are numerous cases where there seems to be a factual basis for these beliefs:

138. De Leon. Bonham, Texas, 1889
'Since twins were a lot of trouble in that time of no conveniences, a sister of our mother, Aunt Sarah, took care of my brother and Mother took care of me. When we were about five, Aunt Sarah died. Bud began to mope: he did not feel well. About two weeks later, Bud and I were playing by the side of the house at twlight. I happened to look up and saw a cloudy, swirling vapour. It became Aunt Sarah, standing there by the house. She had on a dress I had seen her wear many times, and looked just as she always did, except that she never moved. I said "Oh look, Bud, there's Auntie!" When I looked back at Aunt Sarah, I could not see her any more. Bud looked up and saw Auntie and then he began to cry. He ran into the house and told Mother that we had seen Auntie and she said she had come after him. In two days Bud became violently ill and in three more days died.'[174]

We can rationalize this case by guessing that Bud may have already been ill without realizing it, and that his twin brother may have sensed this. But this does not take us far as an explanation of why he, albeit a twin and perhaps sharing the other's feelings, should also have seen their aunt.

Projection with a purpose

We shall be looking more closely into projection in Chapter 8, but this case, where the motivation is self-evident yet clearly spontaneous, shows that it is hardly possible to draw a clear line between projection and some kinds of living ghost cases:

139. Dorothy Carlos. Victoria, British Columbia, July 1969
'At my job at Goodwill Industries I had been reprimanded for taking off too much time and I didn't want to be late. But that morning, after a sleepless night, I was still in bed at 8.30, the time I was supposed to report for work. My guilty knowledge that the store was short-staffed would not let me stay in bed for long, but when I finally reported to Goodwill at eleven I went virtually unnoticed even when

taking my place as clerk-cashier on the second floor. Soon, however, the manager came up to me. He had seen me come in at 8.30, but then he had been unable to find me. "But I just came in a few minutes ago," I explained. He looked at me as if I needed psychiatric attention and stalked away. At lunch time I joked about Mr Keeler's strange delusion with two friends. To my utter amazement both Jessie and Trudy corroborated his statement and reported seeing me come in. Rose, the downstairs cashier, too, insisted that I had entered at 8.30, and that she had greeted me as I came in, "dressed as you usually are". But my daughter-in-law confirmed that she had seen me in bed at 8.30.'[175]

Triggered by guilt, Dorothy's subconscious seems to have projected her extended self to her place of work, where it is seen by her colleagues who suppose it to be her living self. Evidently it conducts itself just as the 'real' Dorothy would have done, which implies that it is either intelligent or intelligently directed. What her colleagues see is, to all intents and purposes, a living ghost. There is some similarity to the *vardøgr* type of case we noted in Chapter 1, in that Dorothy is seen arriving, before her actual arrival. But it seems equally to be a case of projection.

140. Robert Bruce. North Atlantic, 1828

Bruce (a distant connection of the famous Scottish family) is crossing the Atlantic as first mate on a trading barque, when he is surprised to see a stranger sitting writing at the captain's desk. He goes on deck, finds the captain and tells him. The captain accompanies him down to the cabin, but now there is no one there. However, they find writing on the slate on which the stranger had been writing: 'Steer to the nor'west'. The writing does not match that of anyone on board, and the captain decides to comply with the instruction. Some three hours later they come upon an iceberg, which a passenger ship had struck, becoming frozen onto it some weeks before. The survivors, in a desperate state, are brought on board the barque. To the mate's astonishment, he recognizes one of them as the stranger he saw in the captain's cabin. Inquiry reveals that at the time of the sighting the passenger had been asleep, or so it seemed; when he woke, he had assured his companions that they would be rescued that day, for he had dreamed of a ship coming to their rescue. Curiously, he has no recollection of dreaming that he wrote on the slate, but his writing matches that of the message.[176]

If it did not end with a successful rescue, disclosing the survivors' side of the story, this would be a simple and inexplicable ghost experience. But the supplementary information reveals it as more probably a case of projection: the mysterious stranger's projected self becomes Mr Bruce's ghost.

This chapter has shown that ghost experiences can be purposeful in several different ways, and if we possessed more information we would probably find that many seemingly purposeless cases possess a hidden agenda which is withheld from us. The visitation could relate to some factor about either the apparent or the percipient which they are reluctant to disclose – a crime committed, a sexual orientation, a secret vice: anything about which they might feel guilt or remorse.

In virtually every ghost experience the motivation is liable to be personal and domestic. We do not find any larger concerns: ghosts are never interested in helping humanity at large or serving any wider purpose. If they foresee a disaster, their interest is to warn and if possible save the percipient or someone close to him from that disaster. As in the Normandy beach story (no. 128), they don't give a damn about anyone else. Moreover, the ghost is interested only in carrying out its purpose. Once the message has been passed, the warning delivered, the ghost seems to regard the mission as accomplished.

From this we may conclude that the great majority of ghost experiences happen only because someone has a personal need for them to happen. At the start of this chapter we asked: who gains? Most manifestations serve the interests of the percipient, favouring the view that apparitions have a subjective origin. But there are cases where it overwhelmingly seems that it is the apparent who has most to gain, as in the factory-owner case (no. 142). These support the contrary view, that it is the surviving dead who are responsible. So with the 'why' of the ghost experience as with the 'how', the question remains open.

Chapter 5

ON THE MARGINS OF THE GHOST
EXPERIENCE

When a French country girl is visited by Mary, mother of Jesus, or an American housewife is abducted by aliens, we do not think of them as having a ghost experience. Yet what happens to them is no different in kind from what happens to the ghost-seer: they, too, are perceiving beings which have no objective existence in conventional terms. So even if we eventually decide that there are essential differences, we may think that what they have in common is no less important. We may find that it helps us to define what ghosts *are*, by looking at what they are *not*.

Dreams

In the Chaffin will case (no. 112) James is himself uncertain whether he is awake or asleep when his father's ghost appears to him. Should we insist that an entirely different process is involved, depending on whether he was one or the other? Or were the SPR-Group right to think that the same processes are operating whether an apparition is seen in the dreaming or the waking state?

Because dreams are traditionally considered a synonym for unreality, many percipients are at pains to establish that they are not dreaming: they pinch themselves or make other tests to establish that they are awake – Dr H. C. in no. 5, for example. But there are many kinds of waking state, and many kinds of dream state. Here is a striking case which shows how tenuous is the division between them:

141. Miss H. H. M. Britain, c. 1875

'I had gone to sleep . . . Thinking I was awake, I thought I saw standing before my fire, looking into it, with her back turned to me, an elderly woman, rather stout, and dressed like an old-fashioned nurse or housekeeper. Wondering what she was doing there, I sat up in bed to look at her, and the action of doing so woke me. I was fully conscious of suddenly waking, fully conscious that I had been asleep, and had awoken with a shock, yet I still saw the woman distinctly, with my eyes open and wide awake. She faded gradually. I thought it was only the impression of a dream still remaining in my brain that appeared to be seen with my eyes.'[177]

The hypnagogic state between waking and sleeping, and the hypnopompic state between sleeping and waking, are characterized by images of a distinctive kind, a fact that has puzzled many researchers. Evidently the mind is in an exceptional state during this transitional period, and it may be one which facilitates the ghost experience, for Miss H. H. M. is one of many whose ghost-seeing experience occurs at the time of waking.[178] The Burke case cited later in this chapter (no. 163) shows how a dream may merge into a waking sighting, and this next case is indistinguishable from a ghost experience:

142. Mr D. Glasgow, early nineteenth century

Mr. D, a factory owner, dreams one night that Robert Mackenzie, a young employee in whom he has taken a particular interest, appears and tells him 'I wish to tell you, sir, that I am accused of doing a thing I did not do, and that I want you to know it, and to tell you so, and that you are to forgive me for what I am blamed for, because I am innocent.' When asked what thing this was, the young man replies 'Ye'll sune ken'. [You'll soon know.] Very shortly after, his wife bursts into the room with an open letter, containing the news that Mackenzie has committed suicide by taking poison. A subsequent letter corrects the first, establishing that Mackenzie had mistakenly drunk from a bottle of poison.[179]

The dream-figure of Mackenzie bears the characteristic signs of this particular poison – livid colour, sweating, spots on the skin. In short, the figure seen in the dream is as lifelike as a ghost, whereas of course dreams often are not. This raises various possibilities:

131

- some ghost experiences employ the dream mechanism, as opposed to the waking process, perhaps because of the mental qualities of the percipient, or because the apparent prefers this method, or perhaps simply due to circumstances; or
- during *all* ghost experiences, the mind is in an altered state similar to that of dreaming; or
- certain dreams are indistinguishable from the ghost experience except that they are dreamed by the subconscious rather than perceived by the conscious mind.

Augustine of Hippo, in 415, narrates a dream which might have been scripted specifically to demonstrate the blurred distinction between sleeping and waking experiences:

143. Gennadius. Rome, late third century
When still a young man he had doubts as to whether there was any life after death. There appeared to him in sleep a youth of remarkable appearance and commanding presence, who said, 'Follow me.' He was led to a city [which he was given to understand was Paradise]. On a second night, the same youth appeared, and asked whether Gennadius recognized him, to which he replied that he knew him well, and narrated the whole vision. On this the youth inquired whether it was in sleep or when awake. Gennadius answered, 'In sleep'. The youth then said, 'It is true that you saw these things in sleep, but I would have you know that even now you are seeing in sleep . . . the eyes in this body of yours are now bound and closed, at rest, and with these eyes you are seeing nothing. What, then, are the eyes with which you see me? As while you are asleep and lying on your bed these eyes of your body are now unemployed and doing nothing, and yet you have eyes with which you behold me, and enjoy this vision, so, after your death, while your bodily eyes shall be wholly inactive, there shall be in you a life by which you shall still live, and a faculty of perception by which you shall still perceive. Beware, therefore, after this of harbouring doubts as to whether the life of man shall continue after death.'[180]

A substantial number of ghost experiences are shared by a dreamer and a waking percipient:

144. Joseph Wilkins. Gloucestershire, 1754
'One night I dreamed I was going to London. I thought it would not be much out of the way to go through Gloucestershire and call on my

friends there. I came to my father's house and went in: finding all the family were in bed, I went upstairs, where I found my mother awake, to whom I said "Mother, I am going a long journey, and am come to bid you goodbye." Upon which she answered, in a fright, "Oh dear son, thou art dead!" With this I awoke, and took no notice of it more than a common dream, except that it seemed to me very perfect. In a few days I received a letter from my father, addressing me as though I was dead, and gave this as a reason of their fears, that on a certain night, naming it, after they were in bed, my mother awake, I came to her bedside, and spoke the words given above . . . she insisted it was no dream . . .'[181]

In the Durkop case (no. 8) one of the family is asleep and dreaming, one is awake, and one passed out in his car, yet all three are visited by the same apparition at about the same time.

The other crucial lesson we can learn from dreams is the seemingly limitless creativity of our subconscious. Andrew Lang notes:

> As a rule dreams throw everything into a dramatic form. Some one knocks at our door, and the dream bases a little drama on the noise; it constructs an explanatory myth to account for the noise, which is acted out in the theatre of the brain.[182]

This perhaps explains why the author of the ghost experience so often goes to what seems unnecessary trouble – why Elsa Schmidt-Falk, for example, is provided with a Chinese gentleman to show her the way down the mountain (no. 118). Exactly *why* our subconscious is so creatively uninhibited is another matter. Sometimes it is a question of being believed: the more the message is wrapped up in a convincing scenario, the more authoritative it will seem and the more likely it is to be accepted and, where appropriate, acted upon. Compared with the amazing performances which our subconscious stages every night in our dream auditorium, the mounting of even the most elaborate ghost experience cited in this book – the Roe case, for example (no. 119) – would be no more of a challenge than a family game of Charades.

Hallucination

When in 1894 the SPR-Group contemplated the material they had collected, they affirmed:

> this evidence consists largely, though not solely, of apparitions of human beings, who are afterwards ascertained to have been dying, or passing through some crisis other than death . . . the seer not having at the time any knowledge of this fact, other than what is conveyed by the apparition itself. We speak of these phenomena as 'coincidental' or 'veridical' hallucinations.[183]

They faced the fact that this is paradoxical and even a contradiction in terms: indeed, that was for them, as it is still for us a century later, the essence of the problem. A hallucination is, by definition, something that is not real or true; by labelling it veridical, we assert that it does possess *some* reality and *some* truth.

In attempting to resolve this paradox, it seems reasonable to start by accepting the proposition that what all ghosts have in common is that they are hallucinations in which (generally) people who are not objectively present are perceived as if they are present. That having been said, we must recognize that hallucinations can be of many different kinds, and that the processes involved are imperfectly understood. The French psychologist Ey's study alone fills over 1,500 pages, and his is only one contribution – if the weightiest – to an abundant literature. By way of illustrating how psychologists seek to accommodate hallucinations, here is how Ey puts it:

> It is by considering it not as a mythical reflection of culture, but as a real 'shadow' [ombre] resulting from the disorganization of the psychosomatic organization, that we can see the Hallucination for what it is: the apparent reality of the unreal . . . To the manifest content of the Hallucination there does indeed correspond a latent psychic content, but the actualization of that content implies the active disorganization of the psychic self.[184]

No useful purpose would be served by allowing ourselves to be sucked into a discussion of whether psychologists are right to view hallucinations as they do, still less by studying their many and competing hypotheses. For our present purpose, it suffices that psychology recognizes a process whereby we may perceive objects which are not physically present; so that, whatever we may think about the substantiality or otherwise of ghosts, there is at least an accepted psychological niche into which they can be placed. However, there can be no question of thinking that by defining the process of ghost-seeing as hallucination we have explained it to any useful degree. We have simply indicated the type of mental process involved, and we must resist the seductive trap of thinking that the ghost experience is 'nothing but' hallucination as currently understood.

The ghost experience comprises hallucination-plus-content. Simple hallucination would comprise nothing more than the perception of a non-physical being: the identity of the apparent would be accidental, occurring at random. This seems to have been the case in the classic instance of Nicolai, the Berlin librarian who in 1791, following on some personal troubles, finds himself almost constantly in the presence of hallucinated figures,

Hallucination is a recognized symptom of certain medical conditions: this fever victim hallucinates a female figure who is completely unknown to him. Though not a ghost, the figure is produced by the same psychological process

135

some of them distant friends, others complete strangers. So far as he or anyone can tell, these personages come and go entirely at random, unmotivated, unannounced, obscure.[185] By contrast the ghost experience is, as we saw in the previous chapter, rarely random, and generally purposeful. The identity of the apparent is usually known, if not at the time then subsequently, and is determined not in a haphazard way, but by design.

However, to add to the confusion, we find hallucination cases of a kind we would hesitate to classify as ghosts, but where the apparent is clearly recognized. Thus an American mountaineer, climbing solo in the Himalayas, sees standing before him the bartender of New York's '21 Club' who died five years previously.[186] We must suppose that some kind of act of selection took place to determine why this particular individual, from all those in the climber's acquaintance, should be hallucinated, and it is hard to say how this differs from a case like that of Elsa Schmidt-Falk (no. 118). In both cases there is the same ambiguity as to whether the apparition is truly an otherworldly mountain rescuer, or a visualization stemming from the percipient's unconscious, or a guardian angel who chooses this familiar disguise so as not to alarm the endangered person.

But then what are we to say when the hallucinated figure seems to have no individual identity, yet plays an otherwise identical role, as with the 'imaginary companions' frequently described by people in extreme situations? Shackleton and his two fellow explorers in the Antarctic in March/April 1916 later report that they derived comfort from the presence of a fourth man, though none of them mentioned him to one another at the time. A similar figure played a similar role for three escaping prisoners of war in Turkey, at – coincidentally – just the same time.[187] In neither case did the 'fourth man' possess any particular identity, it was simply a comforting presence. There is no reason, therefore, to think that this was a spirit of the dead, returning to give comfort, nor apparently was it anyone living: so we should probably not think of it as a ghost at all. Yet it performed much the same function as many of our reassuring ghosts, and clearly possessed reality of a sort – or how did all the travellers come to have the same impression?

Perhaps it was the creation of only one of the party, who imagined it so strongly that the others also became aware of the presence, rather along the lines of the imaginary *tulpa* which Alexandra David-Neel created as a metaphysical exercise while studying Buddhism in Tibet – a thought-form which she deliberately brought into being and which eventually became so vivid that it could be seen.[188]

Clearly, it would be to halt our quest prematurely to think of hallucination as an experience in itself, or as anything more than a label for a process which occurs as the *modus operandi* of various psychological states related to the percipient's circumstances, pathological or otherwise. Psychological variables of many kinds are the building blocks of the ghost experience: hallucination is no more than the process which enables them to find visual expression as the devil, an extraterrestrial alien or Aunt Jane's ghost. We may think of hallucination as the stage-manager providing the means whereby the mini-drama of the ghost experience can be staged; the actors and the script are supplied by the author's subconscious, either of its own accord or in collaboration with unseen powers. (The drama's audience, of course, is the percipient's conscious self, blissfully unaware of all this trouble being gone to for his benefit.)

Varieties of hallucinatory experience

A notable instance of hallucination:

145. David Fellin, Henry Throne. Sheppton, Pennsylvania, 3–17 August 1963

A disaster trapped two miners 100 metres underground for 14 days. Rescuers were able to contact them on the 6th day, and lights, microphones and food were lowered: they were unhurt, conscious and had some freedom of movement. They had numerous hallucinations, including a doorway leading to marble steps, with people passing through, but when one of them tried to pass through he found it closed. Both saw the Pope in papal dress, a praying woman, and two other miners working with lights. One asked the other, 'Ask them for a light.' But he did not because he was afraid, sensing that they were 'something out of the ordinary': but he insisted he actually saw them, as did his companion. One also told of a 'big garden' with beautiful men and women, and a 'guy' holding a tablet with records on it. He'd have liked to go there, but he wasn't yet ready for it, and he wanted to get back to tell everybody that they should be glad to get there. Though he said there was nothing religious about it, he agreed it was some vision of heaven.[189]

Evidently the stress of the men's situation was responsible for their hallucinations, and dictated their character. The figures were protective – other miners, the Pope (seen by both miners, though only one was a Catholic) – and the visionary scenes were comforting – the doorway, the garden. Of particular importance is that the hallucinations were shared. We may reasonably suppose that the process which enabled both men to see the same visions is similar to that which makes possible collective ghost experiences such as the Barry case (no. 1).

But hallucinations can also result from what seem to be purely physical causes:

146. Unnamed hospital patients. Britain, c. 1980
Patients suffering from eye disease frequently report visual hallucinations such as lines, flashes of light or patterns. Occasionally the hallucinations are more complex:

- A 64-year-old man, while listening to music, sees a brightly coloured circus troupe burst through the window. He sees no such hallucinations if his eyes are closed or it is dark.
- A 75-year-old lady sees brightly-coloured children and other objects.
- A 72-year-old lady sees highly coloured trees, plants and on one occasion gnomes in her garden. The images rapidly change their size and shape.

All three have no doubt their visions are unreal. Each patient's hallucinations are stereotyped, but recurrent so that two give them names: they are not identified with anything in their past experience.[190]

No doubt these hallucinations are a symptom of the eye disease, but the fact that they take these forms shows that even in hallucinations where there is no question of a ghostly manifestation there is more to the experience than the simple process. The disease may supply the hallucination, but its content is contributed by the subconscious.

Hallucinations may be induced by a wide range of factors, ranging from atmospheric conditions to physiological states such as fever, dietary imbalance or fasting, allergy or intoxication. Acting in conjunction with the subject's predispositions, these can put the individual into a hallucinogenic state. A weather-sensitive individual can be precipitated into such a state by meteorological conditions: after a violent thunderstorm which affects him strangely, Colombia farmer Annibale Quintero has an amorous encounter with Extraterrestrials.[191] The seventh-century English hermit Guthlac of Crowland is continually troubled by horrifying visions of demons which are in all probability the consequence of protein and vitamin B deficiency.[192]

Once again we find that, by tracing the experience to its enabling circumstances, we have by no means explained it. The content has still to be accounted for, no less in these cases than in the ghost experience. Guthlac hallucinates demons because they are a significant element in his belief-system: Quintero fantasizes his abduction experience because extraterrestrials are a prevailing folklore in his cultural milieu. But what occasioned this hallucination?:

147. Mr A. England, probably late nineteenth century
On one occasion, when hurrying along a quiet street towards a railway station, Mr A. [who suffered from sight defects] suddenly checked his pace and said to his companion, 'Don't keep me so close to her, rather get in front. I was nearly on her skirt.' He was told that there was no one in front of him and no woman visible at the time on the same pavement. What Mr A. saw as distinctly as anything he had ever seen in his life (if not more so) was the figure of a female walking closely in front of him, so that he could hardly step out without treading on her skirt. The skirt was of red cloth with lines crossing each other, as in a tartan, and over this was a black silk jacket. The dress was beautifully illuminated with sunlight and moved naturally in response to the motion of the figure, while the light jacket was occasionally lifted as if by the breeze. Mr A. made a motion of putting the skirt out of his way with his umbrella, but of course, as he knew, there was nothing there. Having occasion to cross to the shady side of the street, Mr A. lost sight of the figure for a few moments, but it soon reappeared right in front of him, with the sun still shining on it, but this time she had changed her skirt and wore a rich silk tartan, the

prevailing colour of which was green. She was seen not very distinctly in the booking office, and finally disappeared for the day when the platform was reached.[193]

Interestingly, Mr A. sees the hallucination more clearly with his non-functioning eye than with his partially defective one. Honeyman, commenting, says, 'It is not a mere distortion of some object transmitted by the retina to the mind, diverted from its proper course, but a distinct image visualized apparently without the aid of any physical mechanism whatever.'

Yet Mr A.'s lady must come from somewhere! He is adamant that it is not memory – but does that mean it is pure imagination? Whatever Mr A. hallucinates, he perceives in exquisite detail: hallucinating a wall, 'he could see every separate stone and the mortar joints surrounding it, the smooth faces of the water-worn boulders, and the texture of the stones'. Is his subconscious *creating* this image, as it might do in his dreams? Or borrowing it from somewhere? And has his hallucinated lady any psychological significance, or is she just created at random?

Then again, if she is not a ghost, what is she? A subconscious memory of someone he once saw in the street, but cannot consciously recall? Maybe so: but then we must consider the part that memory may be playing in cases which are generally supposed to be ghost experiences. When a widow sees the ghost of her recently deceased husband, could she not be hallucinating in just the same way as Mr A., with the difference that she recognizes her husband whereas he has no recollection of the lady in the tartan dress?

This next hallucination is even closer to a ghost experience:

148. Joseph Kirk. Plumstead, London, England, 1886
'As I descended the stairs to breakfast, I saw Mary (the servant) dressed in her hat and jacket. "So Mary has had to go for milk again," I observed to my wife. "No, she has not." "But I have just seen her, dressed, come from the front door; and besides, I heard the door banged as she went out". "It is your fancy," she returned, "Mary has not been out this morning, and she is now in the breakfast-room." There was no doubt that I had had a very vivid and life-like hallucination.'[194]

No doubt, indeed; but none the less it raises the question *why* Mr Kirk should have so trivial and yet so vivid a hallucination. The content of a hallucination may be purposeless compared with the content of a ghost experience, but it still has to come from somewhere: a choice is made by someone or something. What makes an individual ghost experience specific, and gives it interest apart from that of a clinical symptom or what seems, in Mr Kirk's case, to have been a spontaneous quirk of the mind, is not the process, but the content whose perception is the end-result of that process.

The role of memory seems evident in regard to hallucinations which are deliberately induced: for instance if a hypnotist suggests to her subject that his mother is present in the room. In such a case the visualization is sufficiently 'real' for the subject readily to agree with the hypnotist that, yes, his mother is really there. His memory of his mother is a more likely source for the image than, say, magical evocation, clairvoyance or remote viewing. Even when the suggestion is more general, if the hypnotist asks her subject to 'see' a dancing figure in the room, the subject must first draw on his memories of dancing people to supply the raw material, and then must patch that memory into his present environment. We must consider the possibility that a bereaved wife is employing this cut-and-paste technique when she has the experience of seeing her dead husband.

The fact that the subconscious possesses this power of visualization is a vital element in the ghost experience, for this is likely to be the culminating step of the process: the exteriorization of the image from a mental picture such as you or I can conjure up at any time, to a figure seemingly out there in real space. It is possible that many ghost experiences come about in just the same way as hypnotically induced hallucinations, though whether the role of the hypnotist is taken by the percipient's subconscious or by an external agent is yet to be determined.

A distinction is sometimes made between hallucinations and pseudo-hallucinations, a term for which we have to thank a German named Kandinsky:

> Pseudo-hallucinations may be defined as having all the characteristics of hallucinations, except that of simple externalization. They are unlike the ordinary images of fancy or memory, which we

voluntarily call up, in being spontaneous, and in being more vivid and detailed, and more steady. Like hallucinations, they cannot be called up, nor their form altered, at will. On the other hand, they are unlike hallucinations proper, in not seeming to the percipient to be perceived through the senses. It is with the eye of the mind, not the bodily eye, that he seems to see them; and accordingly they do not even suggest the presence of a corresponding corporeal reality."[195]

Here is an experience offered as a ghost, but which seems as though it might be a pseudo-hallucination:

149. Miss C. B. M. Britain, 1863
'One afternoon, while engaged in some household work, an elderly woman suddenly appeared to me. She stood a few feet below my level, and her face wore a look of anxious inquiry as she tipped back her head to scan me through her spectacles. She remained several minutes with no change of attitude or expression. With my eyes open or closed, she was there.'[196]

Though there is evidently a margin for uncertainty here – we must allow the percipient some say in what sort of experience she is having – it is doubtful if anyone having such an experience would claim it as a ghost if they knew of an alternative explanation. The fact that Miss C. B. M. continues to see the figure with her eyes closed suggests that the experience is subjective. But where does the image of the figure originate and why does it manifest just now and why does it seem to be located in real as opposed to mental space?

Recording hallucinations

Like any brain process, hallucinations are essentially electrical; so in principle they can be recorded. In 1982 a group of Russian researchers claimed to have done just that: they had filmed hallucinations. G. P. Krokhalev, a researcher into *psicotronica* (optical phenomena) reported that they were working on the hypothesis that 'visible images produced by hallucinations are located in a definite space (so-called hallucinatory space) and have a certain succession in time. These images should occur in measurable top-ological space, although this is most probably not Euclidean space . . . the brain radiates in the same manner as the technique which creates holographical representations.' Even allowing for inadequate translation, this sounds more than a little woolly, but they claim practical results, offering photographs taken of sub-jects' eyes at the time they were hallucinating, and which were claimed to be images radiated into space by the psyche.[197] Unfortunately, the images obtained are as ill-defined as ink-blots and fall far short of the lifelike images reported by ghost perci-pients. If these researchers are ever truly able to photograph hal-lucinations, it will take us a giant step forward towards understanding the process of the ghost experience. But for the moment, it seems yet another blind alley.

Religious visions

150. Dora Howell. Paola, Kansas, 30 March 1970
'I was in Miami County Hospital giving birth to my third child. Suddenly I felt my spiritual self leave my body and rise upward. About two metres above my body I stopped and hovered. I looked down and saw my physical body below, seemingly lifeless. Then my spiritual body continued to ascend . . . I knew I must have died. Then I saw God, accompanied by three spirits. I recognized one spirit as my cousin Jo, who had died in a car wreck the previous August. I pleaded with God to allow me to return to my husband and children. Instantly I was back in my physical body . . .'[198]

Homer's audience took it for granted that divine beings could manifest to their Earthly subjects at will. Gods and goddesses participate in the Trojan War, the more readily because they know themselves invulnerable. Zeus is only one deity among many who visits Earth to seduce an attractive Earthperson, while the Old Testament tells of countless otherworldly visits. Nor does this cease with the New Testament: when, in the Acts of the Apostles, Paul and Barnabas perform wonders, they are taken to be gods by the populace eager to believe that wonderworking deities may walk among them.

None of this has much relevance for our inquiry, except as an indication of a stratum of popular acceptance which facilitates the acceptance of stories which, without such sanction, would be beyond belief. But when Christians began to experience visions of their own hierarchy of beings – God himself, Jesus, Mary and other saints – these visions acquired a here-and-now actuality which the old myths had lacked. In particular, many Roman Catholics believe that the Blessed Virgin Mary appears in her physical form to privileged percipients such as Bernadette Soubirous, the visionary of Lourdes.

On the face of it, a recurring religious vision might seem to be much the same kind of experience as a haunting. However, it is an awkward characteristic of religious encounters that though many see the same apparent, no two visionaries see her in precisely the same way. For example, the Mary described by Bernadette at Lourdes in 1858[199] is quite different from the Mary seen by Lucia dos Santos and her companions at Fatima in 1917.[200] This can be variously interpreted. Some might find it reasonable to suppose that it is Mary who decides how she will be perceived on any particular occasion. Others will think it more likely that it is the visionary who decides, drawing upon the store of imagery she has accumulated from her cultural milieu. Because religious visions tend to be public events, instances of established tradition, the individual visionary does not have the same proprietorial hold on the apparition as in a private hallucination. Consequently, there is likely to be an archetypal image – 'this is what the Virgin looks like!' – of which the visionary will be more or less aware, and to which her perception will conform to some degree.

This melding of culturally derived imagery and individual creativity may be playing a part, albeit a less conspicuous one, in some ghost experiences. But even if we set aside the hypothesis entertained by Catholic teaching – that it is the real Mary, descended in her physical body from Heaven, who appears in some at least of the many thousands of purported sightings – the fact that the vision relates specifically to the individual percipient, who seems to have been specially chosen, tells us that the vision is closer to a revenant, targeting a specific percipient, than to a haunter who may be seen by a casual passer-by.

Religious visions are generally perceived by a single person, but this isn't always the case: of the classic Virgin Mary sightings, those at Pontmain (1870), Fatima (1917), Garabandal (1961) and Medjugorje (1981 and continuing) are all collective cases. But there is good reason to believe that at Garabandal and Medjugorje a degree of pretence was involved, and the fact that all these cases involved children – very young children at Pontmain and Fatima – suggests that we might do well to look for a psychological explanation, in which expectation and suggestion trigger a shared fantasy. But if this is true of some, could it be true of all?

Comparison with religious visions may help us understand those ghost experiences where the entity perceived is a folklore figure such as a cowled monk or a woman in white. At both Lourdes and Fatima the entities described by the visionaries differ markedly from the traditional stereotype: this encourages us to think that they are imposing their own image on their experience rather than drawing upon folklore. When a statue is made purporting to represent Bernadette's Virgin, she protests that it doesn't look at all like the figure she saw:[201] indeed to begin with she hadn't been sure her figure was the Virgin, for it didn't resemble the statues she was familiar with from her churchgoing. Only after several visions, when she had time to be influenced by others, did she challenge the figure to reveal its identity and confirm that it was indeed Mary.

At Fatima, the figure as described is a quite bizarre one, very different indeed from the conventional Virgin whose statue is reproduced round the world as 'Our Lady of Fatima'.[202] But this raises a paradox. If a visionary describes a figure which resembles the accepted stereotype – for instance the statues and paintings of Mary familiar from church attendance or devotional reading – then we can reasonably consider it a fantasy formed by expectation and suggestion. But if the figure seen does *not* resemble the images with which she is familiar, then we have to look elsewhere for its source. Paradoxically, the *less* the religious vision resembles the consensus stereotype, the *more* believable is the visionary experience. That both Bernadette and the Fatima children describe something quite different from the stereotype encourages us to think they had a genuine experience of some kind.

Religious figures appear quite often in the role of healer, either predicting a cure or even performing one:

151. Esther Siefker. Long Beach, California, about 1954
'In the early fall I was stricken with double pneumonia and influenza. I heard the doctor say "I don't expect her to live till morning." I was shocked, but not afraid to die. I lay there and prayed, "Not my will, dear Lord, but Thine be done." Then Jesus appeared at my bedside, clad in a long white garment. He leaned over me and smiled. He took a step forward and, like a priest, lifted his right hand about half a metre from my body, directly over my chest. To my astonishment, I sensed balls or pellets of all sizes being released from his hand. While they were not actually visible, the air around them was of a different vibration; thus the pellets were revealed. I felt the heat and shock of them as they went through my skin into my bones and muscles. My body felt light again. I could breathe without difficulty and felt no pain. My fever was gone. The next morning I awoke feeling fresh as a lily and hungry as a bear . . .'[203]

Spontaneous remission of this kind remains a medical mystery. Religious believers see it as miraculous, as Esther herself evidently does. Non-believers might prefer to think that her body achieves the cure by auto-suggestion, in which case we can suppose that she fantasizes a stereotype Jesus as guarantor just as Elsa Schmidt-Falk, astray on her mountain, may have created the oriental gentleman who rescues her (no. 118). That the healing should come in the form of 'pellets' may simply be the consequence of something she once read. And so we can, if we will, opt for a scenario which does not involve Jesus or any external helper. Yet we might think that the healing does indeed come from outside, from some force of nature which chooses to manifest in the form of Jesus so as to conform with Esther's beliefs.

Battlefield helpers

Poised somewhere between religious visions and folklore entities, battlefield helpers may take the form of individuals – Jesus, Jeanne d'Arc or Saint Michael – or they may be categories such as the 'Angels' of Mons. The tradition whereby such beings mani-

146

fest, and sometimes intervene, in the course of human conflict goes back to the earliest forms of religious belief in which the separation of human and divine was less absolute than it has become. Gods and goddesses assist both armies in Homer's account of the Trojan war, and tutelary saints – Saint George, Saint-Denis and others – are invoked by the Crusaders and other armies of the Middle Ages. Apart from Napoleon's personal

'Battlefield helpers' are a picturesque category of apparition. In 1916, during World War One, the figure of Thérèse Martin guides French stretcher bearers to where a soldier lies wounded: it is by doing good deeds of this kind that she gets to be canonized as Saint Thérèse of Lisieux in 1925

demon, otherworldly beings do not seem to have taken part in the wars of the eighteenth and nineteenth centuries, but World War One saw a variety of battlefield helpers ranging from the bowmen of Crécy to the 'Comrade in White' who brought help at critical moments.

Re-emerging as they do at times of national crisis, it is tempting to attribute them to that universal scapegoat, 'mass hysteria', but this does not mean we can exclude such helpers from our inquiry, for here too, as with Virgin Mary sightings, we find individual visions shaped by cultural patterns. Few but the most credulous would believe that Thérèse Martin of Lisieux would physically show up on a battlefield to guide stretcher-bearers to where a soldier is lying wounded; nevertheless, this was reported as a real event.[204] How different is this from ghost experiences in which a relative 'returns' to comfort or even heal the percipient?

Folklore entities

The entities encountered in folklore contexts are like hauntings in that they are recurrent, and like religious visions in that they refer to a cultural tradition, though here there is not even a Jesus or a Mary to provide a degree of identity. Easy enough, then, to attribute the banshee or the vampire to cultural expectation and suggestion. But reality seems determined to reassert itself, even with that archetypal contemporary legend, the phantom hitchhiker:

152. French. Palavas, France, 1981
One night four young people are returning from Palavas beach to Montpellier in a two-door Renault, when they see a woman standing by the roadside. Knowing there will be no public transport at this hour, they stop to give her a lift. Room is found for her between the two girls on the back seat, which necessitates the front passenger getting out to let her in. They drive on: then, as they approach a bend, their passenger cries out 'Mind the bend! You are risking your life!' The driver slows down, safely negotiates the bend, and turns to remark that they are safe when a cry from the girls in the back announces that the passenger has disappeared. Though there is no way in which she can have left the car, a search is made. Then, shaken, the party go to Montpellier police station to report the incident.[205]

No one goes to the French police without good reason: that alone vouches for the sincerity of the witnesses. Commissaire Lopez was impressed that their panic was genuine. But which is the less improbable explanation: that the four are lying, for some reason? that some kind of *folie à quatre* takes place, so convincingly lifelike that they feel the need to report it to the authorities as fact? or that a ghost – perhaps that of a woman who was killed at that location – actually manifests, in sufficiently substantial form to arouse no suspicion on the girls' part that they are sharing the seat with any-thing other than a living person?

153. Ian Sharpe. Bluebell Hill, Kent, England, 8 November 1992
Driving alone on country road A229, about midnight, Ian sees the figure of a young woman run in front of his car. He has no time to brake before hitting her, but stops as soon as he can and hurries back to the body he expects to find. But there is no body, either on the road or nearby: and no mark on his car. After trying in vain to flag down two passing cars, he drives into Maidstone to report the 'accident' to the police. Though they accompany him to the scene to make sure, they tell him that the location is notorious for this type of incident. And indeed, exactly two weeks later, Christopher Dawkins has a similar experience. Though a tentative identification of the girl has been made, it is not certain.[206]

Like haunters, phantom hitchhikers are generally seen repeat-edly in the same place. But not always:

154. Chester E. Hall. Los Angeles, California, 1961?
'I was waiting for a traffic light when I saw the girl. She was hitch-hiking and both the raised thumb and her wistful look were saying she wanted a ride. "No time tonight," I thought. Anyway, no one could want to go the route I intended to take. So with a sheepish feeling and eyes cast down to miss her, I whizzed through the inter-sections to the freeway. As I slowed down to take my place in the traffic, there was the same girl again! This time I stopped. In a moment she was in. I told her where I was heading and gathered this was fine with her. Then I began to think, How could this girl have arrived at the freeway before me? It was 12 kilometres from where I had seen her before, and I had taken every short cut and driven over the speed limit. I decided to ask my passenger some questions, but first I had to give my attention to my driving. When I turned to talk

to my passenger, she was gone. We had been going 90 k.p.h. on a crowded three-lane freeway.'[207]

Even if we can find a plausible explanation of why the girl's ghost should haunt a place where perhaps she underwent a traumatic experience, it is tricky to formulate a scenario whereby it would appear twice, in different places, to the same stranger.

Phantom hitchhikers straddle the line dividing folklore from the ghost experience – or rather, they show that there is no such line. By every criterion, the hitchhikers are as truly ghosts as any others cited in our inquiry.

Angels and women in white

A quite different type of entity encounter experience which nevertheless displays many of the same enigmatic features is the angel. Angels are reported in a wide variety of forms, many of which we can reasonably classify as religious visions. But others seem more appropriately categorized as folklore archetypes:

155. Joy Snell. c. 1919
[Joy is working as a hospital nurse when she sees a figure moving about at one end of the long and dimly lit ward.] 'I thought that it was some patient who had got out of her bed, but when I approached near I perceived that it was not a patient, but an angel. The figure was tall and slender, the features were those of a woman of middle age . . . She went to three or four beds, pausing for a brief space at each one of them and laying her right hand on the heads of the patients occupying them. As long as I remained at the hospital, scarcely a day passed that I did not see this angel ministering to the sick . . . Ofttimes the healing angel helped me when I was attending a patient; at other times, incredible as this may seem, she actually assisted me to raise or shift some heavy and helpless victim of disease or accident . . . I often saw a dark, veiled form standing at the foot of a bed in which lay some patient whose condition was critical. I came to recognize that it portended the speedy death of the patient.'[208]

Although Snell speaks confidently of the figure as an angel, this should not blind us to the similarities with many ghost experiences. Her helpful visitor is unusual in being recurrent: most angel encounters are one-of-a-kind, generally involving rescues or other crisis interventions. Possibly it was not an angel at all but a haunter, perhaps a former nurse at the hospital.

By classifying such manifestations as 'folklore' we may be missing the point. The psychologist Carl Jung has alerted us to the concept of 'archetypes', which he perceives as persistent symbols which recur in our subconscious minds, significantly and meaningfully to those who have the ability to recognize their

The figure of the 'Woman in White' is usually benevolent, but she may appear to reproach a German hunter for shooting a fox

151

significance and meaning.[209] However, archetypes can mean different things to different people, and it would be unwise to see them as universal symbols of anything whatever; for the purpose of our study, though, it is worth considering that archetypal images may have an explanatory value. Aniela Jaffé has collected many instances of the 'woman in white' playing the role of messenger of death in experiences which are unmistakably ghost experiences, and relates them to Jung's theories.[210] Conceivably archetypes provide a kind of shorthand, like the icons that tell you where to find the toilets: perhaps the subconscious, when it has no specific information as to the appearance of a ghost but wishes to make a death announcement, chooses from the available figures the one it considers most appropriate. With the result that the percipient sees a cowled monk, an angel, a woman in white or a man in black, according to her cultural expectations:

156. Rose Hervey. 1871
As a girl of 14 at school, she saw an angel (like the angel in the picture called 'The Reaper and the Flowers', with which she was familiar) carrying one of her schoolfellows in his arms. The vision is believed to have coincided with the death, but the child was known to be dying.[211]

Rose had other veridical visions, so she is perhaps one of those people who appear to have a gift for such things. The fact that her schoolfellow is known to be dying would mean that she is likely to be in Rose's thoughts, and the timing could be coincidental. However, this in no way detracts from the interest of the fact that her feeling – whatever its nature – expresses itself in this form.

But not all angels come in the traditional shape:

157. Silvia B. Alaniz. Alice, Texas, March 1965
'My brother had left his rifles on his bed and I started to move them to the closet. The rifle instantly exploded in my face. The bullet entered my neck . . . I remember men kneeling beside me: ambulance attendants, my father, a deputy. Near the bed, however, was a man dressed in a white suit and in his left hand was something black that resembled a book or a Bible. When I saw him my fear vanished, calmness took its place. As I was being carried out to the ambulance, I saw the man again. He stood on my right-hand side, by the door . . . later

my father and my sister told me there had been no man in a white suit . . .'[212]

If Silvia's man in a white suit wasn't an angel, he was surely doing an angel's job. But how likely is it that Silvia would visualize an angel in this form?

The most frequently reported folklore entity is the 'woman in white', who manifests in several of the cases cited in our study. Aniela Jaffé regards them, reasonably enough, as archetypal figures, representing the 'anima', a kind of super-being defined by Jung as personifying our higher self. If so, encounters with the woman in white are likely to be related to the individual's spiritual development. But we need not, for that reason, suppose them irrelevant to our inquiry: though their *raison d'être* may be different, they may be produced in exactly the same way as ghosts.

Demons and men in black

Demonic entities would be categorized by many as folklore, but this is probably a minority opinion. A substantial proportion of mankind, and not only in primitive cultures, disagree, believing that evil powers physically exist as individual, autonomous entities. Many Catholic theologians maintain the objective reality of the demon apparitions which made life uncomfortable for so many saints, from seventh-century Guthlac whom we met earlier in this chapter to poor old Jean-Baptiste Vianney, the *curé* d'Ars, who was horribly harassed by demons as recently as the nineteenth century.[213] If those theologians are correct who hold that all apparitions, apart from those which are manifestly divine, are of diabolical origin, there is an end to the matter. We can write off the ghost experience entirely as a trick of the Evil One. However, though his existence has been proclaimed for two millennia, the evidence that it was Satan himself who, for instance, individually possessed countless nuns from the Middle Ages through the seventeenth century, is circumstantial at best.

It is not always self-evident whether religious visions are true or false. The continuing visitations of Mary to a group of young people at Medjugorje (Croatia) have been interpreted as diabolical by those, including the bishop of the diocese, who are understandably sceptical that Mary would make daily visitations to a group of not very remarkable teenagers over more than twenty years.[214] When Bernadette Soubirous met Mary in 1858, many other young people of Lourdes claimed that the Virgin had visited them, too. The Church decided that Bernadette's was the only real Mary, the rest were impostors sent by the Evil One. From our point of view, that doesn't really matter: the interest is that so many people believe they inhabit a demon-haunted world.

Somewhat related to demons on the one hand, to extraterrestrials on the other, are those entities known as 'men in black' (MIB) who, as it were, live in both worlds. Ostensibly human, with archetypal characteristics, the men in black, whether or not specifically associated with the devil, are recurrent actors in folklore: they feature in lycanthropy cases in seventeenth-century

The author's rough sketch of one of the three men. The eyes glowed like two flashlight bulbs.

The Man in Black is the counterpart of the Woman in White: a sinister figure who is generally lifelike but with strange behaviour. This is American ufologist Albert K. Bender's drawing of one of the Men in Black who visit him to dissuade him from pursuing research into UFOs

France, and in religious revivals in twentieth-century Wales. Fundamentalist Christians would doubtless perceive them as demonic, whereas they feature prominently in the secular mythology of that remarkable twentieth-century phenomenon, the flying saucer.

However, to assume that today's men in black are no more than a modern variant of the folklore archetype would be simplistic. The MIB are among the most 'real' of all perceived entities, frequently passing themselves off successfully as official investigators and the like. It is only later, after they have driven away in their sinister black Cadillac, that their uncanny nature is recognized by the percipients.[215]

None the less, their behaviour is frequently obscure to the point of being bizarre, which argues against their being a generalized stereotype and supports the view that the experience is directed towards the individual percipient.

In the Middle Ages the following case would surely have been seen as an encounter with the Evil One, yet it is from the SPR's 1894 *Census of Hallucinations*:

> *158. Charlotte and May Goodhall. Country road near Bedford, England, 1873 or 1874*
> 'I was being driven by my daughter in a pony carriage, when I suddenly saw a figure, dressed in black from head to foot, advancing; it appeared to glide along. I said to my daughter, "Oh, do look at that strange figure!" It passed on our left, on the grass, within two metres of us; as it did so, it turned its face directly our way, and of all the fiendish faces it was the most horrible you can imagine; its garments seemed to train behind it. My daughter looked back after it as it passed us; she says it turned its face over its shoulder and looked towards us. I myself turned round immediately – it was gone.'[216]

By contrast, this 'man in black' seems to have been both benevolent and purposeful:

> *159. Barbara Carrothers. Kalamazoo, Michigan, 1935 or 1936*
> 'When I was a teenager, I was playing with my younger sisters and several neighbor girls a game that consisted mostly of chasing each other and screaming a lot. A storm was brewing, lightning crackled overhead and thunder sounded: we decided we had time to make

only one more dash before the rain came. We had run only a short way when we all came to a sudden halt. Directly in front of us under the biggest tree was a man dressed all in black. His wide-brimmed hat and ankle-length coat were from a long-ago past. His hat shaded his face so we could not see his features. Seconds before he had not been there and we couldn't understand where he had come from. Yet there he was, arm and palm held outward as if to warn us to go back. And go back we did, racing and stumbling onto our front porch. We had just reached the steps when a bolt of lightning blazed downward and with an earsplitting crash struck the pavement where we would have been if the man in black had not frightened us into racing home. Screaming, we turned to where the man in black was. But there was no man!'[217]

Can we avoid the conclusion that a folklore entity manifested there, precisely at the right moment to save the girls? Not easily: but let's try. Suppose that one of the girls had a psychic premonition of the impending strike. Her subconscious would project the image of an authority-figure – perhaps drawn from her history studies at school – as the most effective way of halting the girls in their rush towards the place of danger. She might temporarily create a figure, or she might share her visual projection with her companions by mutual suggestion.

Such an explanation involves several unknown processes whose scientific status is questionable: the premonition, the projection of the image, the transmission by suggestion. But it does offer an escape lane for those who would rather not think that a fantasy figure might step out of the pages of *Folklore* to perform a very real rescue.

The next case might be a simple revenant, except that the ghost is chaperoned, like Dante visiting the Inferno with Virgil as tour guide:

160. Unnamed man. Switzerland, 1940
'Six weeks after my friend's death in an accident, I was lying in bed at seven in the morning. Bright daylight flooded the room. Suddenly I saw a completely unknown man standing at the foot of my bed. He looked steadily at me with a smile. I was terrified and wide awake at once. But the man went on standing in the same place and smiling at me. Suddenly he came straight up to me, as if the bed were not there,

and without a word to me, passed by on my right, then through the wall, and disappeared. When I turned back to the foot of my bed I saw, to my great astonishment, my dead friend standing there. He did not smile, but gazed at me for a long time, then went the same way through the wall and disappeared.'[218]

The 'unknown man' seems to be simply an assistant, helping the dead friend to visit the survivor. But is he too a ghost, or a folklore entity performing the function?

Bedroom visitors

Encounters with 'bedroom visitors' seem, at first sight, to form no more than a sub-type of folklore experiences, whether they take the shape of the 'old hag' explored by Hufford,[219] or that of ostensible extraterrestrials such as those that penetrate abductee Whitley Strieber's bedroom despite his elaborate security system.[220] Unlike fairies or guardian angels, bedroom visitors are not an established category whose long history has enabled a consensus stereotype to be constructed. Yet as Hufford found, notwithstanding the absence of any 'authorized' model for them to refer to, many people in many cultures have shared the sensation that an 'old hag', or some such entity, comes to them during the night and perches on them in bed. At Willington Mill (no. 49) members of the Procter family experience pressure on their bodies at night – the classic form of this experience.

This conformity suggests a degree of objective reality, and to some extent this is substantiated by reports. Not only those who experience bedroom visitors themselves, but also observers, have reported the sound of walking footsteps, of furniture being thrown about, and so on, in circumstances which seem to exclude the possibility that it is the experiencer himself who is doing the walking/throwing. In other words, ghosts of a kind are involved in some cases, if not in all.

Do the 'old hags' possess individual identity? So many 'little old ladies' crop up in ghost accounts that it is natural to wonder if the bedroom visitors are simply haunters who make themselves felt but not seen. They certainly have an affinity with the 'resentful residents' we considered in Chapter 4, and perhaps more forcibly than any other folklore entity they require us to ask where, if anywhere, can we draw the line between individual (particular) and collective (general) experience?

This key question arises in connection with certain types of event which experts say cannot and therefore do not happen (for example baby-snatching by eagles and attacks on humans by wolves), but which are periodically reported by the popular media as specific instances, complete with details of who, when and where.[221] Folklorists are not, as a rule, interested in whether the stories they study have any grounding in fact: they analyse them as artefacts and are fascinated by the way they are modified, but the process of origination tends to be overlooked. Yet the question of how it comes about that 'impossible' events are reported as here-and-now cases that occur to named people in identified locations on specific occasions, is crucial to our understanding of the bedroom visitor, the phantom hitchhiker, and the entire spectrum of folklore entities, and of how these experiences relate to the ghost experience.

Extraterrestrial beings

The occupants of unidentified flying objects appear to be the extraterrestrial equivalent of our own astronauts, and no less physically real. Though it is not known for certain that any other inhabited worlds exist, it is logical to suppose that they may do, and if so that their inhabitants are as interested in exploring the universe as we humans are. However, contact with them has been elusive and on an individual basis, so all we have is subjective testimony. Claims are periodically made that there is objective evidence to support that testimony, in the form of landing marks (for the alien spacecraft) or scoop marks (for monitoring devices implanted subcutaneously in human bodies by the extraterrestrials) but the evidence that these are what they are claimed to be is ambiguous. The physical reality of extraterrestrials remains in doubt, and there are reasons to consider the alternative view that they may be no more substantial than ghosts.

Many of those who have studied the subject most closely, such as David Jacobs,[222] insist on the physical reality of the interactions with extraterrestrials which are currently being reported in such numbers from the United States, and to a lesser degree elsewhere. So, of course, do those most closely concerned, who claim to have been contacted and/or abducted by extraterrestrials. For others, these experiences are part of a twentieth-century folklore, and the extraterrestrials themselves should be classified as folklore entities. Both on a biological level – for example, their surprising adaptability to the Earth's environment – and on a behavioural level – for example, their preference for clandestinely contacting private individuals under cover of darkness rather than 'landing on the White House lawn' – they challenge our expectations of how real-life extraterrestrials might be expected to behave.

With rare exceptions, extraterrestrials do not manifest individual identity. American researcher Patrick Huyghe has created a provisional taxonomy which identifies and labels a variety of extraterrestrials, [223] but there is seldom any question of individuals within those types even when they identify themselves by name. The exceptions are those extraterrestrials encountered by the contactees: among others, George Adamski tells of meeting an individual Venusian named Orthon who takes him on interplanetary journeys,[224] and Elizabeth Klarer conceives and bears a child by Akon, a visiting scientist from Meton.[225] (Extraterrestrial names tend to end in '-on'.) However, there are reasons for us to hesitate before accepting either account as literal fact.

Whether myth or reality, extraterrestrials have become a familiar popular concept, and there now exists a consensus agreement as to the forms in which they appear: by and large, the descriptions given us by those who claim to encounter them conform to this stereotype. At the same time, whatever their status, they display attributes which either presuppose the acquisition of skills that we on earth have yet to master, or suggest that their physical nature is not altogether the same as ours. For example, they are periodically reported as passing through walls, windows and other solid objects: this is not something that human beings can do, but it is something that ghosts can do.

While this may be no more than coincidence, clearly ghosts and extraterrestrials have some characteristics in common, and it may be that they share considerably more than that. Many ghosts manifest in response to the needs of the percipient – needs of which she may not be aware on the conscious level. Some researchers (and I am one of them) believe that most if not all apparitions of extraterrestrial beings manifest for just the same reasons.[226]

Seance-room materializations

Spirits of the dead who visit seance rooms in response to spiritualist invitations present us with different problems than the other figures we have been contemplating. On the face of it, they are doing the same thing as revenants: both are the dead returning. But they go about it in such different ways that it is tempting to say that if revenants are what they seem to be, seance-room spirits are not, or vice versa.

However, the differences between them may result from differences in the circumstances in which they are seen: revenants are ostensibly spontaneous, whereas seance-room spirits, however willingly they accept the invitation to participate, are under some degree of constraint to conform to spiritualist protocol. Everyday percipients, if they expect to see anything at all, expect the revenant to be natural and lifelike; seance-room sitters are conditioned to see a figure draped in white robes, shrouded and turbaned, and lo! that is what they get to see.

Materializing spirits almost invariably appear in long, flowing white garments covering all but the minimum of the body beneath, often culminating in massive headgear like a cream topping. Why choose clothing that seems purpose-made to facilitate fraud? Why appear in any clothes at all? Why materialize so fleetingly? Why do most of them dislike to be touched, whereas a few, such as Sir William Crookes's 'Katie King', cheerfully walk round the room arm in arm with the living?[227] To all these questions, the spiritualists are ready to provide answers, but their explanations have an air of being improvised to meet difficulties rather than derived from absolute knowledge.

Yet the possibility must be considered that some, at least, of the figures seen in the seance room are what they seem to be: physical materializations. But materializations of what? Are they in any way, in their physical form or in the mental forces that inform them, related to the dead? Or are they created by the medium, or by the sitters, by some kind of collective 'force'?

Outrageous though this suggestion may seem, the literature of spirit encounters offers a small number of cases which suggest that this is not altogether impossible. In 1912 a Russian occult society, the Brotherhood of the Rising Sun, claimed to have created an *egrigor*, a thought-form brought into being by an assembled gathering, which nevertheless briefly had sufficient physical substance for all present to see it.[228] Something approximating to a man-made ghost, in fact.

When the dead materialize in the seance-room, they choose, or are obliged, to do so swathed in white from head to foot. Queen Astrid of Belgium, killed in a car crash in 1935, is no exception when she reappears in Denmark three years later at a seance with Einer Nielsen

The first seance-room materializations were in the form of wraith-like figures of no obvious shape or identity. Like some of the ghosts we noted in Chapter 3, they would gradually form themselves from wisps of smoke. Then someone, on that side or on this, hit on ectoplasm, which ever since has been the material of choice for materializing spirits. Though its presence in the human anatomy has yet to be established biologically, it has been photographed in the act of emerging from the orifices of the body; and but for modesty, no doubt we would have more evidence still.

Substantial quantities of ectoplasm seem to be required to create a lifesize materialization, swathed in enveloping garments. If it is indeed contained in the human body, it must be capable of very great compaction. It may be that only some people possess ectoplasm, and that it is this which empowers them as material-ization mediums, but you would think that, sooner or later, there would be occasion to conduct a post-mortem of such a person, in which case the ectoplasm, even in compacted state, should have been detected. No such discovery has ever been made.

So far as is known, ectoplasm exists for no other purpose than to provide construction material for spirits of the dead return-ing to visit spirit seances. (The only exception I know is when Belfast medium Katherine Goligher used it to tip tables, by way of demonstrating the spirits' power to investigator Crawford.)[229] It seems unlikely that nature would devise a sub-stance with so limited an application. However, if we speculate on whether ectoplasm may also be used to enable the dead to return to Earth as revenants, we realize that it won't do at all. In the first place, ectoplasm has never knowingly been observed outside the seance room. Then again, the fact that it is exuded from the physical anatomy of the medium herself seems to place it apart from any other category of entity encounter experience: none of our ghosts would be seen dead in the stuff.

A seance-room materialization is invariably visible to every-one present, so ectoplasm is unsuitable for the apparition who wants to be seen selectively rather than collectively. But the mere existence of ectoplasm raises a more fundamental objection: if the dead can return to Earth as ghosts, retaining close if not perfect resemblance to their Earthly selves and thus gaining immediate and unambiguous recognition by percipients, why when they manifest in seance rooms do they go through the cumbersome process of forming a pseudo-body made of ectoplasm, shrouding themselves in swathes of drapery which inhibit recognition? The spirit who manifests as a seance-room materialization does not seem to have any advantage over the spirit that manifests as a ghost: and the drawbacks are many.

Despite these substantial differences, seance room materializations and ghosts do have some attributes in common. For example, both have a tendency to form from a small shapeless source – a luminous ball, a wisp of smoke or some such:

161. Charles Richet. Villa Carmen, France, 1904
[While working with medium Marthe Béraud] 'I see something like a white vapour, about 40 centimetres from me. It is like a white veil or handkerchief on the ground. This whiteness rises, becomes rounded. Soon it is a head, level with the ground: it rises further, grows, and becomes a human figure, a short man, wearing a turban and a white robe, with a beard . . .'[230]

162. N. Heintze. Moscow, Russia, 15 April 1884
'I was lying on a divan, reading, at about 5 p.m., when I saw at the doorway a little luminous circle, like the reflection of a mirror. I could see nothing that would cause such a light. The luminous circle became larger, and when it was as big as the door itself, a kind of dark shadow appeared in the middle of it. A human figure formed more and more distinctly, then detached itself from the wall and advanced towards me. I recognized the figure as my father, who died four years earlier.'[231]

The first is a mediumistic materialization, the second a ghost: so perhaps the two kinds of apparition are not entirely separate phenomena. Or perhaps what seems to be an objective process, taking place outside ourselves, is in fact a subjective one – our minds gradually creating an image from the data they receive? But the fact remains that, while both materializations and revenants are indications of a will to return on someone's part, they set about their task in totally different ways. Seance-room spirits help us to understand the ghost experience precisely because they seem to pursue the same ends using such utterly different means.

Common factors

Here is a case which demonstrates how uncertain is the distinction between folklore entities and ghosts:

163. Pat Burke. New York City, 1964
'I was sleeping in my apartment when I had a terrifying nightmare in which my father appeared in the form of Death. Horrified, I awoke in a cold sweat. There, staring at me from the end of the bed, was a skeleton dressed in a black cape, pointing its bony right forefinger at me – the very figure I had seen in what I thought was a dream. Across its face was a transparent oval form with black marks. I took this to be my father's soul. The figure was making a pitiful, suffering sound. "Daddy, is that you?" "Yes." "'What do you want?" "I'm in a dark, dark place where there's no light ever. Total darkness. I can't get out unless you pray for me. Please, Pat, pray for me. Have masses said. It's the only way I can get out of here." "Where are you?" "I don't know. It's black, just blackness." As suddenly as the apparition appeared, it faded, leaving me confused and shaken. The next day I went to our neighbourhood church and requested masses . . . my father never appeared again. Fourteen years later his sister Bea told him she had had exactly the same experience at the same time.'[232]

Ghost or folklore? Most of the experiences we have considered in this chapter would not be classified as ghost experiences, yet each has something in common with them. To study the ghost experience without taking into account this wider context is to deprive ourselves of much valuable insight. The spectrum of entity encounter experiences, of which ghosts are only one group, shares psychological, physiological, cultural and numinous components. But they do not all have them, or have them in the same degree, which suggests that each kind of experience performs a different psychological function, serves a specific purpose, in our lives.

These marginal entities remind us that apparitions are not the only way we can receive information seemingly known to no living person: even our most private experiences, our dreams, can be invaded from the beyond. Angels may protect us, demons harass us; imaginary companions may reassure us, bedroom visitors oppress us. And each of them, like ghosts, confronts us with the same dilemma: does the protection and the harassment, the reassurance and the warning, come from within ourselves or from without? Does each of us contain within himself the resources to create these richly diverse entities? Or are we surrounded by otherworldly beings who watch over us, unseen and unremarked, intruding into our lives only on rare occasions?

Chapter 6

INVESTIGATING THE GHOST EXPERIENCE

When we consider that humankind have been investigating ghosts for more than 2,000 years, we have to concede that we haven't made a very good job of it. The man and woman in today's streets have pretty well the same idea of ghosts as did their forerunners in those of ancient Rome. The experts are as divided as they have ever been. Few aspects of human experience have resisted explanation so obstinately.

Ghost experiences have almost always been perceived as paranormal events; consequently those who had them, and those who heard their stories, have from the start looked for explanations beyond the normal range of natural causes and daily experience. As each community cobbled together its belief-system, ghosts were accepted as part of the divinely ordered nature of things. The shades of deceased heroes who flit between this world and the next in Homer's *Iliad* are not the anomalous entities of today, but creatures who fit comfortably into the world picture their author shared with his audience.

The majority of people, throughout the earlier centuries of human history, held religious beliefs which allowed for the possibility of the ghost experience. This is because virtually every early culture seems to have held in some form the idea of a separable self which can act autonomously: the notion that each of us possesses, in addition to our physical self, a *non-physical* self – a soul, a spirit, a second or astral self – which exists together with our physical body but is not restricted by its physical limitations. After death this second self shakes the dust of Earth from its non-

166

physical feet and proceeds to some other level of existence: 'Communication with human ghosts was possible only when one imagined that man was composed of two separable entities, the spirit and the body, and that the former had a substantial exis-tence apart from the latter,' writes Professor Shirley Jackson Case.[233]

If the living dead survive somewhere, then it is reasonable to think that, under exceptional circumstances if not as a matter of

Ghosts have been part of human experience since many centuries before the Common Era. An episode of the Trojan War tells how Achilles tries – in vain – to prevent the ghost of his friend Patroclus from leaving for a life elsewhere

course, they may be able to revisit Earth. The belief that ghosts are returning spirits of the dead is not confined to theological religion: it is widespread among unsophisticated peoples. Anthropologists have attested that 'this belief is universal throughout the islands of the South Seas. At the same time it is hardly probable that it came from the Ancient World . . . the inhabitants of the Mariana Islands were convinced that the spirits of the dead return: they had a great fear of the *anitis* (souls of the dead) and they complained of being molested by spirits'.[234]

Once such a concept has come into acceptance, it can be embodied in a variety of beliefs and stimulates a bewildering diversity of ethnic practices. The dead must be appeased, so a king in Dahomey is buried along with his wives and servants, Egyptian VIPs are mummified and provided with food in the tomb, Antigone risks her life to give her brothers honourable burial. Most primitive practices concerning the dead are concerned to encourage them to stay where they are, and not return to trouble the living. For the dead acquire additional powers, most of them unpleasant: the ancient Egyptians believed that the dead were responsible for plagues and illnesses, which they could inflict at will. By and large, ghosts are not welcomed by the living.

Many cultures, besides Christianity, suppose there to be a choice of destinations to which we are sent according to the way we have conducted ourselves in our lifetime. A Greek hero, dying heroically, could expect better treatment than the common lot; but though the dead Achilles enjoys royalty status in the underworld, he confides to the visiting Odysseus that he would rather be the servant of a poor peasant than a king ruling over the breathless dead.[235] From this world, no permanent escape is countenanced, and even when the gods are persuaded to relent, they impose fatal conditions, as when Orpheus is thwarted in his attempt to lead his dead wife Eurydice back into the world of the living. However, occasional return visits are allowed to the privileged few in exceptional circumstances and this gives support to the ghost belief. Contrariwise, the living – again, in exceptional circumstances – might visit the world of the dead and obtain, as it were, a preview of the fate that awaits us. Homer's Odysseus and Virgil's Aeneas both visit the Infernal Regions, where life is not very enjoyable. Jesus visits Hell at the outset of his ministry, as do Zoroaster, Osiris, Horus, Adonis, Baldur, Quetzalcoatl and many others.[236] All of these encounter the dead in human and recognizable shape: this, too, supports the ghost belief by showing that in the afterlife, we shall retain our human form and earthly identity.

Sad to say, there were unbelievers then as now, who reason that the entire concept of ghostly visitations is philosophically absurd. The fourth-century BCE Greek philosopher Democritus is a sceptic who does not believe in the immortality of the soul. Yet like generations of sceptics to follow, he acknowledges that those who report ghost experiences do so in good faith, and consequently philosophers like himself have an obligation to explain them. So he offers an alternative model: that the supposed spirits of the dead are nothing but atoms, detaching from the body at the time of death, which proceed to take the shape of the defunct person. Which is not such a far-fetched idea at that.[237]

The danger of generalizing about what our ancestors believed is demonstrated by the variety of teachings they offered. We find the Epicurean philosophers denying the existence of a soul altogether and therefore rejecting the possibility of returning spirits. Not so, say the Stoics, not only does the soul exist, but it has real material existence: so when you die your spirit can travel as freely as it did during your lifetime. But only so long as you retain your personal identity. This identity will gradually fade and your soul will be absorbed back into the primal essence, after which point there is nothing of you left to form a ghost. Plato and his followers also accept the soul, but for them it is something which pre-exists your body, and unlike your body is pure and perfect: in fact, only because it is contaminated by the body can it be seen. Ghosts then, by definition, are impure – and this explains why they cling to the world of sense. We noted earlier that Socrates regards haunters as impure souls, sullied with traces of their physical self; but for which they would be invisible.[238]

Clearly, from this multiplicity of teachings, some of which directly contradict others, there is no way we can form a single, unified model. But these are the teachings of the few, the elite: ordinary people, then as now, were unconcerned with the disputes of the scholars. They knew that people experience ghosts, and they saw no reason to question that they are what they claim to be: spirits of the dead. And Plutarch, writing in the first century with the lucid common sense which characterizes his writings, dismisses a priori doctrines and trusts the ghost experiencers:

> Although there are people who utterly deny any such thing, and say that no man in his right senses ever yet saw any supernatural phantom or apparition, but that children only, and silly women, or men disordered by sickness, in some aberration of the mind or distemperature of the body, have had empty and extravagant imaginations, whilst the real evil genius, superstition, was in themselves; yet if Dion and Brutus, men of solid understanding and philosophers, not to be easily deluded by fancy or discomposed by any sudden apprehension, were thus affected by visions that they forthwith declared to their friends what they had seen, I know not how we can avoid admitting again the utterly exploded opinion of the ancient times, that evil and beguiling spirits, out of envy to good men, and a desire of impeding their good deeds, make efforts to excite in them feelings of terror and distraction.[239]

When religious doctrines began to be formalized, theologians adopted a more sophisticated approach. In the early centuries of the Christian era we find the Church Fathers arguing the matter this way and that, calling up theological doctrines to support their views. Needless to say, this is all academic stuff: there are virtually no reports of anything resembling an investigation. Most of the apparition accounts are written by clerics and tend to appear in lives of the saints, where the primary concern of the writer is to glorify his subject and hit the reader with a moral. These tiresomely repetitive stories have little or no value as accounts of ghost experiences: what is important is the fact that they are told at all, showing us that return visits by souls in Purgatory are regarded as a reality as much by the Church as by the general population.

When the Protestants break away from Rome, they take a different line, corresponding with their different conception of the afterlife. We find Louis Lavater in 1572 claiming that any 'true' ghost is a delusion created by the devil, because there is no possibility that spirits might return from the dead. So 'it is the Devil who for the most part is the worker of these things, for he can change himself into all shapes and fashions'.[240] Speaking to the contrary, the Catholic writer Pierre LeLoyer (1605) insists that ghosts *are* generally spirits of the dead, who have obtained permission to return temporarily to Earth to perform a mission – to set right a wrong or to expiate their guilt for some misdeed, and it is this – not the person himself, but a phantasmal look-alike – that the witness generally sees. But not always: in some cases the supposed spirit is a fabrication by the Evil One to serve some sinister purpose. It takes an experienced priest to distinguish the one from the other.[241]

Academic interest apart, what is important to us is that so many authorities feel obliged to come up with an explanation for ghosts. It is by no means an abstract matter for them, but one of immediate, day-to-day concern. People are experiencing ghosts, and they look to the priests to tell them what they are experiencing, as did the people of Alais in the story below.

The ghost stories that are recorded are written by priests and monks, who have a virtual monopoly of the necessary skills. Naturally they use them to serve their own purposes: to warn against evil as well as to encourage their audience to do good, to make donations to the Church, to honour and protect the ecclesiastical establishment. So even when names and places are provided, they are seldom equivalent to today's ghost stories. These are moral tales, *exempla*, told for a reason: the stock situations, the formal moralizing, tell us this is a kind of theological folklore, on a par with the miraculous stories told of the saints in order to encourage veneration.[242]

Yet we can be fairly sure that ordinary people are experiencing ghosts in more believable circumstances, otherwise the priests would not find their audiences ready to listen to them. They get away with their pious fables only because their hearers are familiar with the concept of ghost-seeing: and ordinary people can be familiar with the idea of ghost-seeing only if some among them are, indeed, seeing ghosts. Moreover, every now and again we come across a story which seems to have no hidden agenda, which seems to be narrated with no other motive than that of chronicling a remarkable event. When this happens, we find that people of past times, though working within a specific belief-system, did not permit their beliefs to overrule their common sense. In many cases the events are narrated in sufficient detail for us to see that the incident was investigated as thoroughly as in our own day.

For example, in 1323, in the town of Alès (then Alais) in the Gard, France, an incident occurred which was reported by the investigator:

> On Christmas day in the year 1323, I, Frère Jean Goby, Prior of the Order of Preachers, in our friary of Alais, in the province of Provence, was requested by the principal inhabitants of Alais to go to the house of Guy de Torno, in which house, for eight days together since his death, a certain voice had been heard by many people of consequence in the town. Although I went reluctantly, still, to see whether it was an imposture or some diabolical illusion, I set off, taking with me three of the community [names given]. Besides these there accompanied us more than a hundred laymen, to wit, the Lord of Alais, William de Cadoena, etc. When we came to the dwelling, in order to take precautions against fraud, we very carefully searched the house and even under the tiles, and not only that, but all the neighbouring buildings. And in all those which we examined we left the best of the townsmen to keep watch, men whom we could thoroughly trust, turning out all the usual occupants. Further, in two places of the house itself which might offer facilities for fraud, that is on the flat roof (solarium) over the room in which the said voice was heard, and also in the middle of the rafters, we stationed other picked townsmen. And lest perhaps the wife of the said dead man might play us any trick, we arranged that a worthy and elderly woman should sleep in the same bed with her. The doors then being shut, I asked the wife at which of the beds the voice was particularly heard. She answered that, so far as she could tell, it was at the bed in which he had died. And so I, with my three companions, each of us having his lantern lit, sat down upon the bed of the dead man. [Though nothing is seen on this first occasion, subsequently a luminous form appears, claiming to be the dead Guy, suffering the pains of Purgatory and requesting human prayers.][243]

'It would almost seem,' Father Thurston comments, 'as if Prior John Goby could give points to the Society for Psychical Research in the thoroughness of the precautions he had taken against fraud.'

We can be sure that there were, in all societies and at all times, individuals open-minded enough to pursue the facts in defiance of any imposed theories. But it is not until the seventeenth century that the intellectual climate allows a more open approach in which doctrine is no longer allowed to dominate inquiry. Reading Balthasar Becker in the Netherlands,[244] and Joseph Glanvil in England,[245] we feel that these authors, even if they cannot altogether throw off traditional thinking, are doing their best to judge the cases on the evidence. Now, at last, ghosts can be evaluated for what they are, rather than what the theologians insist they must be.

Early in the eighteenth century, in *The Secrets of the Invisible World Disclos'd*, the book he wrote as 'Andrew Moreton', Daniel Defoe suggests that ghosts can be distinguished as 'Angelical, Diabolical, or Human Souls departed'. As the two cases cited in Chapter 4 (nos. 110 and 111) demonstrate, his ghosts still serve a moral purpose, but the moralizing is no longer sanctimonious.

Now collections of amazing stories, aimed at the general public, start to make their appearance: typical is Tregortha's *News from the Invisible World* which is subtitled *Interesting Anecdotes of the dead, containing a particular survey of the most remarkable and well-authenticated accounts of Apparitions, Ghosts, Spectres, Dreams and Visions*, (1808).[246] While the book is of little value in itself, its popularity – my copy is a third edition and there were more to come – tells us that there was a popular demand for ghost stories, and many such collections were published alongside the Gothick novels in which ghosts are a recurring and Romantic feature.

The night side of nature

Meanwhile, serious inquirers began to search for secular solutions. While we may applaud their intentions, it is unfortunate that the theorists tended to try to impose their theories on what they perceived as the problem, without going to any great trouble to discern what *really* had to be explained. Here is Samuel Hibbert, Secretary to the Society of Scottish Antiquaries, for example:

> When the head is filled with many stories which others have related to us of the ghosts of monks, nuns, etc, a man takes what he has perceived for a true apparition. Imagination then heats him; intense and terrible images present themselves to his mind; the circulation of the blood is deranged, and he is affected with a frightful agitation.[247]

This is hardly an accurate description of a single case quoted in our inquiry. But on the basis of it, he constructs his theory that 'Apparitions are nothing more than ideas, or the recollected images of the mind, which have been rendered as vivid as actual impressions'.[248] By which he means to suggest that all ghost experiences are simply the result of our reading or hearing of fantastic folk-tales, which work on our imagination so that we suppose them to be reality. By what process these 'images of the mind' are rendered 'as vivid as actual impressions', he does not explain.

Sceptics like Hibbert are among those blamed in the book which marks the turning point in attitudes towards ghosts: the popular English novelist Catherine Crowe's *The Night Side of Nature* can be read with pleasure and profit today.[249] Published in 1848, this is the year when the Fox sisters in New England are having the experiences which led to the creation of modern spiritualism, but Crowe's approach to the spirit world takes quite the opposite direction. She considers it a scandal that, all around her, people are having paranormal experiences yet the scientists do nothing to explain to them what those experiences are:

> In undertaking to treat of the phenomena in question, I do not propose to consider them as supernatural; on the contrary, I am persuaded that the time will come, when they will be reduced strictly within the bounds of science. It was the tendency of the last age to reject and *deny* every thing they did not understand; I hope it is the growing tendency of the present time, to *examine* what we do not understand. Equally disposed with our predecessors of the eighteenth century to reject the supernatural, and to believe the order of nature inviolable, we are disposed to extend the bounds of nature and science, till they comprise within their limits all the phenomena, ordinary and extraordinary, by which we are surrounded.[250]

174

The impact of spiritualism

I don't know of any scientist who took up Crowe's challenge: but the rise of spiritualism, in the wake of the claims by the Fox sisters, roused widespread public interest, and scientists felt obliged to take an interest if only to debunk the fashionable mania. Here at last, the spiritualists claimed, was evidence that spirits exist, that there is another world to which we shall pass when we die. In fact there was nothing new about spiritualism except that from isolated practitioners, enjoying a social status equivalent to that of today's fortune-tellers, they now constituted a worldwide movement who soon formed their own associations, developed a literature, and established modes of practice. And some, at least, were sufficiently methodical in their approach that it seemed appropriate for intelligent people to take a serious interest.

Ghosts had traditionally been associated with spirits of the dead: so the news that the latter were alive and well and living in another world, and communicating with this world, inevitably had an impact on the belief in ghosts. They were no longer to be dismissed; now they must be explained. To take one example to stand for all, we find French researcher Adolphe d'Assier in 1887 insisting, like Crowe, that there is no reason to suppose that ghosts have anything of the supernatural or the occult about them: rather, he looks for a 'scientific' explanation.[251] He does so first by establishing what attributes a ghost would need to have in order to do what is reported, and then setting out to create a *modus operandi* which would do this. An eminently sensible procedure, but Assier suffered from writing at a time when standards of verification were non-existent, so that his ideas lack the support of convincing case histories.

What he proposes is that a ghost is a secondary persona of the individual, which during that person's lifetime is able to detach itself and manifest as a projected apparition, and which continues to exist after death, enabling the individual to become a haunter or a revenant, as he chooses. This second self is a material thing, though gaseous and with many attributes which the primary physical body lacks, such as the ability to pass through doors. While the individual is alive, the secondary self derives its

175

energy from the primary self; and, like a battery-powered torch, has enough energy to keep going after death, though gradually fading. Sometimes, though, it can, as it were, recharge its batteries by draining energy from the living, or from other sources: he suggests that vampires may do this.

It is tempting to dismiss this as an ingenious but ultimately speculative scenario, yet it contains several interesting ideas which we shall find echoing in other theories and indeed in our own inquiry.

Spirits and hallucinations

The spiritualists, convinced that at last a regular channel of communication had been constructed between this world and the next, felt little need to seek scientific backing though they welcomed the interest of authoritative figures from the scientific world. The claims, if true, were of such a fundamental interest that conscientious inquiring minds, even if repelled by the spiritualist milieu, felt they should at least be aware of what was going on. All kinds of people attended seances, and a climate was created in which reputable scientists could feel they were not risking their reputations unduly if they showed a cautious interest. In 1862 a group of such people formed the Ghost Club, an institution which still exists today. In 1871 the London Dialectical Society, another 'gentlemen's club' for inquiring minds, conducted an excellent inquiry into spiritualism which can still be read with profit.[252]

When the Society for Psychical Research was founded in 1882, the fact that its founders were respected academics encouraged other eminent persons to join. By far the greatest contribution to ghost research ever made was the Gurney/ Podmore/ Myers *Phantasms of the Living* of 1886,[253] together with the 1894 *Census of Hallucinations* for which the same researchers were joined by Professor and Mrs Sidgwick and a host of investigators.[254] For the first, nearly 6,000, and for the second, 17,000 people were questioned. *Phantasms* contains over 700 cases of various kinds; the *Census* includes 352 apparitions of living persons, 163 of the dead.

What is of the greatest value today is the unique collection of case histories, all of which were double-checked. While this does not mean that each and every one necessarily occurred as reported, it does mean that they were examined far more rigorously than the typical anecdotal collection where the percipient's claim may be accepted on nothing more than her say-so. The compilers of these two reports go to great lengths to explain how they excluded many cases, not because they doubted the witness but because there was no way to substantiate the claim. Nothing approaching this effort, which involved countless hours of dedicated labour, has ever been carried out since, and the cases in these collections remain the finest evidence ever presented for the diversity of the ghost experience.

Here is an example of the care taken by the SPR before they would include a case in their *Census*. Mr S. Walker-Anderson writes from Australia that on 17 November 1890, 'An aunt of mine, who died in England, appeared before me in Australia, and I knew before I received the letter of her death that she was dead. I took a note of it at the time.'[255] First, this is confirmed in writing by the percipient's wife; secondly, on 19 December 1891 Professor Sidgwick personally interviews Mr Anderson, to check on details; thirdly, on 20 March 1892 he questions both the percipient and his wife; finally, the date of the aunt's death is independently confirmed.

But there is more to *Phantasms of the Living* and the *Census* than case histories: there are the comments made by the authors. The SPR-Group adopted a cautious and thoughtful approach which set the standard for all future research. But they were working at a moment of transition, which is perhaps best expressed by Andrew Lang, himself a member of the SPR and a prolific inquirer into the ghost phenomenon:

> The old doctrine of 'ghosts' regarded them as actual 'spirits' of the living or the dead, freed from the flesh or from the grave. This view, whatever else may be said for it, represents the simple philosophy of the savage, which may be correct or erroneous . . . The modern doctrine is that every ghost is a hallucination: it gives the impression of the presence of a real person, in flesh, blood, and usually clothes, though no such person in flesh, blood and clothes is

actually there ... The difficulty begins when we ask whether these appearances ever have any provoking mental cause outside the minds of the people who experience them – any cause arising in the minds of others, alive or dead.[256]

Lang quotes the American psychologist William James (another prominent SPR member), and we shall do the same, for no one has more lucidly expressed the difficulties that challenge us:

Sporadic cases of hallucination, visiting people only once in a life-time (which seem to be by far the most frequent type), are on any theory hard to understand in detail. They are often extraordinarily complete; and the fact that many of them are reported as *veridical*, that is, as coinciding with real events, such as accidents, deaths, etc. of the persons seen, is an additional complication.[257]

The SPR-Group were determined to drag psychical research into the scientific age, and did not question that hallucination offers a better explanation of the ghost experience than spirit visitation. Yet the testimony they collected spoke eloquently in support of involvement by 'the minds of others, alive or dead'. The solution then, the *only* viable solution, was telepathy (and other forms of ESP). In the very first paragraph of *Phantasms* they write:

We propose to deal with all classes of cases where there is reason to suppose that the mind of one human being has affected the mind of another, without speech uttered or word written, or sign made; – has affected it, that is to say, by other means than through the recognized channels of sense.[258]

The same assumption prevails in the *Census*, where the authors reveal their approach in such a comment as this: 'If all hallucinations are sensory manifestations of conscious or subconscious ideas, all that telepathy has to do is to introduce the idea.'[259] The assumption that every apparition of the living can be classified as telepathic bogged down their inquiry by closing the authors' minds to wider implications. We shall see in Chapter 8 that, for all the perception and intelligence the SPR-Group brought to the subject, their attempt to classify every such apparition as an instance of thought-transference is inadequate to explain so complex a phenomenon.

Investigation after 1900

The investigator of ghosts is rarely a witness: Rosina Despard, heroine of the Cheltenham case (no. 14), is very much the exception. Almost always the investigation of ghosts is a second-hand affair: what the investigator is investigating is a story told by someone else about what they have experienced.

The two monuments of SPR research, *Phantoms* and the *Census*, are mainly concerned with apparitions of the living or crisis apparitions (which they classify as apparitions of the living); by far the majority are once-only cases. The SPR-Group make little distinction between haunters and living ghosts, assuming them to be fundamentally the same phenomenon, but since their time on the two fields of research diverge. Just as ghosts are divided into two broad categories – those which manifest repeatedly, such as haunters; and spontaneous ghosts which appear once or twice only, such as crisis apparitions – so investigation of them is of two kinds: the approach is altogether different in each case. Haunters, being an on-going affair, are open to field investigation of the site: historical research can provide clues, and the ghost-buster can go into action with a full panoply of cameras, recorders and detectors. Once-only apparitions, on the other hand, are not available for investigation, so attention is focused on the percipient and the attendant circumstances.

If you look in library or bookshop for books about ghosts, you will find that the great majority fall into the category of 'A Ghost-hunter's Casebook', dealing almost entirely with hauntings, and generally written by enthusiastic amateurs. Investigating haunted houses is an enjoyable group activity, providing participants with the opportunity to exercise their talents without the need to get emotionally involved. In the investigation of once-only apparitions, on the other hand, questioning witnesses is often the only line of approach. It is laborious and potentially embarrassing; the issues are less clear-cut, there is little scope for detective work, and the results are liable to be ambiguous. Which is why such research is more often conducted by professional bodies such as the SPR and ASPR.

The early twentieth century was the era of the private investigator, usually an author who when he has collected sufficient cases to fill a book, writes one. The literature of ghosts is vast, but the great majority consists of collections of anecdotes: interesting in their way, and providing food for thought, but not helping us much along the way to understanding. Typical is Elliott O'Donnell (1872–1965): I have more than thirty of his books on my shelves, but I have quoted from none of them in this inquiry. The lack of any real evidence and the flamboyant style make for tedious reading despite the sensational detail with which he spices the stories. The 1930s saw a proliferation of such collections: Lord Halifax's two volumes boast reputable sources but their evidential value is slight. Harry Price, for all his shortcomings, did more than any other individual to sustain serious interest. He paid some attention to ghosts, but most of his time was spent investigating mediums; as for the case with which he is most widely associated, Borley Rectory, it has become so embedded in controversy that the original ghost story – which seems to have contained authentic episodes (no. 46) – is lost among the modern fun and games.

A handful of thoughtful investigators, Andrew Green and Peter Underwood in Britain, Scott Rogo and Raymond Bayless in America, have maintained a serious level of investigation standards. But the investigators who have best honoured the precedent set by the SPR-Group are Andrew Mackenzie, whose examination of such cases as that of Cheltenham is a model of thoughtful research,[260] and his colleagues Alan Gauld and Tony Cornell (whose failure to see a ghost is recounted in no. 61).

Exorcists and 'ghost-busters'

In the popular mind the investigation of ghosts tends to be equated with 'ghost-busting'. The only type of ghost which is directly susceptible to investigation is the haunter, and it is widely assumed that the haunter is some kind of pest which one should seek to expel as one would woodworm or rats.

There is of course an element of truth in this. People moving into a new house are rarely pleased to find it is haunted, even by a little old grey-haired lady who doesn't harm anyone. Some households accept their ghost, and may even take a proprietorial pride – Oh goodness, they say to the guest who comes down ashen-faced to the breakfast table after a disturbed night, you mustn't mind her, she's almost a friend of the family!

But most haunters, even if they are not malevolent, are disturbing, and it is understandable that families should wish to be rid of them. So there are countless investigators, working singly or in groups, who offer to clear houses of unwanted residents. They often include those claiming psychic gifts, who can detect the presence of the ghost. Once its identity is established, a dialogue is set up and the ghost is talked into leaving.

Is this what is actually taking place? Or is something less specific being dispelled, some kind of psychic atmosphere? Could it even be that it is the percipients themselves who are purged of their fears, real or imagined?

Those who would have us accept the reality of demons point to the frequent success of exorcism in rescuing victims of possession. Psychologists, on the other hand, prefer to think that if exorcism succeeds it is because it is driving out not a demon but the *idea* of the demon. For them, the supposed demon is a fantasy creature who exists only in the mind of the victim, and what the exorcist is doing is using one fantasy to dispel another. Consider this admirably honest account by Father Trabold, Professor of Comparative Religion at St Bonaventure University, in New York State, USA:

> Only on very rare occasions have I ever performed an exorcism, and even in those cases I am not absolutely sure whether or not these were cases of true possession, or if there was some other explanation. At the time of this particular case, I felt there was an emergency situation. The girl had experienced a period of infestation in her apartment, which was witnessed also by the girl who roomed with her. She believed Satan was appearing to her and talking to her, threatening to take her over completely. I tried to use psychological methods such as suggestion, counselling, etc., but I could not make any headway. She believed she had sold herself to the Devil, with the consequences of poltergeist or infestation

phenomena, visions or hallucinations of the Devil or demons. [I reached the point where] the only action I felt would help her would be some form of prayer and exorcism. I felt if the girl did not receive help immediately, she could become psychologically unbalanced and might very likely have tried suicide. We are dealing here with a person in great need. Whether or not we are dealing with a true diabolical being or whether we are dealing with a demon created by the mind of the person, it is extremely real for the person. So if an exorcism helps, either in a supernatural way of actually driving out a real demon, or psychologically, simply by removing the demon from their mind, it is for me an act of healing.

When performing the exorcism, I did have a feeling of an evil presence. The opposition was very strong, the battle continued for quite some time. Finally the girl opened her eyes and a beautiful smile came on her face. 'Is he gone? Is he really gone?' While I have no absolute proof the exorcism was successful, the indication is that it was.

I must in all honesty call attention to a possible alternative explanation from the point of view of psychology. If she were suffering from merely a psychological delusion, you could overcome this through a counter-suggestion. If the person is so convinced the Devil is real, the only way you can help her, even on a psychological level, is to come down to her level of belief. Even if we are dealing with a case purely of a psychological state, the exorcism becomes a form of healing.[261]

This has relevance for our inquiry in that some apparitions may be, like the delusions of demonic victims, fantasies which are given a quasi-existence by the percipient to serve some psychological need of her own. If all those saints who have wrestled with demons throughout history were in fact fighting nothing more than a fantasy construct created by their subconscious to give substance to their beliefs, then so it may be with a proportion of our ghosts.

The same ambiguity arises when it's a matter of expelling a haunter from a house. Much will depend on the beliefs of the investigator. An unprejudiced investigator such as Andrew MacKenzie will investigate a case such as the Cheltenham haunting in a dispassionate manner, his sole concern being to establish the facts. Others, on the other hand, may work from a particular belief system: if they subscribe to the belief that the haunter is an unhappy spirit, for instance, they will proceed accordingly. There is a class of people, variously known as 'psychics' or 'sensitives', who consider themselves closer to other dimensions of reality than the rest of us, and to be in a position to make contact with beings who inhabit those dimensions. Such people, if invited to investigate a haunted house, claim to detect presences. Some will go further, and undertake to persuade earthbound spirits to let go their hold on things of this world and make their way to the next.

For example, self-described 'soul rescuer' Terry O'Sullivan describes a visit to the Black Swan inn at Pluckley, Kent:

164. O'Sullivan. Black Swan Inn, Pluckley, late twentieth century
[In the corridor leading to the toilets] I became aware of a quiet voice calling . . . I could hear the voice clearly, I realized that it was crying mournfully as it pleaded: 'Simon, Simon, it's me. Please, please, where are you? It's Matilda. Please, talk to me – it's been too long, please!' I asked the landlord if any ghosts had ever been seen or heard in the pub itself. 'Oh yes,' he said without hesitation, 'we've got Matilda! The story is she's haunting the pub looking for her husband, who was arrested on a charge of treason by Cromwell's Roundheads. It seems they took him away to Rochester Castle where they tortured him. Some of the soldiers took her down to the cellar where they raped her.' [He goes down to the cellar.] I only had to wait a few minutes before Matilda's disembodied form appeared. I was expecting a young woman, so I was surprised when Matilda turned out to be in her sixties. At first she was disappointed that I wasn't Simon, but I reassured her that I would help her find him . . . Luckily Simon wanted to be called forward. As Matilda had been searching for him, so he too had been looking for her. I only had to chant for a matter of minutes before he began to appear . . . Even though Simon and Matilda were in the cellar with me they were unable to see each other because they were in separate time zones; Matilda had died over 40 years after Simon . . . All I had to do was ask each of them to focus and visualize on an important event in their lives and then to trust in each other's love. Both chose their wedding day . . . all three of us prayed for their reunion. I was so happy for them, reunited on their wedding day and then able to move into the spirit realms.[262]

It's a heart-warming story, and perhaps this is exactly what took place – but we have no confirming evidence, and a lot of questions. Should we believe that Matilda has been hanging around that pub for 350 years, crying mournfully night after night, until the happy day comes when she is rescued by someone who happens to know how to contact earthbound spirits? We can surely sympathize with her comment that 'it's been too long'.

A sceptic might wonder that, if Simon and Matilda couldn't see each other because 'they were in separate time zones', how come O'Sullivan could see either of them? He might further point out that popular books refer to Pluckley as 'the most haunted village in England', and that a professional soul rescuer would be aware of its reputation and be primed to expect ghostly encounters. The entire episode could be a fantasy: though if Matilda's sighs are never again heard at the Black Swan, that would tend to confirm O'Sullivan's claim.

One problem with 'ghost-busting' is that the ghost-busters tend to work to an agenda. Whether they start from a specific belief-system – for instance, that ghosts are demons, or spirits of the dead – or whether their ideas develop as a result of their experience, they sooner or later establish a formularized procedure. While they may be right, what we have seen of the ghost experience in our inquiry suggests that the adoption of any formula is likely to be premature. Consequently we should look at the claims of the ghost-busting individuals and groups with scepticism, if not disquiet.

For example, Robin Furman, described as a psychologist and one of Britain's few lecturers in parapsychology, heads a team of psychic investigators that includes a microbiologist, a computer consultant and an electronics engineer, which sounds as if they are going about things in a properly scientific spirit. So, when they investigate a haunting at Grange Farm, Lincolnshire,

> our first task was to disrupt the earth's magnetic forces around the house, so we took our rope and completely encircled Grange Farm. The rope was no ordinary rope. Entwined in it was a flexible wire so that when the two ends met it formed a continuous, unbroken circle. This formed a 'ring of power' – a shape that has historically been found effective against unpleasant forces . . . At the four points of the compass we erected cardboard pyramids . . . We drew a double circle in white chalk on the bare floor of the lounge . . . inside the circle we wrote a few magic words, the sort of words

which have been used since time immemorial . . . To complete this traditional magical scene we all dressed up, covering our everyday clothes with black, monk-like robes . . . We lit a brass brazier of incense . . .[263]

Mr Furman and his colleagues would doubtless justify these means by the successful ends. They claim a high success rate in busting ghosts, and if rings of power, monks' robes and incense help, who's arguing?

Well, one who would want to argue with that approach would be the housewife in a case I helped investigate, who told me 'I don't want to get rid of it, I want to *understand* it.' The ghost experience is often a shared affair, in which the percipient is as much involved as the apparent. It may be that all ghost-busting does is to remove one part of the collaboration. The manifestations cease when the percipients – believing the ghost 'busted' – withdraw their involuntary contribution to the experience.

If all ghost-busting groups employed the same methods and worked to the same criteria, one might have more respect for them. But each has its own protocol, and the inference is that it is not the procedure but the individuals operating it, which count for most in the affair. If by their carryings-on they are able to rid houses of unwanted disturbances and put people's minds at rest, perhaps the ends do justify the means. There is no doubt but that some ghost-busters and exorcists are successful: after their ministrations the activities cease. But by curing symptoms rather than identifying causes, they don't take us a step towards understanding the ghost experience.

A physical basis for ghosts

Not all investigative groups operate with predetermined belief-systems. Many ghost investigators focus on the material aspects of haunting. Is there a physical aspect to the haunter which can be established independently of human observation? To this end, groups such as Britain's ASSAP (Association for the Scientific Study of Anomalous Phenomena), which have no preconceived viewpoint, visit haunted sites armed with as much equipment as

Today's ghost investigators occasionally obtain inexplicable results. Just before the Association for the Scientific Study of Anomalous Phenomena commenced an all-night ghostwatch at the Ancient Ram Inn, Wotton-under-Edge, Gloucestershire, England, on 5 June 1999, this anomalous shape was photographed on the staircase where, some years earlier, a murder had been committed

they can afford to buy or borrow. The Ghost Research Society of Chicago, going into action in an allegedly haunted house, took with them a negative-ion detector to search for static electricity; an infrared-based non-contact thermometer 'gun' to gauge fluctuations in temperature; a Geiger counter to detect unusual radiation; and a tri-field meter to recognize disturbances in electromagnetic fields.[264]

Some investigators claim positive findings. Filmed for a television documentary, investigators headed by William Roll and Andrew Nichols, both of them professors of parapsychology in American universities, found significant electromagnetic readings in houses where hauntings were claimed. In the Johnson home in Indiana, the electromagnetic field level measured 130 milligauss where the norm would be between 2 and 10, the geomagnetic field 440 compared with 50.[265] Significant – but signifying what, exactly? Is this what conditions have to be like in order that a haunter may haunt? Would any home with such configurations bring the haunters out of the woodwork? Would your home or mine be haunted if it met the specification?

Surely there is more to a haunting than the electrical properties of the site; yet it may be that such coordinates are requisite before a sighting may occur. But then again, another question arises: who are they requisite for, the haunter or the haunted? Perhaps the haunters are there all the time, ready to perform, but only if the energy levels are conducive is the living percipient able to detect them. And even then it may be necessary for the percipient to be an exceptional person: the victim of the Indiana home, Doretta Johnson, was able to enter an altered state of consciousness very rapidly, 'indicative of the type of brain configuration that we find in people who are psychically sensitive'. Well, but how do you evaluate someone's psychic sensitivity? By her ability to detect ghosts? We are into a circular logic that doesn't seem likely to take us very far.

Nor are haunted houses the only locations where geophysical conditions may give rise to apparitions. In 1997–98, according to a posting on the internet, Bob Schott, a television producer, using a night-vision camera in the supposedly haunted Bell Witch Cave at Adams, Tennessee, recorded 'an energy pattern emerging from a crevice . . . as the light rose, it floated to the right, growing into an image that resembled a face'. A drop in temperature was simultaneously recorded.

It is difficult to know how seriously to take this – the account is as vague as the apparition itself seems to have been. However, similar cases have been reported elsewhere:

165. Eastman, Woodew. London, c. 1930?
Eastman, Chief Engineer at the Rhodes Electrical Company, London, was working with his colleague Harold Woodew in a darkened room, arranging high-tension wires to form a magnetic field. To their astonishment, a luminous blue sphere began to form over a dynamo revolving near them. Then, as the light grew brighter, they saw a form resembling a human hand appear in the centre of the sphere. They watched it for several minutes, until it faded away. For four days, the two men worked to re-create the conditions in which the phenomenon had occurred. When they eventually succeeded, the sphere again appeared, but this time the form which appeared in the magnetic field resembled a human head, white in colour and slowly revolving. Eastman is said to have photographed the form before it vanished.[266]

166. Unnamed workers. LaCrosse, Wisconsin, 1931
Workers at the Northern State Power Company's generating plant observed a similar display, though even more distinctly. A standby turbine had just been brought on line when a cloud began to form above it. The engineers thought the turbine must be overheating, but when they checked their gauges, everything seemed normal. Then within the cloud there appeared, clearly and distinctly, the image of a woman lying on a couch. One of her arms was covered with jewels, and there were rings on her fingers. The men watched it for about twenty seconds before it faded out.[267]

These tantalizing anecdotes could lead the way to establishing the physical basis of hauntings, if we only had the relevant data. As it is, we don't. Bob Schott also found unusual temperature fluctuations in Hermitage Castle, a thirteenth-century Scottish building where child sacrifices are said to have been made, though when and by whom is undisclosed. For good measure, balls of light have also been seen. Should we conclude from this that the spirits of the murdered children are still haunting the place, perhaps disguised as balls of light – balls which may perhaps swell into person-size figures if the electromagnetic levels are favourable (see nos. 161 and 162)? Does the temperature drop when they manifest? Again, there are so many undetermined factors that the heart sinks in frustration.

Well, but there may be a similarity here to the Gestalt theory, or class of theories. Such theory suggests that 'groups of thoughts common to many minds may form autonomous, mind-like, conscious, active psychical entities, with telepathic, clairvoyant, precognitive and telekinetic powers.'[268] Which could be responsible for *egrigors*, *tulpas* and other deliberately created entities. Except that we don't even have a testable model, let alone scientific evidence that anything of the sort takes place.

Another approach is to focus on the haunted location. Two serious American researchers, Michaeleen C. Maher and George P. Hansen, have published detailed accounts of their investigations of haunted sites, taking with them a team of sensitives and a team of sceptics, as well as instruments of various kinds. They found that the sensitives were able to identify, at an above-chance level, the precise locations associated with apparitions, performing significantly better than the sceptics. On the other hand, 'three witnesses each chose a different likeness from a series of photographs as the image that most closely resembled an apparition each had reported'. Conceivably, they speculate, more than one ghost was haunting the site . . .[269] Their findings strongly support the belief that there is something 'psychic' about the site, but they fail to confirm a particular haunter, let alone provide any indication of who the apparent might be, what her purpose is and why anything at all should be happening.

The experimental investigation of the ghost percipient

The percipient in the Johnson haunt possessed an exceptional brain configuration, which may have made her more liable than the rest of us to detect the presence of a haunter. For the most part, however, in spontaneous cases – revenants, crisis apparitions, living ghosts – field investigation is generally irrelevant: the approach can only be through the percipient's own account of the experience, together with a study of the attendant circumstances.

This is rarely a field in which an amateur investigator has any competence, so research of this kind tends to be professional, conducted by behavioural scientists.

Since the ghost-seeing process is almost universally considered to be, or to involve, hallucination, this is the area which has been most studied. Experimental efforts to determine what is involved in hallucination have been made for a long time. One experiment sought to find out whether the body responds to hypnotically induced hallucinations, but no conclusive findings were obtained. The effect of drugs is another approach: it has been found that drugs can inhibit REM sleep, and therefore dreams (or at any rate, any memory by the subject that he has dreamed). So, do drugs affect our ghost-seeing potential? The level of serotonin in the body can inhibit hypnagogic visions. All of this may throw light on the neurological processes involved; but just as emerged when we considered hallucinations in Chapter 5, it is unlikely to illumine the element that defines the ghost experience: the ghost itself.

The situation today

One of the most thoughtful present-day commentators on ghosts is Emily Peach and it is difficult to argue with her when she writes:

> The scientific theories have a pleasant, polished, and very satisfactory, unsuperstitious and down-to-earth appearance. Unfortunately, although they do cover some cases very well indeed, they fail to function adequately in others. Primarily, this is because the theorists are reluctant to admit in any category of case, whether collectively perceived or not, that some thing or being external to the percipient(s) might be objectively present, preferring to postulate instead that percipients of veridical hallucinations, having obtained information by telepathy, then proceed (for obscure psychological reasons that are never really satisfactorily explained), to convert that information into a hallucination. Further, while some of the theories allow the possibility that the information itself might have been conveyed by a deceased person, others will not countenance even that, and in all cases they demand extraordinary feats of the human mind.[270]

She proposes instead an 'occult' theory. (The label is unfortunate, because it conjures up ideas of Blavatsky and Crowley, which could discourage people from taking her ideas seriously.) I think she means one which assumes that the facts can be explained only by taking on board either a spiritist scenario, or one which assumes the existence of a secondary self of the kind we have already encountered in our own inquiry. This is not far from Jungian psychologist Aniela Jaffé's summing-up:

> Parapsychology has two possible explanations of the phenomenon of ghostly apparitions. One is the so-called *spiritist theory*, according to which ghosts are self-existing beings (whatever their nature) external to the human psyche. The other is the *animist theory* according to which ghostly apparitions are visible or auditory, exteriorized or projected contents of the psyche, that is, hallucinations.[271]

We shall see in Chapter 8 how this matches up with our own findings.

Chapter 7

THOSE WHO HAVE THE GHOST EXPERIENCE

When the newly created Society for Psychical Research carried out its Census of Hallucinations in the 1890s, they found that approximately one person in ten of their sample had undergone some kind of hallucinatory experience.[272] And since they saw no reason to doubt their sample was representative of the population as a whole, they reckoned that one in ten of us hallucinate at least once in our lives.

There is no reason to question these figures, or the intentions of those who interpreted them. But is it legitimate to extrapolate from them as though the ghost experience is the same among the nomads of Outer Mongolia or office workers in Nairobi? Indeed, we might wonder whether the survey is representative even of the people of Britain. We are told that the intelligence and educational status of the percipients were taken into account, but what statistics could evaluate the likelihood of seeing a ghost among East Anglian farmworkers as compared with Welsh miners?

But these are relatively trivial questions compared to the far greater one: are people who have the ghost experience typical members of the population, or are they 'special' in some way – more gifted, more suggestible, more open-minded, more anything? By and large, the SPR-Group do not seem to have faced this question, but Mrs Sidgwick, one-time President, made this comment:

As to the seers of ghosts, we can lay down no rules. The power does not, so far as has yet been ascertained, depend on any obvious conditions of health, temperament, intellect, or emotion. It is not even

192

certain that it is possessed by some persons and not by others, although there are reasons for thinking this probable . . . Perhaps the truth may be that we all have potentially the power of seeing such things, but that it requires a special state of mind, or body in us, to coincide with some external cause, and that the coincidence rarely, and, in the case of most individuals, never, occurs. [273]

A few years later her thoughts were to some extent supported by this remarkable case:

167. *Miss M. W. Scott, her sister Louisa and another sister, and Miss Irvine. St Boswell's, Scotland, 1892–93*
Three sisters on several occasions encounter the figure of a tall man, wearing somewhat old-fashioned clothing 'like the dress of Scottish clergymen about a century ago', in the same stretch of a country road. They all see it, and moreover, each sees it in appropriate perspective – once, when two of them are walking apart, it appears between them so that one sees it from the front, the other from the back. Miss Irvine, a governess, also sees the figure. Yet on two occasions there are other people in the vicinity, who by any normal supposition should see the figure, but who see nobody. To make things even more complicated, sometimes one sister will see the figure, while another does not.[274]

This selective visibility is generally explained by the supposition that the ghost chooses to whom it will appear. In this case, it is apparently willing to be seen by the Scott sisters (though not always by them), but not by men working in nearby fields or tending the hedge in the lane along which the figure walks.

But the apparent is not known to the sisters, and presumably they are not known to it: so what grounds exist for the apparent's choice, if it is his? A possible identification is made with a vicar who is said to have murdered his servant, some 150 years earlier, but this is far from certain, and in any case offers us no reason why the apparition should choose to be seen by these particular ladies. Alternatively, had the sister who failed to see what her sister saw eaten something for lunch which inhibited her perception?

Three options offer themselves: the ghost chooses to be seen only by certain people, or the percipients possess some special faculty, or they are in an appropriate state of body and/or mind.

There are features of this case to support each of these approaches. On one occasion at least the figure shows that it is aware of the percipients: 'He turned round and gazed at me with a vacant expression and the same ghastly, pallid features . . . he looked at me intently for a few seconds, then resumed his former position. Moving on a few steps he again stood and looked back for the second time, finally fading from view at his usual spot . . .'

So the percipients aren't simply chance observers of a spectacle that might have happened in the same way whether they were present or not. They are, however slightly, involved in the ghost's actions, for those actions are modified by their presence. *The ghost behaves as if it knows it is being seen.* The implication is that it possesses at least some degree of conscious awareness.

At the same time, the fact that only certain people see the figure implies that they possess some special attribute, or are in some way exceptionally suitable. Is this something the ghost itself senses, which perhaps triggers it to make an appearance when otherwise it would not have done? But then it's ridiculous to picture the ghost waiting around until someone suitable happens to come along!

Furthermore, even the ghost's most persistent witnesses see it only now and again, which suggests that even if they do possess some special faculty, they also need to be in a particular frame of mind. Miss M. W. Scott comments: 'The ghost always appears when our thoughts are bound up in something else, but if the opposite, then we are sure not to see him.'

This seems to have been a haunting ghost, and ghosts usually haunt places, rather than people, and it is not unusual for them to be seen by several people unconnected with one another. This ghost, though not seen by many, was certainly seen by the governess, and by two other people, stepsisters, who lived nearby. Were they gifted with the same faculty as the Scott sisters possessed?

Exceptional people

Although nearly all the percipients cited in this book believed they had a ghost experience, this is by no means the same as saying that they believed in ghosts. Probably most of them would have strongly denied any such belief, at any rate until after their experience.

Sceptics are apt to assume that ghosts are seen by people who believe in them, but there is no evidence that this is so. At various periods and in various cultures, that the dead can return as ghosts has indeed been part of the prevailing belief-system; and it could be argued that anyone living at that time and in that culture would be a 'believer'. But this is to confuse two levels of belief: *passive* belief, where one is a member of the community which shares a doctrine that ghosts exist, is by no means the same as the *active* belief of an individual which is based on personal experience. During the last two centuries we have increasingly chosen to make our own decisions on what and what not to believe. The most we could say of most of our ghost-seers would be that they were prepared to accept ghosts as a possibility.

In any case, in this study we are not particularly concerned with belief, one way or the other. For most of our percipients, their ghost experience was a once-in-a-lifetime event, and many insist that 'nothing of the sort ever happened to me before'. Of course an acceptance that ghosts may exist, however passive and unformulated, may be a facilitating or enabling factor, as it were *easing* the ghost experience to occur; and in the more subjective type of experience, we must consider the possibility that it might actually *cause* the experience to occur. It may even be true that no one can have a ghost experience if they do not accept – if only at the subconscious level – that such a thing can happen. But there is little reason to think that the majority of ghost experiencers are believers in the active sense.

In the Cornell case (no. 61) the ghost is seen by the householder and by one of the investigators, but not by the other. What blinded Tony Cornell? What is it that enables some people to see ghosts but prevents others? This next case is especially revealing:

168. May Clerke. Barbados, August, 1864
'About 3 or 4 o'clock in the afternoon, I was sitting reading in the verandah of our house in Barbadoes. My black nurse was driving my little girl in her perambulator in the garden. After some time I got up to go into the house, when this woman said to me, "'Missis, who was that gentleman that was talking to you just now?" "There was no one

talking to me," I said. "Oh, yes, dere was, Missis, a very pale gentle-man, very tall, and he talked to you, and you was very rude, for you never answered him." I repeated there was no one, and got rather cross with the woman, and she begged me to write down the day, for she knew she had seen someone. I did, and in a few days I heard of the death of my brother in Tobago. Now, the curious part is this, that I did not see him, but she a stranger to him did; and she said that he seemed very anxious for me to notice him.'[275]

There is a clear implication here that the nurse has an ability to see ghosts that May lacks. It is certainly May and none other that her brother's ghost is intent on contacting, and it continues to make ineffectual efforts to win her attention: it is here for that purpose. We might think that the apparent, frustrated by the ghost's failure to reach his target of preference, would seek around for the next best thing, and direct the ghost to the nurse who can be expected to relay the sighting to her employer; but the ghost shows no sign of realizing that the nurse has observed it. But if the apparent is purposely targeting his sister, rather than sending out a general distress call, how does the nurse get to see it? The fact that she sees it when May doesn't supports the notion that some people are more gifted than others in ghost-seeing.

The case also throws light on who must be responsible for the apparition. It can't be the intended target, May, because she sees nothing. It can't be the maid, because she doesn't know the apparent. So it can only be the brother himself. If the maid hadn't been close by, presumably his ghost would not have been seen by anyone. Which makes us wonder, how many ghosts fail to find someone to see them? Perhaps full many a ghost is born to haunt unseen . . .

In 1998 American researcher Sylvia Hart Wright interviewed 61 men and women who felt they had seen deceased relatives or acquaintances, or had some other kind of posthumous communi-cation with them.[276] Following through on the details they sup-plied, she questioned 56 of them about their childhoods, and found that 21 had parents who made excessive use of alcohol or drugs, and that 19 had parents who were authoritarian, prone to excessive anger, or who abused their children. It would seem that these childhood experiences formed the percipients in some way. She writes: 'it would appear that children with alcoholic parents are particularly likely to develop sensitivity to paranormal phenomena'. These figures are much higher than the average – approximately 34 per cent where somewhere in the region of 7 per cent would be expected. (The figures are necessarily vague since 'excessive' drinking is a matter of subjective judgement.)

Another factor which seems to play a part is whether the percipient's family is familiar with, and accepts, the paranormal, or the reverse. Eighteen of her 56 interviewees indicated a previous familiarity with the paranormal. Here again, there is no way this can be precisely measured, and it would surely vary hugely from one culture to another. Nevertheless her figures are striking, and we should take into consideration that these could be preconditioning factors which could make someone more likely to have a ghost experience. But perhaps indirectly rather than directly: Wright herself suggests that such childhood experiences make the subject more 'sensitive', a term which may or may not be interchangeable with 'suggestible'. While this is not a parameter easily recognized by psychologists, nor easily measured if recognized, it is a matter of everyday experience, and encourages us to stick our necks out and say that some people seem to be constitutionally or circumstantially more likely than others to see a ghost.

There are reasons to think, too, that a person may be prone to a particular *type* of ghost experience. Aniela Jaffé cites a correspondent who on three separate occasions saw a lifelike living ghost of a person – one her daughter, another a sister – who died within a few months. However we interpret her experiences, she evidently possessed a 'gift' for this kind of experience.[277]

One thing seems certain: there is no evidence to support the notion that anyone who sees 'something that isn't there' is mentally afflicted. Even now, this is a prevailing belief among many doctors and behavioural scientists, especially in the United States. If someone reports seeing a non-real figure, they say, that person is hallucinating, and that means she is mentally ill to some degree. Yet while it is true that some illnesses, both physical and mental, cause hallucination, it does not follow that all hallucinations are caused by illness. We shall see that a very great variety of circumstances – ranging from the weather to diet, from driving alone in the dark to taking drink or drugs – can trigger the entity-seeing process.

But could there be *physiological* characteristics differentiating ghost-seers from the rest of the population? Adam Bhuman-Wiggs, a clinical psychologist at the University of Kansas, proposes that ghost-seers do see differently from other people.

It is fairly well established that the ability to see without using the eyes – a phenomenon frequently reported but just as frequently dismissed – could in fact be related to an alternative form of sight, using not the thalamus but the colliculus. Though not as precise as normal sight, it could provide quite a bit of information to those who get used to interpreting its signals.

Bhuman-Wiggs speculates that this facility could be the path whereby some people, and not others, get to see ghosts and such. At the time of writing, he was advertising for experiencers to step forward and permit themselves to be examined to discover whether they possess this gift. Even if he gets his volunteers, that is a long way from establishing that everyone who has ever seen a ghost belongs to the segment of the population who are thus gifted.[278]

Another differential is offered by researcher Whately Carington, albeit very tentatively: that apparitions are seen only by those who are capable of 'eidetic imagery'. Unfortunately this too is a difficult matter to establish. First, a talent for eidetic imagery is not a thing you either have or don't have; different people have it to different degrees, and perhaps have it more or less according to circumstances, so it would be hard to draw a line and say that if you have less than this then ghosts are not for you, only if you have more of it do you qualify for the ghost-seeing class. Second, it is virtually impossible to test for, since there can be no question of testing every ghost experiencer for their eidetic imaging capability, to say nothing of all those who have in past times made such a claim.[279]

Sensitive people

It is commonly said that 'so and so is exceptionally sensitive', and we usually know what is meant. But sensitivity is not easily measured: to do that, you have to reduce it to performance in hard, clinical experiments. Which is fine up to a point, but hardly measures the individual's ability to pick up a psi-conducive ambiance or latch on to a dead person's earthbound astral self. The advertising pages of New Age magazines are full of people who claim to be psychically gifted, but the only way to test their claims is by trial and error. Certainly no clear-cut profile emerges which would tell us whether sensitive A is more likely than insensitive B to see a ghost, though off the record most of us may have our own intuitive ideas about which of our work colleagues is most likely to see a ghost.

The Clerke case just cited, and some others in this book (nos. 100, 102 and 103, for example) suggest that sometimes the 'wrong' person sees the apparition. The following case is striking because, though there is a link between apparent and percipient, it is so slight that no one could reasonably suppose it sufficient to trigger a visit by a ghost. Indeed, the very slightness of the connection provides a valuable clue to the nature of the ghost-seeing process:

169. Louise McKee. Portland, Oregon, 1940
'My husband and I were planting flowers in our yard. A double-seated swing stood about a metre and a half from the path where I was working. I saw it begin to move slowly. Since the day was hot and windless, I stopped curiously. A lovely old lady in a mauve dress sat in the swing. I said "Hello?" The lady looked at me but did not reply. All this time she propelled the swing back and forth with her foot. I wondered how she got into the swing without me seeing her. I called my husband to come – we had company. He came up the path – but the old lady had vanished. Suddenly I remembered I had met the old lady before, while between trains at St Paul. She had been introduced as Mrs Meyer. I knew a relative of Mrs Meyer so I wrote describing in detail what I had seen. In ten days I received an answering letter telling me that Mrs Meyer had passed away. She had been dressed in her coffin exactly as I had seen and described her.'[280]

Evidently Mrs Meyer is far from being a close friend, and surely has relatives who would be more appropriate witnesses. So why manifest to Louise? The link between them, weak as it is, is surely essential to the sighting, for otherwise Louise could not recognize her at all. But if we are going to set aside the need for a strong link, and accept that the link can be of the weakest, then what about all the countless other people that Mrs Meyer must have met, no less casually, in the course of her life? So is there something special about Louise? Is she especially 'sensitive', has she the appropriate body chemistry, is her mind tuned to the right wavelength? What is it that makes her the only person, so far as we know, in Mrs Meyer's acquaintance to pick up Mrs Meyer's signals? Or is there some more spiritual link: do the threads of their destiny intertwine, will they meet in Heaven as twin souls, is some higher fate weaving a pattern in which both are implicated? Sillier things have been suggested.

Similar considerations arise with hauntings. Haunters don't seem to be particularly choosy about whom they are seen by: they rarely interact with witnesses, and in general go about their business with total indifference to whether anyone sees them or not. And yet not everybody does see them. We do not know whether their apparent air of indifference is in fact feigned, and that if the truth were known they have gone to some considerable trouble to be seen by these particular witnesses. But more often than not those who see haunters are total strangers, and it's anybody's guess why they should be privileged.

One difficulty is that we can't be sure whether we are looking at a cause or an effect. It may be that nephew George is more likely to see his Aunt Jane's ghost because the ability to do so is in his genes, but it is also possible that it is because some prior experience has conditioned him. People who have suffered accidents – Dutch psychic Peter Hurkos fell off a scaffold, Bavarian stigmatic Teresa Neumann was involved in a farm fire – often report consequences which we would categorize as 'psychic', and those who have been traumatized, whether by something as physical as an electric shock or as psychological as witnessing the killing of a parent, may become extra-sensitized to external influences and therefore, perhaps, more liable to have a ghost experience. This area of behaviour has not yet been adequately explored, nor would exploration be easy, but there are many hints that a whole range of factors may affect the individual's suggestibility and render him more liable to have a paranormal experience.

'Encounter-prone' people

New England psychologist Kenneth Ring has shown that individuals who report near-death experiences and encounters with UFOs, while their personality profiles are not usually pathologically distinct from the average, do present a somewhat particular psychological profile which adds up to what he labels 'encounter proneness'.[281] His is the most authoritative input into a long-running debate as to whether near-death experiencers and alien abductees are different from you and me.

The Fund for UFO Research sets great store by findings by psychologists which tend to support the view that those who have UFO-related experiences are typical members of the population,[282] but critics have questioned the legitimacy of the conclusions they draw from those findings. Researcher Robert Bartholomew and colleagues have tried to show that these experiencers are fantasy-prone, but they are not, it seems, by the classic definition.[283] But is the classic definition inadequate or inappropriate in this context? Currently, the debate remains open. For the moment, Ring seems to hold the field with his suggestion that experiencers are constitutionally made, or have been conditioned, to be more likely than the populace at large to have this kind of experience.

Do Ring's findings also apply to ghost-seers? Though American researcher James Houran and his colleagues have made some preliminary probes into the subject,[284] no comprehensive psychological profiling of ghost-percipients has ever been attempted. Perhaps it is assumed that so widespread a phenomenon is unlikely to be confined to this or that sub-category of humankind. Yet if such a study could be made, we might well find that ghost-seers, without being pathologically abnormal, are nevertheless to be found in a particular segment of the total population.

Even then we would have to face the possibility that though some people may be constitutionally better adapted than others to see ghosts, it does not follow that they are necessarily better adapted to see *all* kinds of ghost. It could be that the qualities which enable a person to confect a hallucination from her own internal resources render her *less* likely to perceive a ghost of external origin, or vice versa. So while it is certainly worth seeking to establish the existence of a ghost-prone personality, we must bear in mind that each type of ghost may have its own target audience.

Exceptional states

Fatigue and other circumstances can put a person into a receptive state. Typical of many experiences is that of a woman named Dorothy Scott who, walking home, weak and tired, imagines herself at her destination. When she arrives she finds that the son of the house has already reported her arrival, having seen her living ghost which has gone ahead of her like a *vardøgr*.[285]

A person in an exceptional state is perhaps more likely to see an apparition. Around 1890, an unnamed invalid sees the figure of Death standing behind the visiting doctor: a few days later he dies. Is the apparition a premonition, or does the invalid fall victim to his own imaginary terrors?

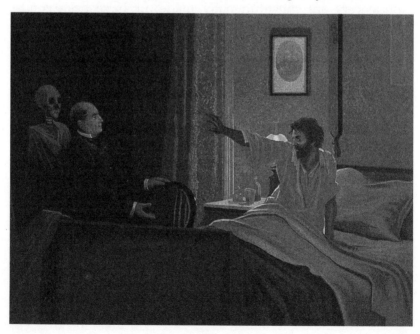

A substantial proportion of visionary experiences occur when the percipient is in something other than his usual state. Since the definition of what constitutes an altered state of consciousness is so uncertain, it would be rash to assert that to be in an altered state is a necessary condition, or even a facilitating one, for the ghost experience. None the less, since some if not all altered states are conducive to hallucination, and since hallucination appears to be the process for some if not all entity encounter experiences, it would be unrealistic for us to ignore the probability that some ghost experiences occur – and are perhaps more likely to occur – when the percipient is in an altered state:

170. *Lynda Houston. Denver, Colorado, 7 July 1965*
[As a result of reading about 'image projection' she determines to try it herself.] 'I decided to try to appear in the house of my neighbors. I imagined myself sitting on the Gholstons' couch . . . then I imagined myself climbing the stairs. As I started to imagine myself going into the bedroom I found I could not move. From this time on I merely observed what took place in my mind as if watching the action on a movie screen and yet somehow being involved in that action. I saw myself turn to look back down the stairs and there I saw a man coming toward me. He was very tall and emaciated and I saw him not in the colors of life but in shades of brown . . . As he came to the top of the stairs he seemed to grow taller and taller and at the same time I felt small and weak . . . He stood over me, his hands on his hips, looking down in disgust. As he glared at me I realized I must get up, run downstairs and home . . . Next morning Mrs Gholston came to tell me she had had a frightening experience.' [sensing some frightening thing outside her bedroom door: the ghost was identified from a photo as a Mr Spiby who had built and lived in their house but died some sixteen years previously][286]

It is safe to say that it is because Lynda is in an altered state – in this instance, a voluntary out-of-body trance – that she is able to meet the ghost next door. A person in an altered state generally becomes much more suggestible. Under hypnosis, the altered state *par excellence*, a subject becomes remarkably open to suggestions from the hypnotist: seeing someone who isn't present, or not seeing someone who is. This could be the crucial factor, for it is becoming more and more clear, as we close in on the nature of the ghost experience, that the crux is that the image of the apparent is imposed – whether by the subconscious, or by an external force, or by an external force acting on the subconscious – on the percipient's conscious; and suggestion of some kind is how the conscious is tricked into subjectively seeing what isn't objectively there. So states that favour suggestion could be all-important, as we saw in the Scott case (no. 167): the sisters sometimes see and sometimes do not see their ghost, according to their state of mind.

Heightened suggestibility is only one of the consequences of altered states which could be relevant to our inquiry. Altered states lead to exceptional behaviour of many kinds. In the excitement of battle, a soldier may fail to notice that he has incurred a wound that in normal circumstances would incapacitate him. Horrified to see her child trapped under a crashed car, a mother will lift a weight she could not possibly raise at other times. The apparent prospect of imminent death may induce the remarkable 'life review' in which one's whole life seems to pass before one.[287,288] Near-death situations lead to out-of-body experiences, and perhaps to the kind of projection where the subject is seen by others. If a person in a critical situation manifests as a crisis apparition, it could be because he has been shocked into an altered state which has provoked a spontaneous projection.

Mystical states

The history of mysticism in the Christian context is rich with accounts of visions of Jesus, Mary and various saints. In any religion, to experience a vision is perceived as an outward indication of spiritual advancement. Setting aside the view of those theologians who hold that these visions are actual manifestations by the divinities concerned, it seems probable that most visionary experiences occur in a mystical state of some kind; and that such a state is probably necessary for the experience to take place.

As with alternate states, we must ask if there is a parallel with the ghost experience. If those who have mystic experiences are divinely privileged to do so, may some such privilege be extended to ghost-seers?

The situation is complicated by the controversy whether one

can have a spiritually meaningful mystical experience outside a formal religious belief-system. The Church insists that you can't; promoters of hallucinogenic substances claim that the insights they offer are no less life-changing. Various experiments have explored the similarities and differences between the two, but it is not clear whether the differences observed are essential, or merely circumstantial: certainly they are not easily quantifiable.[289] We know that both conduce to encounter experiences, but are we justified in lumping together encounters arising from mystical states with those which result from non-religious altered states?

It is one thing to recognize that a wide range of factors can facilitate, and even actually induce, an altered state, ranging from purely physical factors such as diet, through conditions which are partially physical and partially psychological such as sensory deprivation, to precipitating emotional states such as bereavement. But the emotional climate of the altered state is likely to be different if it is induced by LSD taken for kicks, or alcohol imbibed to drown one's sorrows, or fear, or diet, or personal loss, or sleep deprivation; and it would be natural for this to affect the content of any hallucination which resulted. However, this does not necessarily mean that the experience is different *in kind*: it simply tells us that a different set of psychological parameters has conditioned the content of the experience. The actual process whereby the mystic sees his vision may be just the same as that whereby the ghost-seer sees his ghost.

The process of religious conversion frequently involves visionary encounters, in which the percipient believes that he is privileged with a personal intervention by a divine being. A classic case is that of Alphonse Ratisbonne, a prominent French Jew whose conversion to Christianity was hastened by a timely encounter with Mary, mother of Jesus.[290] What makes this relevant to the ghost experience is the implication that religious conversion is either the direct consequence of an otherworldly vision – that is to say, the visionary entity asks or even orders the visionary to change his religion; or that the visionary experience precipitates conversion because it is perceived as providing a kind of legitimization without which the visionary would have hesitated and perhaps refused to take this decisive step.

The distinguishing feature of the conversion experience is the mind-set of the individual. Clearly this provides the motivation, while the cultural milieu which the subject inhabits will provide the form the experience takes. In the case of Ratisbonne, either he had a genuine visitation from Mary, or his mind supplied a stereotype image of her: either way, he had no doubt who she was, and that she was there on his account. So far as the process goes, there seems no reason to distinguish it from that of the ghost experience. Only the intensity of the emotion puts it in a class apart. It tells us that if there is sufficient motivation, if it is fuelled by emotion, lo! a vision can happen.

Once again, we must be on our guard. There are the same two ways of explaining the vision as there are for any other apparition: one, that the vision comes from afar in response to the need; second, that it is created by the individual, who exteriorizes it to give it authority.

Religious conversion has a unique status in theology, but it is not without parallels. Other kinds of experience can bring about a similar modification of the experiencer's values and lifestyle. Near-death experiences are an obvious example, though it could be argued that a close encounter with one's end would sober most people into behaving better. But there is an even closer parallel: encounters with extraterrestrials. A very high proportion of those who believe themselves to have contact with aliens display a striking change for the better in the way they conduct their life – they give up smoking, they take up art, they develop a concern for the environment, undergo an overall replacement of values and redirection of aims.[291] Doubtless the Church would be reluctant to accept that spiritual benefits could be conferred by a close encounter with a flying saucer, but we must remember that for many abductees their experience is far more profoundly 'spiritual' than attending church on Sunday.

By contrast, I do not know of any ghost experience which has led to anything of the kind. In the medieval *exempla*, of course, whenever a ghost appears, a moral is sure to follow: the sinner, either admonished by her visitor from beyond the grave, or driven to reflect upon her sinfulness, mends her ways, and those who hear the story are advised to go and do likewise. The tradition is still alive when Defoe writes early in the eighteenth century, but none of his stories possesses more evidential value than Dickens's *A Christmas Carol*. After that, the pious fictions disappear almost entirely. I cannot recall that a single one of the percipients whose cases were recorded by the SPR ever added a postscript to the effect that he had upgraded his philosophy of life as a consequence, though doubtless many were led to ponder deeply on the implications of what had happened to them.

The inference is that those encounters with extraterrestrials or with religious figures which direct the experiencer to a personal transformation are a different kind from the ghost experience. Conversion experiences, and perhaps alien encounters too, are means to an end – personal transformation. This implies that they are likely to be subjective in nature (though we cannot altogether rule out the possibility that the Virgin Mary, or the aliens, have picked up on the individual's need and have come to her rescue). The ghost experience on the other hand rarely, if ever, aims at anything so profound.

Exceptional circumstances

A healthy, normal person may be put into a hallucinatory state by a wide range of personal factors. We have already noted that some medieval encounters with demons may be attributed to diet deficiency; the sixteenth-century physician Johann Wier diagnosed excessive fasting as the underlying cause of an outbreak of 'convent hysteria' in which nuns believed themselves possessed by the devil and behaved accordingly.[292] Overindulgence in drugs or alcoholic beverages, sensory deprivation or overload, extreme emotional states such as fear or expectation, stress arising from domestic relationships – all of these can provide the springboard for a visionary experience.[293] For example:

171. Starlitt Arrance. Oregon, 1986
When Mrs Arrance misses her way at night on a country road and crashes into a ravine 30 metres below, leaving her unconscious, her five-year-old daughter Starlitt is thrown free. Though bruised and bleeding, she begins to climb the cliff because her father taught her

that if she should find herself in a ravine, there's sure to be a road at the top. Sometime during the night, exhausted, the girl finds a hole in the face of the cliff, and sleeps there for a while before continuing her climb. Next morning she is found walking along the road: with great difficulty rescuers find the van. It takes them three hours, using rock-climbing gear, to reach the unconscious mother and bring her up onto the road. So how did 5-year-old Starlitt climb the cliff in the dark on her own? Well, she was not alone, she explains. During her climb a young boy, holding a puppy, came to her and comforted her.[294]

Hallucination? No doubt: and we may suppose the boy with the puppy is a figure from school or the neighbourhood, or even a character in a story-book, chosen as a guarantor because he is someone Starlitt would trust. But chosen by whom? Her subconscious? Or is the boy her guardian angel disguised in this non-frightening form?

An emotional crisis is most likely to put the percipient into a suitably suggestible state, but it doesn't always have to be so extreme:

172. Mrs Katherine Macquoid. Chelsea, London, 22 December 1880
Mrs Macquoid, herself a novelist, has arranged to visit a neighbour, the writer George Eliot, whom she has never met. A few days before the date arranged, she wakes to see George Eliot standing by her bed, recognizing her from photographs. The figure says a few words then vanishes. Mrs Macquoid returns to sleep, forgetting all of the message except the number 61: next day she learns that Eliot has died at the time of her manifestation, aged 61.[295]

We must suppose that the two novelists, in arranging to meet, set up some kind of rapport: doubtless Mrs Macquoid was excited at the prospect of meeting one of the greatest writers of the age. This, slight as it is, and though the two concerned have never met, is perhaps enough to enable the experience, as seems to have been the case in the garden incident (no. 169).

Violent death and reincarnation

Reincarnation is a very different kind of return from the dead from the ghost experience or the seance-room materialization, but it possesses one characteristic feature that could be relevant to our inquiry. A very high proportion of alleged reincarnation cases concern individuals who died a sudden, violent death. This seems to be paralleled in two categories of ghost experience: hauntings and crisis apparitions.

This disproportion is too great to come about by chance, so we must suppose that violent death, in some cases, prevents the death process from following its normal course. Either the victim is unable to come to terms with her experience, or she has the sense of something not yet resolved. In this state of mind she may be impelled to seek reincarnation, perhaps by way of making up to herself what she's been deprived of by her untimely death. Perhaps returning as a revenant or a haunter is an alternative option, driven by the same motivation.

This may also be a clue to understanding the crisis apparition. On the face of it, crisis apparitions are quite straightforward: the apparent wishes to inform the percipient of what is happening to her. But not everyone in a critical situation manifests as an apparition, or we'd be hearing about hundreds of cases every day. One explanation could be that, though *all* people in critical situations try to manifest as apparitions, only some are capable of it. Or it could be that only some can lay their hands – at such short notice – on a suitable percipient. But the parallel with reincarnation suggests a further possibility: perhaps only some people, finding themselves threatened, feel sufficiently hard done by to want to manifest as apparitions?

There seems little doubt that these are not automatic consequences of the situation. Someone or something *chooses* that this person will remain as a haunter, that person will be reincarnated, yet another will return as a revenant. And who more likely to make that decision than the distressed individual herself, though perhaps she must obtain authorization from the powers that be?

Many theories about hauntings speak of traces left by emotions, which do not necessarily have to be the result of violent death. Ghost-hunter James Wentworth Day reports: 'Mr Clay [a ghost witness] gave me the most logical explanation I have ever heard of why some people see ghosts and others do not. His view was that certain happenings in life – murder, suicide, extreme agony of mind or infinite kindness to others – can leave an

209

impression on what one might describe as "the cinema screen of time". The result is that at certain periods the episodes of the past are thrown up and repeated on, say, the anniversaries of their happening.'[296]

What this explanation noticeably does *not* do, is precisely what Day claims for it, that is, show why some people see them and others don't. The phrase 'the result is' is meaningless, since no process of cause and effect is proposed. As for the 'cinema screen of time', heaven alone knows what he has in mind. Yet, for all that, Mr Clay may well be on to something.

Immediate circumstances

We have considered various 'enabling' circumstances – but what about 'disabling'? Ostensibly the manifestation of a ghost seems to transcend all circumstances – for example, one would not expect a ghost to fail to appear because it's raining, or because the percipient is on the loo, or because it's a Bank Holiday. None the less, such trivial factors do seem to play a part, if only because they may make all the difference in putting the percipient into a suitably receptive or suggestible state. We have already noted cases of people in such situations as mountain climbing and polar exploration, who have fancied they are not alone. It is noteworthy that these percipients were in situations where they were not likely to be distracted. Driving alone in the dark is a notoriously propitious setting for encounters with aliens or phantom hitchhikers, and it was in similar circumstances that this classic vision occurred:

173. Edith Olivier. Avebury, Wiltshire, England, October 1916
Driving alone on a dark October evening during World War One, she found herself passing between the megaliths at Avebury: 'This did not surprise me, for I already knew that the village of Avebury was built actually within the old circle, its cottages standing rather incongruously among the megaliths, from fragments of which they were built. This might be expected to spoil the effect of grandeur which Avebury should give; but on that particular night a village fair happened to be in progress. The grand megaliths and the humble cottages alike were partly obscured by the failing light and the falling rain, but both were fitfully lit by flares and torches from booths and

shows. Some primitive swing boats flew in and out of this circle of light: cocoanuts rolled hairily from the sticks upon which they had been planted: bottles were shivered by gun-shots and tinkled as they fell. And all the time, the little casual crowd of villagers strayed with true Wiltshire indifference from one sight to another. I stood for a short time watching the scene; and then I decided that too much rain was falling down the back of my neck, so I got into the car and drove away.'

It was not until nine years later that, revisiting Avebury, she learnt that the annual fair there had been abolished in 1850. Though at the time all had seemed perfectly normal, 'now there seemed to be no doubt that in October 1916, I had watched a scene which must have taken place at least sixty-six years earlier'. Subsequently she learnt that the avenue of megaliths had disappeared before the year 1800, 'so not only the fair but the whole of my experience had taken me back to some time in the eighteenth century.'[297]

A circumstance of a different kind may be the date of the manifestation. For example, we have two cases occurring at Christmas (nos. 85 and 189). Haunters are often said to appear on anniversaries of their death, though there is little reliable testimony to this. It is possible that the dead retain sufficient awareness of earthly calendar time to appear on significant days, but it seems more likely to be the percipient who is in a heightened emotional state, recalling past Christmas Eves enjoyed during the lifetime of the apparent. The date could even function as a link between apparent and percipient, rendering the latter more suggestible.

Geophysical parameters

Certain individuals may be affected by environmental circumstances – the weather, in particular. Some theorists go further, and attribute the seeing of apparitions to geophysical factors. Writer John Pendragon, in 1954, was struck by the coincidence that East Anglia, much of which has a clay subsoil, has more than its share of ghosts. This led him to put two and two together: 'Essex, as statistics of haunted areas go, is definitely the most ghost-ridden [county] in England, and the subsoil of that county is clay. Therefore may we not deduce that cosmic rays or the deflection

211

of them by soils predominantly of clay does, in some way yet unknown, act as an aid to the production of phenomena?'[298]

Pendragon informs us that he lives in a sandstone area: sandstone is an insulator, and the only local haunting case known to him is where there is a belt of clay. This sounds encouraging for his theory, but a far more exact study is needed to establish a case, and even then we could not be sure the correlation was a direct one. Moreover, the connection between cosmic rays and the ghost experience is, as Pendragon admits, as yet unknown.

A theory of a somewhat similar nature has been advanced by Canadian neuroscientist Michael Persinger, who suggests that geological and geophysical factors may provide a natural environment that facilitates paranormal experiences.[299] He proposes a scenario which would account for the ghost-seeing process so far as the percipient's own body, brain and senses are concerned. As he says, 'all of your experiences are generated within your brain . . . you do not directly respond to the stimulation of your senses, but to signals from your brain, wherever they may be initiated'. So our experience will seem the same to us irrespective of whether it originates within ourselves or is induced from outside. The delusion, illusion or hallucination must be seen as an internal event, even though there may be a stimulus, as yet unidentified, working on us from outside ourselves.

He points out that by stimulating specific areas of the brain, specific types of unreal experience can be evoked. These are not usually direct memories, but clearly the imagery can only be drawn from our personally acquired pool of memories or imaginations. It is, however, beyond the power of the neuroscientist to trigger specific memories.

While this is all fairly interesting, it does not go very far towards helping us understand the ghost experience: it simply puts the explanation at one further remove. We can go along with Persinger so far as to imagine an agent – whether interior or exterior – initiating the ghost process by stimulating the brain in a suitable manner. But this is a long way short of explaining how a particular ghost is seen by a particular person at a particular time; yet ghost-seeing is, far more often than not, a very directed, individualized, and precisely timed affair. Many of our apparitions are motivated, they possess identity, they display awareness;

none of these could come from the mental equivalent of a knee-jerk response.

Many years of research have enabled Persinger to build up an impressive theoretical case, and his subjects have had some weird experiences by letting him do tricksy things to their brains. However, so far as his theory helps us to understand the ghost experience, the most that can be said is that certain natural conditions may provide an environment which may act on the brain to make the individual more suggestible, more liable to have a ghost experience where in other circumstances he might not. But, like Mr Pendragon's clay subsoil, this falls a long way short of accounting for the ghost experience itself.

I do not see that these theories take us anywhere useful, so far as understanding the ghost experience goes. Yet they are valuable in that they remind us that whatever else the ghost experience may be, it is a psychological event; and helpful in that they provide another set of parameters for the mental condition of the percipient. They can be added to the list of conditioning elements which could be acting on the individual, and perhaps help us to understand why some of us have a ghost experience, why some of us have many ghost experiences, and some of us never have a single one.

So, if a person experiences a severe electric shock, or his house is built on clay, or he is susceptible to thunderstorms, or he is laid low by fever, or eats the wrong food or no food, or dallies with drugs or abuses alcoholic beverages, or pushes himself too hard at the office, or drives alone at night or sails alone across an ocean, or undergoes a spiritual transformation or quarrels with his partner at the breakfast table – in these or a hundred other situations, he may be rendered more likely to have a ghost experience.

This seems a long way from the 'psychic gifts' that some people claim to possess. Or is it that such people are interacting with these other factors? Is the 'second sight' mediated by the rocky terrain of the Scottish Highlands? Are ghosts discouraged by houses which have been arranged strictly on feng shui principles? Are more phantoms seen at the full moon? Do organic foods make us more or less likely to see a ghost? The fact is, we humans are such complex beings, and so delicately balanced on the tightrope of 'normality', that too much or too little of virtually anything can destabilize us.

It does not seem likely that any of these things, or even a combination of them, would of themselves *cause* a ghost experience to occur. They might induce hallucination, indeed, and perhaps our subconscious might take advantage of the occurrence to superimpose on the hallucination a meaningful ghost experience of its own devising. So we could accept that one or other of these factors – Pendragon's and Persinger's included – might trigger some of the types of ghost experience which seem to have their origin entirely in the mind of the percipient.

Some other types of ghost experience do seem to depend on favouring external circumstances. Louise McKee is working quietly in her garden when she sees Mrs Meyer (no. 169): she might not have noticed her if she'd been at Tesco's at that moment. Edith Olivier (no. 173) is driving alone at night when she sees Avebury *en fête*: if she had made the same journey on a bright summer afternoon, she probably wouldn't have seen anything.

On the basis of what we've looked at in this chapter we must conclude that pretty well everyone *can* see a ghost, but some of us may be psychologically constituted in a way which favours or inhibits seeing one. And where you are and what you are doing, the state of your health and the state of your mind and the state of the weather – these and a thousand other factors can help make you one of those who have the ghost experience.

Chapter 8

UNDERSTANDING THE GHOST EXPERIENCE

In our daily lives, we learn that if we disregard the limits set by science, we do so at our peril: the guidelines which the scientists have painstakingly laid down are not lightly set aside. However, faced with phenomena for which science cannot provide a convincing explanation, we are justified in adopting – if only as working hypotheses – concepts that jump the guidelines. This is the case with the ghost experience, which confronts us with paradoxes that defy current scientific paradigms. If we suppose we can resolve those paradoxes without embracing one or more concepts which lie outside those paradigms, we are deluding ourselves.

Can conventional science really not explain the ghost? Desperate not to invoke any kind of break-out from conventional paradigms, most of those who seek to explain the ghost experience have sought to do so in psychological terms. If it could be shown that the ghost experience is 'all in the mind' of the percipient, we might have no need to quit the beaten track; for the human mind remains largely uncharted and science grudgingly recognizes that it has a seemingly limitless capacity for erratic behaviour.

So really the big, the fundamental question is this: can the ghost experience be confined to the workings of the percipient's mind, without any intrusion from outside?

And the answer is yes, it can. We can devise a scenario by which all ghosts emanate from within the mind of the percipient, and we can forget about spirits returning from the grave, crisis victims sending out distress calls, warning messengers and all.

Yes, we can do this – but only by attributing to the mind powers that are hardly less paradigm-busting than accepting other-worldly intrusions. For there is no way that the mind, as commonly understood, can be responsible for the ghost experience.

That a good many ghost experiences are purely mental creations is undoubtedly true. And there can be no disputing that the ghost experience is fundamentally a psychological process, involving either the senses or a masquerade of the senses. But the findings we have accumulated in the course of our inquiry leave us with no doubt that we have either to dismiss the testimony as unreliable, or to accept the extension of our mental activities beyond currently prescribed limits.

Even if we grant that we humans possess unlimited powers of self-delusion; that we can hallucinate apparitions of relatives, friends, strangers and even ourselves; that we can mistake these hallucinations for real; that two or three of us – unknown to one another – can experience the same hallucination either simultaneously or on separate occasions; even if we grant that we can have the illusion of visiting a friend at the same time that that friend has the illusion that he is visited by us – even if we grant that all these can be explained according to our existing knowledge of behaviour, we have yet to explain how we can obtain, through the ghost experience, information and personal details that should, by any normal expectation, be inaccessible to us.

Whichever scenario we ultimately adopt – whether we conclude that the ghost experience is best explained in terms of enhanced powers of the mind, or of manifestation by other-worldly beings, or a combination of the two – there are certain concepts which have stood on the sidelines throughout our inquiry, awaiting our attention. It is now time to turn to them.

Our sense organs

Our general conclusion is that the great bulk of the hallucinations included in our Census are not in any way dependent on the condition of the sense-organs of the percipients. The view that many – if not most – hallucinations are originated centrally, in the brain

216

and not in the sense organs, is that now generally held by physiologists, as well as by psychologists.[300]

So, a hundred years ago, concluded the SPR-Group. More recently, researcher Scott Rogo has written:

> We are not seeing apparitions with our eyes. Perhaps the apparition, appearing in some sort of fourth dimension, is actually not affecting our optic nerves but rather is igniting our clairvoyance. Thus an apparition, if a conscious aware entity, might *cause us* to see it as clothed or accompanied by a physical object . . . An apparition is actually *somehow psychically causing us to see it.*[301]

To support this view he cites the fact that some apparitions are seen in total darkness while others are seen glowing.

It is certainly true that the process of seeing an apparition is not the same as the process of seeing someone in normal daily life. Something or someone is putting on a show. But it is not evident that our sense organs are bypassed. They are clearly *ostensibly* involved in the process of perceiving a ghost. We have seen cases where the percipients close their eyes and the ghost disappears, they open them again and the ghost reappears. They look away to another part of the room, but the ghost does not move; when the percipient looks back to the original location, the ghost is still where it was. If the light goes out, the ghost is not seen: if the light is restored, so is the ghost.

A good many percipients go to considerable trouble to establish that they are really and truly seeing something. Insofar as it is possible for a person, in the grip of an illusion, to persuade himself that he is not in the grip of an illusion, they do so. But then this ostensible involvement of the senses, and even the testing, may be part of the illusion. If we take the ghost experience to be a hallucinatory artefact created by the percipient's own subconscious, then the shooting script could include the illusion of looking away, and so on. Similarly, in cases where the ghost is seen even though the room is in total darkness, this could be because, as Rogo suggests, it is a subjective image created by the mind and so requires no illumination.

Anyone who sees a ghost is being deceived. Whether it is her subconscious or an outside agent that is responsible, a drama is being enacted for her benefit. Just as a hypnotist can suggest to his subject the idea that her mother is in the room when she isn't, so the percipient can have the apparition suggested to her sub-conscious, which then visualizes the apparition in such a way as to deceive the conscious mind. This is a known and frequently observed psychological process, and it means that we can com-fortably attribute this much of the ghost experience to a known faculty of the human mind. The question, are the sense organs involved?, is virtually impossible to resolve when such sophisti-cated processes are being employed. There is evidence pointing either way. When Morton Schatzmann experimented with his subject Ruth, who was able to call up apparitions at will, he estab-lished that her brain acted as though the apparitions were real, but that they did not affect the retina of her eyes (which are not controlled by the brain's cerebral cortex).[302]

The inference is that the subconscious is using alternative path-ways. And since the subconscious seems to be masterminding the game, and is responsible for so much, it is reasonable to wonder if *all* of the ghost experience – both *what* is perceived and *the way* it is perceived – is initiated and executed by the subconscious.

In principle that sounds fine – but in practice? When we apply this to actual cases, we hesitate. Look again at Mr and Mrs P. (no. 114): can we be happy with the thought that an internally gener-ated subjective hallucination on Mrs P.'s part (who has never seen her father-in-law, and who doesn't know her husband is in finan-cial difficulties) causes her husband to wake and speak to the apparition which he sees just where his wife sees it? Or take the Cheltenham case (no. 14): on occasion the dogs would bark at nothing which just happens to be situated where Rosina is seeing the apparition. Were they picking up her thought-process? or sharing the subconscious suggestion that is causing Rosina herself to hallucinate?

As soon as we try to force our experiences to fit ready-made theories, we realize that it is one thing to formulate a process but quite another to apply it to the individual instance. If we want to make sense of Rosina's ghost experience, the default scenario must be that if the dogs bark at something on the stairs, it is because there is something on the stairs for them to bark at. While we cannot absolutely deny the alternative possibility that they are barking at Rosina's subjective illusion, this is so very much less plausible than the barking-at-something scenario as to be little more than a theoretical option.

But the dogs at Cheltenham don't help us to understand the dog at Menton (no. 50). As we examine one case after another we realize that no blanket theory is going to do for all. One requires one kind of explanation, another demands another. Between them, they force us to accept that a variety of processes may lead to a ghost experience. That sometimes the subconscious can manage on its own, sometimes it needs help from outside – from another living person, or possibly from one who is dead. The sense organs may play a part – or they may not. Sometimes a material or quasi-material apparition may be physically present, in which case we may suppose the percipient sees it with his everyday eyesight. But when the apparition is no more than a hallucination emanating from a suggestion, either from the percipient's own subconscious or from an outside agent, the sense organs may be bypassed.

Psi

One incontrovertible feature of the ghost experience is that frequently the percipient obtains information of which no one living is aware. This information, whether it is a visual detail or a spoken instruction, can be obtained in one of only two ways: either by extra-sensory (psi) perception of some kind, or by direct communication from the apparent, who may or may not be living. (This communication, of course, may also involve psi.)

Price has set out the difficulties with a physical explanation for ghosts, and explains why the SPR-Group preferred to look to a psychological theory with 'telepathic hallucinations' as the *modus operandi*:

> In the crisis-apparition a telepathically-received impression makes use of the psycho-physical machinery of hallucination 'to get itself across' – to make itself consciously known to the percipient and thereby to influence his emotions and his actions.[303]

219

However, he goes on to emphasize that while this may go part of the way towards an explanation, in that telepathy or something like it is almost certainly involved, the psi-only hypothesis is inadequate as the total explanation that the SPR-Group hoped it would be, even if it is accepted – as they somewhat reluctantly recognized they had to accept – that sometimes it may be necessary to extrapolate from telepathy with the living to telepathy with the dead.

According to their scenario, the percipient's mind, conscious or subconscious, receives from an agent, living or dead, a telepathically received impulse which it proceeds to 'translate' into the externalized image of the apparent. Here, from their casebook, is an instance which favours their interpretation:

174. Mrs K. E. Malleson. Littlehampton, Sussex, England, 1874–75
'My husband and one of our sons, about 16, were to take the night boat to the French coast, returning in a few days. With no cause for special anxiety, I felt lonely and depressed, and went to bed. I had slept for some hours when I was suddenly awakened by feeling someone bending over me. I felt no doubt that it was my husband. "Oh, Willie, you have come back!" I put out my arms and felt his coat. He answered,"Yes! I am come back." The tone was very solemn and my fears were aroused. I asked, "Has anything happened?" He replied in the same peculiar low, solemn tone, "Yes! something has happened." Then I thought of the boy and asked eagerly, "Where is Eddy?" There was no answer, and after a moment's pause I felt that I was alone. In an instant came the conviction that it was not in his ordinary bodily presence that he had been there . . . I remained restless, anxious and miserable until I received a letter from my husband. When he returned I told him of my vision: he was vexed and merely said, "Well, you see I was in no danger, so I hope you will never believe in visions or presentiments any more!"'

However, Malleson was not being strictly correct when he gave his wife the impression that nothing had happened. [He writes:]

'My son and I left Littlehampton by a steam boat to cross in the night to Honfleur. We stayed some time on deck, then I went below to try to get some sleep, while he preferred to remain in the fresh air. I fell asleep, until I was awakened by two men talking. Presently they rose to go, and I said, "I have left a boy of mine on deck. Would you mind seeing how he is getting on?" They returned, and said they had not noticed him anywhere. My imagination began to work upon their answer, and I pictured myself searching for my son all over the deck in vain, and questioning the sailors, and getting to hear nothing about him . . . After a little time my imagination gained greater hold of me, and I found myself pacing woefully along the lonely sea road to our cottage with the terrible news to tell my wife that our boy was gone – fallen overboard, no doubt, and no one had even seen or heard him. The story had now taken possession of me – the thought of what I should say – what answer was I to make to the inevitable question "Where is Eddy?" . . . I rose and went on deck. For a time I could not find Eddy anywhere, but before I had become seriously uneasy I discovered him snugly hidden under a great sheet of tarpaulin . . . I refrained from telling my wife my half of the experience. She was not strong, and I feared the excitement of so strange a corroboration of her vision.'[304]

What is interesting is that the danger is imaginary, yet Malleson's imagination creates a visionary experience which seems not to differ in any way from a crisis apparition where the danger is real. Since the cause resides so clearly in his mind rather than in the actual situation of their son, it is well nigh certain that his mind is the originator, and that telepathy, or at any rate some form of psi, is involved. (Though there is just the possibility that an out-of-body experience is taking place.)

Telepathy can be credited in this next case, too, but here something more is involved:

175. D. Doris Pogue. Carlisle, Cumbria, England, 25 December 1952
'My husband John served on an aircraft carrier somewhere in the Mediterranean. On Christmas Day I felt lonely all day. That night, in the bathroom while brushing my teeth I happened to glance in the mirror where to my amazement I saw my husband standing behind me. I spun round, overjoyed to see him, and through a mouthful of toothpaste asked, "How did you get here?" "I don't know. I wanted to see you so badly and somehow I'm here." I moved towards him – and suddenly I was back in bed. It must have been a dream . . . The following day I wrote John to tell him about my odd dream. In his letter, which I received about a week later, he described his strange experience on Christmas night. For a few minutes he thought he was standing behind me in the bathroom, watching me brush my teeth. I had seen him reflected in the mirror and turned to speak to him. The short exchange of words that followed was identical to the one I remembered. Then suddenly he found himself back aboard ship.

221

Maybe it was coincidence but the fact that we independently recalled the same minor details – right down to my bare feet – makes that a dubious explanation.'[305]

So far as Doris is concerned, this is a very vivid ghost experience; but John seems to be enjoying something resembling a spontaneous projection, no doubt activated by his feelings and perhaps drawn by hers. That he is in some manner in the bathroom, not just his image but his conscious self, seems certain – for she sees him, they exchange words which both recall, small details are remembered. If this is psi, it is psi of an exceptionally sophisticated kind.

Could the entire ghost experience be the consequence of telepathy between the agent and the percipient? American researcher Loyd Auerbach proposes that the process of ghost-seeing goes something like this:

Ghosts, or more appropriately apparitions, are ostensibly the spirits (soul or consciousness) of previously living people. If they exist, their existence is likely to be a form of energy. Their ability to communicate, to be seen, heard, felt, or even smelled, has to do with telepathy. That is, the apparition communicates with and projects information into the minds of us living folks. When a person 'sees' a ghost, he or she is actually receiving information from the apparition which gets translated into visual data in the perceptual process. It gets added to the data already coming through the eyes – superimposed.[306]

Such a scenario would account for Doris's side of the incident, but it is not really satisfying as an explanation for John's part – not to mention that he is living, not 'previously' but right now. Since we have no right to set any limits to how much information can be communicated via psi, we have to accept that this could conceivably be a psi-only event. But John's sense of being present forcibly suggests that he *is* present in some more real sense than merely as an image visualized by Doris.

Nor do psi theories explain why visualization takes place at all. Wouldn't a mental, or at most a verbal message suffice? Well, perhaps the agent doesn't want there to be any misunderstanding. Left to himself, the percipient might simply dismiss the message: the surest way to ensure that he doesn't is to deliver it in person, as it were. Doubtless Tyrrell has this in mind when he suggests that telepathy *per se* is simply not enough; there has to be a sharing between the mind of the percipient and that of the agent.[307]

This next case puts even more strain on the psi-only hypothesis:

176. Jeanie Gwynne Bettany. Mid-nineteenth century
'When I was about 10 years old, I was walking in a country lane. I was reading geometry as I walked along, a subject little likely to produce fancies or morbid phenomena of any kind, when, in a moment, I saw a bedroom known as the White Room in my home, and upon the floor lay my mother, to all appearance dead. The vision must have remained some minutes, during which time my real surroundings appeared to pale and die out; but as the vision faded, actual surroundings came back, at first dimly, and then clearly. I could not doubt that what I had seen was real, so, instead of going home, I went to the house of our medical man. He at once set out with me, on the way putting questions I could not answer, as my mother was to all appearance well when I left home. I led the doctor straight to the White Room, where we found my mother lying as in my vision. This was true even to minute details. She had been seized suddenly by an attack at the heart, and would soon have breathed her last but for the doctor's timely advent.'[308]

We can see why the SPR-Group would be content to give this as an example of telepathy, but we would want them to explain how it comes about that Jeanie sees the entire scene. Does the mother, though lying unconscious on the floor, send Jeanie a complete visual image of the room? Surely not. Well, does she send her a telepathic SOS on to which Jeanie's subconscious superimposes her own mental picture of the room, to give the message greater impact? That too will hardly do, because Jeanie later finds she has pictured the scene in accurate detail, the room and her mother's body lying just so. So has she, somehow alerted by her mother, visualized the scene by clairvoyance?

Whatever the scenario, the mother has to play *some* part, for (unless we drag in the super-psi scanning we shall be looking at in a moment) it needs her heart attack to trigger Jeanie's vision.

But Jeanie's visual impression is probably best explained by clair-voyance: so we could, just possibly, hypothesize that the mechan-ics of the case are clairvoyance triggered by telepathy. Not one, but *two* processes which science hesitates to recognize!

The psi-only hypothesis has some difficulty, too, in coping with cases where more than one ghost is seen. To account for the fol-lowing case, in which three ghosts are seen together by several people on several occasions, we would have to invoke something like collective telepathy:

177. Elaine McGee. Farm near Richmond, Virginia, September 1926
'My father and I were having dinner when, glancing out of the window, I saw three men walking up the lane past our house. We got up to see who they were, but by the time we reached the yard the men had vanished, apparently into thin air. We both remembered the oddity of their clothing – a checkered cap, a coat over one arm, and unusual trousers. After I married, we moved away, then my husband John and I bought back a small part of the old place and built a home there. One night, driving home, a car approached us with its head-lights on full. Just before it reached us we saw three men walking along our side of the road. I told John to watch out, he might hit them. My two nieces, in the rumble seat, not having heard what I said, leaned round and cried, "Look out, Uncle John! There's three men walking up ahead!" The men were dressed exactly as the ones Dad and I had seen seven years before. When we reached the spot where the men should have been, they were not there. There was no place they could have hidden. Several years later my two nieces, riding along the same route about the same time of year, saw those same three men at exactly the same spot. I have heard that there were others besides my family who have seen them, but I cannot vouch for this.'[309]

It seems almost as though it is the entire scene, rather than the ghosts as individuals, which is the essential aspect of the sighting. So perhaps we should class it as a time slip rather than a haunting case. But changing the label doesn't get rid of the problem.

Research on telepathy has developed considerably since the SPR-Group published their *Census* in the 1890s, and a more sophisticated version of the telepathy theory may be applicable. Murphy and Klemme, investigating the Buterbaugh case (no. 42), wondered if Coleen's vision of the past could have been triggered by her psychological make-up, and if the process might involve something like Whately Carington's association theory of telepathy. He suggests that associations of ideas in one mind may be accessible to another mind. Thus if agent A is thinking of a subject and percipient P is thinking along similar lines, P's mind could 'jump' to A's mind and pick up not simply the immediate link, but also whatever associations the idea has for A.

While this doesn't actually take us any farther towards explaining the process, it does give us a useful analogy to work from with regard to ghost-seeing. The basis would be laid by P's mind working around a particular idea: her mind would then form an association with a similar pattern of thought in A's mind, thus leading to the transfer of information so that P would learn things that, ostensibly, no one but A knows. Carington gives an example:

> A and P are two friends or acquaintances, or perhaps more closely related. A is drowned, and at or about the time of that event P, who has no normal knowledge of it, experiences a crisis apparition involving an hallucinatory vision representing A with contorted features and dripping clothes. The basic fact is that P has paranormally become aware of an event in the life of A, namely his death. The form in which this awareness is, so to say, dressed up by P is a different matter altogether. The experience of being drowned would be responsible for the appearance of sensations of wet, struggling, choking, etc.: all these images, making up the idea of 'death-by-drowning' will be present in A's mind. If P happens to think of A at an appropriate moment, there will be a tendency for the idea of 'A-drowning' to come to P's mind. Whether it actually does so is a different matter, depending on local factors, notably the degree of competition from P's immediate environment.[310]

This is a plausible scenario: its shortcoming, though, is in the phrase 'If P happens to think . . .' Are we to suppose that crisis apparitions happen by mere chance – that, of all the million and one things P might be thinking of, he happens to think of A at just the time that A is in drowning situation? Surely this is stretching chance too far! We may grant with Carington that, *once linked*, P's mind might access A's and that an apparition might be the consequence, but he fails to show convincingly how they get linked in the first place.

While it is hard to avoid the conclusion that psi plays a crucial part in the ghost experience, it is also evident that, as tradition-ally understood, it is certainly not the master-key which opens every door. Which leads to the further thought that perhaps the notion of psi – which even though it is not accepted by science is a commonplace concept to psychical researchers and has a sort of comfortable familiarity – perhaps it is precisely this which is holding us back, as it held back the SPR-Group a century ago.

We may even find it more productive to set aside the notion of psi, as generally conceived, and to think not of simple communi-cation but of a merging of minds, a process which may be anala-gous to psi and even include it, but which is holistic rather than partial.

Projection and the extended self

The question whether or not we each possess a superphysical body in addition to the physical body we are aware of is a crucial one for our inquiry. Consider this famous case:

178. S. R. Wilmot. Mid-Atlantic, 3 October 1863
Mr Wilmot, an American, is crossing the Atlantic from Liverpool to New York in the steamer *City of Limerick*. One night he dreams he sees his wife – back home in Connecticut – approaching his state-room. At the door she seems to realize he is not the only person in the cabin, and hesitates: then she steps forward, bends over him and kisses him. Next morning, Mr Tait, his fellow passenger, says 'You're a pretty fellow to have a lady come and visit you in this way!', explaining that he witnessed the whole incident. Clearly, it had been more than a dream. When Wilmot reaches home, his wife asks if he received a visit from her a week before? He tells her he was at sea then; she explains that she was worried about him because another ship had recently run aground. On that night she had lain awake, thinking of him, and it seemed to her that she went out to visit him. She crossed a stormy sea, came to a steamship, passed below decks till she came to his cabin. She then noticed that there was a man in the upper berth, observing her. After a moment's hesitation, she bent down and embraced her husband.[311]

226

This case resembles that of Doris Pogue (no. 175), which we cited when considering the role of psi. It raises the same problems, with the additional complication that Mrs Wilmot's ghost is seen by her husband in a dream but also by a stranger who is awake. So the one apparition is three different kinds of experience: for Tait a ghost experience, for Wilmot a dream, while for his wife, though she thinks it only a dream, it is evidently a case of spontaneous out-of-the-body (OBE) projection.

There are so many cases on record in which projection of the extended self seems to be taking place that it is hard to maintain the sceptical view that such experiences are entirely subjective. It's not as though the only evidence is the story told by the projected person (indeed, she is often unaware that she has projected!). OBE travellers frequently describe things they have seen when out of the body, which they could not otherwise know except by clairvoyance. But even clairvoyance is inadequate to explain how the extended self comes to be perceived by others:

179. Barry Brown. Toronto, 1960
'One night, dozing off to sleep, around midnight, I suddenly found myself outside my parents' house . . . I had heard of astral projection and my first thoughts were, "Hey, I've astral projected." I decided to test this out by walking to my girlfriend's home . . . Suddenly, there I was in the bedroom she shared with her grandmother . . . I stood beside Laura. Her brow was furrowed as if she was having a bad dream. Then, as she stirred as if to wake up, I abruptly found myself back in my own bed . . .' Next day he describes to Laura the room which he had never seen, and she tells him, 'I woke up at midnight because I thought someone was there.'[312]

180. Pat Kosharek. Milwaukee, Wisconsin, 21 November 1975
'When I came home from work, my husband told me that both of our children had been running high temperatures. Annoyed because I was exhausted, yet concerned, I peeked into their room to check on them. Both were breathing heavily from congested chest. I wandered back into the kitchen to chat with my husband but he had fallen alseep on the couch. Suddenly I heard a low groan followed by a crash. Again I peeked into the children's room. There, immediately above my son Jimmy's bed, frolicked a white figure that resembled him exactly. It jumped and bounced like an excited child at play. I

rushed forward in panic. The form jumped over the boy but was still attached to him through the top of his head. It swayed for a moment and then was pulled back through the skull like a genie into a lamp. Carefully I lay down next to my boy and fell asleep . . . Bright light suddenly invaded the room, waking me: it hung directly above me. As soon as my eyes adjusted, I again saw the detached figure of Jimmy. I lay frozen by terror. Fascinated, I watched the figure jump off Jimmy's bed and onto my son Alex's bed where it began to tug at his body as if to wake him. In childish glee it pulled off the covers and proceeded to nudge Alex, then it noticed I was awake. Quickly, in one move, it returned to Jimmy's body and I never saw it again. I lay wondering if I had seen a ghost or if I was merely overtired and having a strange dream? My question was answered when I saw my husband in the doorway with eyes as big as saucers . . .'[313]

The question of what happens when the 'self' separates is complex, and would be a distraction from our purpose here, which is to establish whether or not the extended self could be responsible for many ghost experiences. However, we must recognize that projection is not simply another word for the OBE. Consider this case (which does not involve a ghost):

181. Norman F. Ellison. Arras, France, 20 February 1916
'On sentry duty in the worst trenches we had ever been in. Too utterly fed up to curse. Exhausted, sodden, chilled to the bone with icy sleet, hungry, not a dry square inch to sit upon . . . several hours of this misery, and then I became conscious that I was outside myself: that the real "me" – the ego, spirit or what you like – was entirely separate and outside my fleshly body. I was looking in a wholly detached and impersonal way upon the discomforts of a khaki-clad body, which whilst I realized it was my own, might easily have belonged to somebody else for all the direct connection I seemed to have with it. I knew that my body must be feeling acutely cold and miserable but I, my spirit part, felt nothing. In the morning H remarked to me upon my behaviour during the night. For a long time I had been grimly silent and then suddenly changed. My wit and humour under such trying circumstances, had amazed him. I had chatted away as unconcernedly as if we had been warm and comfortable "as if there was no War on" were his exact words. Nothing will shake my inward belief that my soul and body were entirely separated.'[314]

'Entirely?' Enough of Norman remains behind to converse with wit and humour – that is, his physical self retains a capability for more than robot-like behaviour. Yet it seems not to feel the cold and hunger, while self-awareness seems to have been transferred to the separated self, invisible to his companions. This fascinating experience warns us that we must not suppose that the extended self, when activated, monopolizes the individual's personal faculties: *both* bodies may display intelligence, if not necessarily of the same kind.

Some – though not nearly enough – research has been conducted to determine if projection has a material basis. Experiments with Al Tanous in 1972 seemed to detect, using photomultiplier tubes, his presence at the remote location synchronous with his projection attempt. Later experiments with Ingo Swann produced significant psychokinetic effects at a distance of 1000 kilometres.[315] It is deplorable that lack of funding hampers research in this important field: valuable as eyewitness testimony is, instrumental confirmation is always a comfort.

Why are intentional projectors more frequently seen by others than spontaneous OBErs? Perhaps because, though both are 'managed' by the subconscious, the intentional projector adds the force of conscious purpose, in contrast with spontaneous, involuntary projection. In the Brown case cited above, Barry might not have been sensed by Laura at all if he hadn't turned his spontaneous OBE into a purposeful projection. But whether seen, sensed or unnoticed by the person visited, it is hard to see how these experiences can be accounted for as anything other than an actual visit by the extended self; nor can we deny the evidence they present that the extended self has visual sense, awareness and intelligence.

The Sagée case (no. 31) showed us the extended self in the form often labelled bi-location. Here is another example of the kind:

182. John F. Kissinger. New Castle, Pennsylvania, summer 1935
'Father invited me to a lecture at the Scottish Rite Cathedral. As we sat listening to the discourse I became aware that, centimetres away from the lecturer's form stood another distinct form, identical to the first but more ethereal, composed of a finer "atmosphere" than his solid physical self. As he gestured the ethereal image also gestured;

it appeared to be completely synchronized with him, with each casual movement of his material body. When he opened his mouth, the phantom double's mouth moved in unison. I had watched this phenomenon for at least 10 minutes before gathering enough courage to ask father whether he could see what I was seeing. He hastily assured me he certainly could.'[316]

Here, as in no. 27, there is duplication of both the figure and its movements, but the extended self shows no sign of awareness or intelligence, or even of independent behaviour. It is tempting to think of this doubling as an unintentional mistake on someone/thing's part. But the mere fact that the extended self can manifest in so rudimentary a fashion is itself instructive, for it is an indication that it doesn't appear only when specifically invoked, but has a kind of unconscious or autonomous existence of its own.

One feature of intentional projection is particularly relevant to the ghost experience: even when the projector has never previously visited the destination of his projection, he manifests there in a natural way, for instance on a space of open floor rather than embedded in an item of furniture. The projector will subsequently claim that he was fully aware of his surroundings, and this claim is confirmed by the percipients. This is equally true of the great majority of ghost experiences and it would be unrealistic not to adopt, as a working hypothesis, the presumption that a similar process is at work in both cases. That is to say, we should take seriously the possibility that some categories of ghosts are the extended selves of their apparents.

But there is a complication, as this case illustrates:

183. Clarence Godfrey. England, 16 November 1886
Godfrey made two (out of three) successful attempts to project to the home of a friend. She had the feeling that someone had come into her room. She went downstairs, and on the staircase 'I saw Mr Godfrey standing, dressed in his usual style . . . I held up the candle and gazed at him for three or four seconds in utter amazement, and then he disappeared. . .'[317]

The complication is that the primary, physical Godfrey was not dressed 'in his usual style' at the time, but in his nightwear. As Podmore comments, 'The dress and surroundings of the phantasm represent, not the dress and surroundings of the agent at the time, but those with which the percipient is familiar.' He concludes: 'If other proof were wanting, this fact would in itself seem a sufficient argument that we have to deal, not with ghosts but with hallucinations.' But the notion of the extended self, which had not been clearly formulated in Podmore's day, offers a third and, we may feel, a more acceptable alternative.

The apparition which Godfrey's friend sees is not the image of the physical Godfrey as he currently is, but a modified image. The modification may be the work of her subconscious, reluctant to see him in his nightclothes; or that of Godfrey's subconscious, unwilling that he should appear before her improperly dressed. When Godfrey's extended self leaves the physical Godfrey and travels to his friend's home, it takes with it awareness and intelligence, for it behaves naturally in a place it has never been before, it is aware of its surroundings and carries back memories of what takes place.

We may think that the simplest explanation is that Godfrey's subconscious is temporarily 'housed' in his extended self. If so, if the extended self can take with it the full panoply of abilities possessed by the owner, independent of his physical body, during his lifetime, we may be prepared to go the whole hog and face the possibility that it can also do this in the event that, after his death, the extended self survives the physical self.

The existence of a surviving extended self, and if it exists, its nature, have been debated for centuries, often naively but sometimes thoughtfully. The Italian/French researcher Cesar De Vesme (1862–1938) offers an interesting model: the *'larve'* is a duplicate self which appears after death in the form of a phantom body, generally invisible and made from a 'fluidic' substance, taking the form of the human body, possessing only rudimentary intelligence and with the instincts of a living animal. It comes into being because life has not altogether abandoned the somatic (physical) body: it is not yet completely dematerialized. But as life drains out of the somatic body, so the larval body gradually deteriorates, mixing its elements with those of the environment until it is completely disintegrated. 'For many peoples, this larval self lasts about three days; for others, it lasts as long as the memory of those to whom it was connected. It is only more developed peoples that have accorded it a longer life, of undefined limit.'[318]

Price felt that the notion of some kind of extended self is essential to explain hauntings. He suggests that every living being may possess a 'psychic atmosphere' which surrounds the physical body: 'a man's psychic atmosphere will be a kind of secondary body, related to his mind in the same kind of way as the ordinary physical body is, though perhaps more intimately.' He accepts that 'the notion of a "spiritual body" additional to the physical body is an old and familiar one: what is new is only the suggestion that it is composed of unconsciously projected images, or at any rate of image-like stuff.'[319]

What happens when a witness perceives a haunter, in Price's view, is that there takes place an 'overlapping or interpenetration of two psychic atmospheres, the one which surrounds the percipient's body and the one which pervades the room' (which he supposes has been, as it were, left behind by the haunter after her death). This is somewhat akin to Carington's proposal, mentioned earlier, except that Carington is speaking of a psi relationship between two minds, whereas Price is speaking of a relationship between two atmospheres. Both seem to be groping towards the holistic merging – a rapport which is something deeper than telepathic contact – which we already began to suspect when considering psi.

Super-psi and the accessibility of all knowledge

'Where does the uttered music go?' a poet once wondered; and it is an awe-inspiring thought that every word you have ever spoken, every TV game show ever screened, may float around the universe for ever.

Along the same lines is the thought that all knowledge continues to exist somewhere; and the wonder of the internet encourages the science-fantasy notion that it may be recoverable and accessible. Theosophists had the same idea long before computers were invented. They conceive that every event, thought and action makes an impression upon the *akasha*, a subtle ether, where it is permanently stored – the 'Akashic Records' – and whence it can be retrieved by suitably credentialed persons. Christians traditionally expect to be confronted, come Judgment Day, by St Peter with an end-of-term report listing all their sins. Some near-death experiences support this notion, providing an instant play-back during which, in a few brief seconds if not instantaneously, our entire life unrolls before us.[320]

There seems no limit to the information which can be retrieved by the memory – though, alas, it cannot do it to order. But we have all had the experience of entirely trivial memories suddenly rising from the past – a schoolfellow we have not thought of for forty years suddenly appears in a dream. Does memory die with us, or can we think that, if we survive, we carry our memories with us? The problem arises very specifically in reincarnation and in all those categories of the ghost experience which seem to involve the dead.

The accessibility of all knowledge would be one way of accounting for the fact that when Uncle Jack manifests to his nephew George as a crisis apparition he may be wearing an overcoat purchased only last week and which George could not know of (as in no. 76). Clairvoyance? Well, but what is clairvoyance, if not a tapping of the Akashic Record? Similarly, the well-established phenomenon of psychometry, in which a sensitive holds an object belonging to you and seems to obtain access to information about you, past, present and future, puts a considerable strain on the psi explanation.

One way of accounting for the crisis apparition would be if our subconscious is continually scanning the cosmos, like the radar scanner at an airfield, and picks up on happenings relevant to itself – of which the involvement of our Uncle Jack in an accident might be one. Or we could make an analogy with the search facility on this computer, which will in a fraction of a second find every use I have made of the word 'ghost' in this book. Our subconscious would be programmed to detect anything related to Jack – well no, more likely not everything. Jack brushing his teeth could be screened out; it would have to be things which merit our attention. But would Jack's accident be sufficient on its own, or would he have to play a positive role, emitting a distress call, either vague or explicit, to catch the scanner's attention?

Which brings us to the 'super-psi' hypothesis. Many researchers have toyed with this concept in varying forms, but so far as it applies to the ghost experience, it is summed up by researcher Hornell Hart as follows (I have taken the liberty of substituting 'psi' for Hart's 'ESP'):

> The dramatizing powers of the unconscious, making use of a com-prehensive form of telepathy, clairvoyance, precognition and retrocognition (which I shall call *super-psi*) may create pseudo spirit personalities, which convince wishful believers, but which give no genuine evidence of survival . . . a similar process might create apparitions of the dead . . . [super-psi] operates in ways which can gather pertinent information from anywhere in the world . . . the information thus gathered is organized into plausible pseudo-communicator form by the dramatizing capacity of the . . . unconscious mind.[321]

The concept of super-psi has been welcomed by those who, whether or not they have a personal belief in survival, are uncon-vinced by the evidence. It is not really a theory, because it has no specific tenets: it is simply a recognition that, since there are no known limits to the capabilities of the mind, we cannot exclude the possibility that the creativity of the subconscious is capable both of creating apparitions and of investing them with informa-tion content of which no living person is aware.

The weakness of the super-psi concept is that it explains nothing: it simply states the possibility that an explanation for certain phenomena may be found without requiring us to take on board the notion of survival. By contrast, the various survival hypotheses explain the matter much more simply and straight-forwardly. But we must not, for that reason, think that survival is more probable than super-psi. A good many of the cases cited in this inquiry are more plausibly explained by super-psi than by traditional ghosts: for example, the Malleson case (no. 174), and the following:

184. Canadian POW. German–Dutch border, 1914–18
During WW1 a Canadian prisoner-of-war in Germany manages to escape, eventually arriving at night, during a snowstorm, at a cross-roads where one road leads to Holland and probable safety, the other to probable recapture. He hesitates, then makes his choice. Suddenly there appears before him the apparition of his brother, utterly clear

and lifelike, who says 'No, Dick, not that way. Take the other road, you damned fool!' He takes the other road and reaches safety.[322]

His brother is in England, living, and probably asleep. This would not prevent us theorizing that their two minds had merged in some way. It is conceivable that the sleeping brother might suddenly become aware, through psi, of his brother's predicament, and seeing (thanks to super-psi) which is the right road, hurries to save him, appearing as an apparition thanks to visualization on the prisoner's part. But why bring the sleeping brother into the matter at all? Isn't it more probable that it is the prisoner himself who obtains access to the information (again, by super-psi), and whose subconscious, needing a guarantor for the information so that it will carry weight, conscripts his brother – that is, the *image* of his brother – into the act?

The notion of super-psi, and in particular the access to all knowledge, is attractive because it enables us to resolve, at one stroke, the supreme problem of the ghost experience: that the percipient frequently obtains information of which no one living is aware. As we saw earlier, this information can be obtained in one of only two ways: either by extra-sensory perception of some kind, or by direct communication from someone no longer living. Super-psi offers us a way of avoiding the survival issue: the living mind can do it all. Yet there remain strong arguments for the contrary point of view. The case for super-psi is not so strong that we can exclude the alternative possibility of external agency.

Understanding the ghost experience

We have reached the point when we should bring these various threads of thought together and weave them into something like an explanation of what is happening when someone has a ghost experience.

We have basically two models for the experience:

- The *subjective model*, originating with the subconscious of the percipient. Either of its own accord, or in response to information obtained via psi or super-psi – comprising telepathy, clairvoyance, and unlimited access to information including precognition and retrocognition – the subconscious initiates a visualization process whereby it exteriorizes an image which can be perceived consciously by the percipient, and perhaps by others, as an apparition.

- The *external model*, originating with an external agent – by which we generally mean the extended self of a person still living, or the surviving extended self of a person once living but now dead – which is able either to manifest as an apparition, or to impose an image by suggestion on to the subconscious of the percipient(s) and cause it to exteriorize an apparition

We should not rule out the possibility that both processes could conceivably work together: for instance, in a crisis apparition, Uncle Jack, undergoing a crisis, may stimulate nephew George into the super-psi/visualization process.

Granted that none of the notions presented earlier in this chapter – of the extended self and its ability to project, of super-psi, of the accessibility of all knowledge – granted that none of these is proven, let us nevertheless see how, by taking them on board, they can help us understand the specific categories of ghost experience.

Understanding revenants

It seems likely that a good many ostensible revenants are nothing of the sort. When a deceased relative appears to comfort or reassure the living, it could be a wish-fulfilling fantasy created by the percipient's subconscious, without any external intervention by the apparent.

There are other cases, though, where the motivation seems to stem from the apparent, where we must consider the possibility that what is seen is a projection by her surviving extended self. This may be seen directly, as a quasi-material apparition; or it may be imposed by suggestion on the subconscious of the percipient which then visualizes it: or conceivably by some kind of mind-merging collaboration between the two.

Many revenant cases involve the transmission of information to which the percipient would not normally have access. This information could be communicated by someone now dead, or the percipient could obtain it via super-psi. Some cases appear to make more sense on the survival hypothesis: the Chaffin will case (no. 112), for example, while it could conceivably be a super-psi case, seems better explained as originating with the dead father. It is unlikely, though not impossible, that the son's subconscious would, after a period of years, suddenly deploy super-psi to ascertain the whereabouts of a missing will of whose existence he has no conscious awareness.

Revenants: the bottom line. Many revenants are likely to be creations of the percipient's own subconscious, visualized as apparitions. But for those willing to contemplate the possibility of survival, the case is strong that many are visitations by the surviving extended self of the apparent.

Understanding crisis apparitions

There are two parts to the crisis apparition: the setting up of a link between apparent and percipient, and the conveying of sufficient information for the apparition to be created. Consider this case:

185. Paul Stewart. Denver, Colorado, April 1925
'My wife and I were entertaining friends at bridge. In the midst of a game, I unexpectedly felt impelled to go outside for a breath of fresh air. I had stepped only a few paces into the garden when I heard a voice calling my name. I turned, and there was my father . . . I spoke to him but he stood silent for a brief moment and then vanished. His death had occurred while vacationing in Greece almost exactly when I saw his ghost.'[323]

Paul feels *impelled* – strongly enough to quit his game and his guests – to go to where his father's ghost is awaiting him. While it is not impossible that his subconscious, using super-psi, is alerted to his father's death, it is surely far more likely that the impulse comes from the dying father. From then on, admittedly, super-psi could play a part, and the staging of the meeting could be the result either of super-psi on the father's part, combined with a suggestion compelling his son to visualize his ghost; or the apparition could be his extended self. Like the Zurich case (no. 98) and so many others, this crisis apparition gives no indication of why it is happening. The apparition is all.

We can say with some degree of confidence that the apparent does not consciously choose to manifest as an apparition. So it's either an uncontrolled event, a kind of by-product of the mental state of the apparent; or it is a deliberate process initiated by something other than his conscious mind. This could conceivably be the percipient's subconscious, but is surely more likely to be the apparent's subconscious. Perhaps it is a last, desperate effort

Crisis apparitions provide the strongest reason to accept the reality of ghosts. In 1894 the ghost of a former librarian of Leeds Library, Vincent Sternberg, is seen by his sucessor, John MacAlister, at about the time of his death

on the part of the living apparent to communicate, and there is no further survival. Alternatively, and perhaps more probably, it is the apparent's extended self, liberated by the shock of the crisis and now acting autonomously. If the apparent survives the crisis, the extended self will rejoin the physical self; if he dies, then it may continue its independent existence.

What can we say about the process whereby a crisis apparition is perceived? Is the apparent sending out a general distress call, or is it targeting a specific individual? Some cases, for instance the Clerke case (no. 168), seem clearly to indicate selection; in others, though, the call is picked up only by someone who may be a very remote acquaintance, as in this case:

186. Lois J. Myers. New Brunswick, c. 1950

'My mother sent me to town to do some shopping. I was taking a short cut when I met the father of a girl friend, Mr Aldrich. I remarked how well he looked. He drank considerably and never kept up his appearance, but on this particular day he was all dressed up. I spoke with him for a while and went on my way. That evening a friend asked me if I knew Mr Aldrich was dead. I told her I had seen him about two o'clock that afternoon. She said that was impossible as he was buried at two o'clock. She asked me what he was wearing, and said that was just what he was buried in.'[324]

Lois is not a close connection of the apparent, and surely not his first choice of the person he would most like his ghost to be seen by. Yet she not only sees him, wearing clothes she could not expect but which his physical body is indeed wearing at the time, but speaks with him 'for a while', implying that he is participating in the exchange. What would a passer-by see – a girl standing in the street talking to nobody?

If we look to super-psi for an explanation, we would have to consider something like Carington's hypothesis, of a cluster of associations linking to another of the same. While Lois is not a close acquaintance of Mr Aldrich, a link exists: and perhaps this is enough to bring about the encounter. Louise McKee's case (no. 169) is another instance where an extremely fragile link seems to be sufficient to induce the apparition, while the Money case (no. 22), where the apparition is seen by the babysitter, seems to clinch the matter, for how could she conceivably originate the apparition?

But just when it seems self-evident that the crisis apparition originates with the apparent we come across a case such as this:

187. Etta Benson. Kennett, Missouri, summer 1938
'While walking home from a revival meeting, late one night, my mother-in-law saw a small child all alone in the circle of illumination formed by a street light. The baby, playing in waist-high grass, wore a little pink dress and bonnet. Knowing that the nearest house was one of ill repute, she thought the child had been left by some visitor. She walked on past, then worried why the child was out so late, turned back. When she reached the spot she found it deserted. She decided the child had been taken in. Next morning she received the news that her sister-in-law's baby, a child she had never seen, had died. When she saw the child in its casket, she recognized it at once as the child she had seen, even to the pink dress and bonnet.'[325]

We can hardly classify this as anything but a crisis apparition. But even if we suppose that the child is somehow responsible for the apparition, she can hardly have Etta in mind as a percipient. Yet the apparition occurs in a place where Etta, alone of her relatives, would be at this time. The alternatives are: Etta has an instance of super-psi, which her subconscious translates into an apparition; or the child sends out a generalized distress call which anyone psychically attuned might pick up; or the child's mother aims the message at Etta, wherever she may be, supplying the details that Etta's subconscious needs if it is to collaborate in creating the apparition – which she does, then and there. But why the lack of information? It is noteworthy that crisis apparitions very rarely present a picture of the crisis scene – the rail crash or whatever. Why does the apparent project only his image, with no more than a hint and often not even that of the crisis event, leaving it to the percipient to exclaim, Hey, there's Uncle Jack, looks like he's in some kind of trouble!

This next case, like many, teases by offering partial clues, yet still stops short of telling the percipient what has actually happened:

188. Louisa Shaw (née Rogers). Tewksbury, Massachusetts, February 1938
'The roads were covered with ice: no one went outside their home unless they had an important errand. My father, the town lawyer, felt

he must deliver some legal papers, and left the house. Later in the afternoon I was standing at the top of the stairs combing my hair in front of a mirror, not thinking about anything in particular. Slowly my reflexion changed into the face of my father. He did not have his glasses on, which was very unusual, and there seemed to be a cut above his right eyebrow. Gradually his face faded and I again saw my own face looking out. I was so frightened my flesh had goosebumps although the house was cozy and warm. I ran downstairs and tried to explain to Mother what I had just seen. She did not believe me and nonchalantly went back to playing the piano. 15 or 20 minutes later I heard the back door open. I flew down the stairs in time to see my father come into the kitchen. He did not have his glasses on and blood was running down his face from a gash over his right eyebrow. His car had skidded, hit a telephone pole and landed in the ditch. He had bumped his head on the steering wheel, breaking his glasses and cutting his forehead. He had walked home, and this had taken 15 or 20 minutes. So I had seen him in the mirror at about the same time the accident had occurred or very shortly afterwards.'[326]

This simple but intriguing case reminds us that the crisis in crisis-apparition cases need not always be fatal; but of course Mr Rogers may well have thought his life was threatened when his car skidded. But why does he appear only as an image, admittedly with two telling details, yet still holding back on Louisa as to why she is seeing the apparition at all?

And then there is the way he appears. Does his subconscious – or Louise's if she is responsible for the apparition – choose the mirror as a convenient way of appearing? One or other of them must be responsible. These things don't just happen, someone or something initiated the process and decided how it should be done. But suppose Louise had not looked in a mirror that afternoon: would her father have appeared as a conventional apparition? Or did her subconscious prompt her to look in the mirror, having set up the process?

There is a curious parallel to this incident in the story of Ruth, the patient treated by psychiatrist Morton Schatzman who could deliberately create lifelike apparitions. She was able to look into a mirror and transform her reflection into an image of her father.[327] Perhaps the subconscious makes use of mirrors as it does crystal balls, as a way of channelling the visualization process. (For another case where the mirror-image changes see no. 133.)

With crisis apparitions, the best alternative to super-psi is projection on the part of the apparent's extended self. We have already wondered whether the crisis in which the individual finds herself may be sufficient to induce an altered state; and there is no doubt that in such states projection can occur, either spontaneously or as the result of suggestion. 'Animal magnetizers' in nineteenth-century France found that some of their subjects could, under instruction, 'travel' to a distant place and report on what they saw; there are too many examples of this, too rich in detail, for us to attribute them to chance or coincidence.[328]

The projection option is supported by such a case as the Obalecheff case (no. 76) in which Aimée sees the ghost of her brother-in-law Nicolai wearing a dressing-gown which she does not know he possesses – but which he is indeed wearing at the time. Either Aimée has a clairvoyant perception of him at Tver, or he is projecting his image to Odessa. If we prefer the psi option, we have to accept that she not only sees Nicolai in his dressing-gown, but stages the scenario whereby he comes into her room, stepping over Claudine's legs to sit in the chair. No doubt this is well within the capability of the subconscious: however, if we prefer the projection option, it is natural that he should be aware of the position of the furniture, and also the need to step over the servant's legs. The fact that Nicolai has a motive for projecting to Odessa, whereas Aimée has no particular reason for conjuring up a clairvoyant vision of her brother-in-law, is further reason to prefer the projection scenario.

Neither way of explaining the crisis apparition – super-psi or projection – can be ruled out. In the majority of cases, projection seems the more plausible if only for the simple reason that it is the apparent who is having the crisis, not the percipient. For those who prefer the super-psi explanation this is not an insuperable obstacle, because it is part of the charm of the super-psi hypothesis that is has no known limits.

A third possibility is that the crisis apparition results from a collaboration between the two parties concerned. Gurney, back in the 1890s, and Tyrrell sixty years later, thought it likely that crisis apparitions are created by a collaboration between agent and per-cipient, the two working together to produce an 'idea-pattern' which is satisfactory to both parties.

Crisis apparitions: the bottom line. It seems likely that the major-ity of crisis apparitions originate with the apparent who is under-going the crisis, shocked into an altered state which leads her to spontaneously and subconsciously project her extended self either towards targeted individuals or to anyone it can find who is in an appropriate state to see it. In some cases there seems a def-inite intention to inform the percipient (e.g. the Barbados case, no. 168), but in as many others the ghost makes no effort to convey a message (e.g. the garden swing case no. 169).

The projection hypothesis can be avoided by supposing a kind of super-psi sweep on the part of the percipient's subconscious, whereby it picks up on the apparent's distress, zeroes in to see what's happening and then informs the conscious mind by visu-alizing an apparition. The weakness of the super-psi hypothesis is the unaccountable failure of apparitions to be specific: if the percipient's super-psi can pick up that the apparent is in a crisis situation, it should be able to tell her the nature of the crisis. This failure is easier to understand if it is the panicking crisis victim who is responsible.

Understanding living ghosts

It is reasonable to think that when the apparition of a living person is seen, it is her extended self, possessed of its senses, awareness and intelligence, spontaneously projecting for reasons that often remain obscure. Thus in the Boulton case (no. 4), not only is the lady seen as a ghost by others, but she herself notes details of the place where she is seen; since she has never visited that place in her physical body, she must either travel there in her extended self, or she must acquire the knowledge by psi. In the Boyd case (no. 24) an explanation in terms of a spontaneous pro-jection by the son's extended self is in many ways more satisfac-tory than telepathy.

An aspect of these cases which favours neither one explanation nor the other arises when we ask *why* Mrs Boulton should travel to obtain knowledge of the house she will one day rent. Is she subconsciously foreseeing that one day she will physically go there? Asking this question warns us that we must not think of super-psi and projection as mutually exclusive explanations: super-psi could be the normal mode of awareness possessed by the extended self. That is to say, it is her/its awareness that she will one day go to the house which prompts Mrs Boulton's extended self to pay these preview visits. But even as we set it out in this way, we feel the absurdity of trying to explain it in every-day human terms. We sense some broader frame of reference that encompasses the dream-visits (which include seeing the house before the changes), the rendering herself visible to the residents via out-of-body projection, and her eventual in-the-body visit.

This next case alerts us to another complication:

189. Laurence Orchard. London, 25 December 1913
'I was in the bathroom, when I heard footsteps and doors being opened and closed quite distinctly, and as I was the only one in the house it surprised me, so I opened the door and looked out, and to my astonishment I saw Mother (or thought I did) in a black dress at her bedroom door and her arms full of parcels. I made an exclamation – "Mother", I think, and I think there was some sort of response, and then all disappeared suddenly . . . it was the noise that attracted my notice first.' [Mrs Orchard was in Canada at the time.][329]

Sounds are rare in ghost experiences; this one is remarkable because it is the sounds which alert the son. If the apparition is the mother's extended self, why should she need to stage so elab-orate a drama, sound-effects and all? – and the same question arises if Laurence's subconscious is the impresario. Probably the most plausible account would be that the mother imagines herself – perhaps in a dream – visiting her London home, and goes through the sequence of opening doors etcetera, all of which is shared by her son, their family rapport strengthened by its being Christmas Day when their thoughts would naturally be with each other. While in principle there is no reason why the event should not be so detailed, the agent seems to have gone to extraordinary lengths to make the visit realistic.

Living ghosts: the bottom line. Spontaneous projection of the extended self seems the explanation of choice for most if not all living ghosts, with the proviso that this may involve psi and even super-psi, and intelligent behaviour on the part of the extended self even though – as is almost always the case – the apparent herself is unaware that her extended self is projecting.

Understanding hauntings

It does not seem plausible that a dead person should choose to manifest as a haunting ghost. If there is no future life, what is this non-life that haunting seems to be? And if there is a future life, why is the haunter hanging around here when he could be getting on with it? Here is a case which presents the problem of hauntings at its simplest:

190. Trudy van Riper. Kerrville, Texas, early 1958
'I was driving to make a business visit to a ranch. It was a beautiful day, and I decided to stop and walk up a mountain beside the road. I did not realize it was so far until I had started to climb. I became tired and stopped under a tree. While I sat there, catching my breath, I heard a whimpering sound. I looked round and there, standing not five metres from me, was a little boy. He looked about eight and had long blond hair and blue eyes. He was crying. "Are you lost?" I asked. He shook his head and said, "I lost my red ball. I threw it up into the air and now I cannot find it." I told him I would help him find his ball. "Do your folks know where you are?" I asked. He nodded and said, "Oh yes, I play here all the time." I suggested looking at the bottom of the hill: I turned and said for him to come on and look here too. He started towards me, stubbed his toe and fell headlong in the dirt. I ran to him and leaned over to help him up. My hand went through him and before my very eyes he vanished. I was so shocked that for a minute or two I couldn't move. When I told my mother, she told me that a German family had lived in a shack there: they had a little boy about eight years old who died of a fever in 1921 and his parents buried him beneath the tree where I stopped to rest. I did not see a grave, for there was nothing under the tree but a pile of stones.'[330]

We can assume that the ghost is that of the dead boy, but consider the difficulties with this seemingly simple case. Trudy knows

245

nothing of the story, so the ghost can have originated in her mind only if we adopt the super-psi hypothesis at its most far-fetched. But has the ghost of the boy been playing there day after day for more than thirty years? Or has he somehow escaped from time? No, that won't do, because his words and actions involve a sequence in time. To play for thirty-seven years with a ball on a mountainside implies something akin to a robot or a zombie, yet the boy interacts with Trudy, behaving and speaking intelligently.

Such questions seem naive, but they are relevant. The mere fact that a ghost is seen haunting a certain location – generally a former home – is evidence of some degree of purpose. And though the majority of haunters are somewhat zombie- or robot-like in their behaviour, this is by no means invariably the case. Several haunters, such as the boy just cited, are recorded as interacting with the percipient, clearly aware of their presence. Moreover, the fact that in the great majority of cases haunters adapt to the physical circumstances of the location – walking along a 'Nun's Walk', negotiating stairs, following country lanes – implies awareness of their physical environment.

So what is this entity which does not seem to have a very clear idea what it is doing, but is sufficiently aware of itself to adapt to the physical environment and to interact with people it happens to meet? Again, it seems plausible that it is the apparent's quasi-material extended self which seems to possess sufficient substance for it to be seen by (some) others.

In his Presidential Address to the SPR in 1939, Price discussed haunting apparitions and showed that there is no way to explain the evidence in terms of existing scientific knowledge. We have no option but to invoke some power as yet unknown to science to explain the phenomenon. A lot of progress has been made since 1939, and if he were making the same analysis today, Price would probably feel less constrained by conventional thinking. But his analysis of the challenge remains insightful and perceptive:

> The haunting apparition is normally a more or less exact copy of the body of some person who formerly lived in the haunted place. But is this at all what we should have expected if the ghost is a persistent and projected image originating in the apparent's mind? Is it not most uncommon to form an image of one's own body – espe-

246

cially an accurate one? The puzzle is increased by the fact that the image would have to represent the visible appearance of one's own body as seen from without. If the image was formed and projected by him in some period of intense emotion, surely the last thing he would be thinking of at such a time would be the outward aspect of his own body?[331]

We came across this difficulty with no. 183, where a projector in his nightclothes is seen in his day clothes. The only way to avoid this dilemma is to recognize that the mental process is overridden, that his manifestation as a ghost is something out of his control. Andrew Lang offered an interesting suggestion in 1897:

> What natural thing most resembles the common idea of a ghost? You are reading alone at night, let us say, the door opens and a human figure glides into the room. To you it pays no manner of attention; it does not answer if you speak; it may trifle with some object in the chamber and then steal quietly out again. *It is the House-maid walking in her sleep.* This perfectly accountable appearance, in its aimlessness, its unconsciousness, its irresponsiveness, is undeniably just like the common notion of a ghost. Now, if ordinary ghosts are not of flesh and blood, like the sleep-walking house-maid, yet are as irresponsive, as unconscious, and as vaguely wandering as she, then a ghost *may* be a hallucination produced in the living by the *unconscious* action of the mind of the dreaming dead.[332]

I think Lang made this delightful suggestion not so much as a serious theory but as a reminder that we should not expect revenants and haunters always to behave in a totally purposeful manner. His suggestion won't do, of course, for many of our encounters, but it warns us not to take it for granted that every case must be explained in the same manner. Ghosts like any other phenomenon may have their exceptions and their variations. Most of us don't walk in our sleep; but some do, sometimes, and perhaps ghosts do, too, sometimes.

By and large, the notion of the surviving extended self effectively meets Price's criteria, and is in many ways our best option, in that it makes use of a process which, even if it lacks scientific approval, has an enormous consensus of popular belief behind it, and which is plausible and satisfying.

What part, if any, does the percipient play? Surely only a passive one, but yet a necessary one. The fact that only some people see a haunter – even if there are others present at the time – implies a degree of collaboration: we may think of it as a collaboration between the extended self of the apparent and the subconscious of the percipient, a collaboration which the haunter is prepared, or able, to make with some, but not with others. Price thought this might be the case:

> Why is it that so few places are haunted? If the haunting of a house is ultimately caused by the emotions or other experiences of persons who formerly lived there, surely any house which has been inhabited for twenty or thirty years ought to be haunted, and indeed haunted by a number of different ghosts? Almost every street corner ought to be packed with apparitions. And what about prisons and law courts, what about railway stations: arrivals and departures often cause extremely strong emotions. So it would seem that there ought to be a great deal more haunting than there actually is. It is of course true that a special type of percipient is required. It is not everyone who can see a ghost, even granting that the requisite conditions are present on the objective side. But percipients exist, and should we not expect them to see vastly more ghosts than they do see?[333]

Price's explanation is that places are indeed haunted by lots of ghosts, but often so many that they cancel one another out and no particular psychic atmosphere can be distinguished from the mass. This is plausible up to a point, but it doesn't really explain why, in a haunted house, the apparition of a little old lady, say, imposes itself so overwhelmingly on all the others that it can be said that the house is haunted solely by that particular haunter. But Price is right to say that the explanation for this difficulty 'will help us to form some notion of the causal process by which ghostseeing is conditioned'. Any explanation of hauntings must confront the problem of why, out of the millions who die, do only some live on – if that's the right phrase – as haunters?

We saw in Chapter 7 that the same problem recurs in reincarnation: even in cultures where reincarnation is accepted, it is a rare happening, but when it happens it tends to occur especially to persons who suffered violent deaths.[334] This could mean that the same factors which cause reincarnation may also lead to haunting: perhaps haunting and reincarnation are alternative strategies for those who find themselves projected into the next phase of being as the result of a violent and untimely death. Without going so far as to picture the newly dead person being debriefed by some kind of selection board, having the options pointed out to him, and saying 'Oh, I think I'll be reincarnated' or 'I guess I'll be a haunter', we can suppose that, on some level of consciousness or subconsciousness, he makes the decision, or has the decision made for him. Consider:

191. Patricia Stirling. Weyburn, Canada, 1938
Patricia and her husband George, spending their first night in their new home, hear a sound like sweeping in the next room. They find nothing to explain it, nevertheless the sounds of a heavy broom swishing over the floor occur night after night. One night Pat and her young son, returning home, are confronted by a tall, slender, white-haired woman, with a mole on her cheek, busily sweeping the lino-leum floor. They flee to neighbours who identify her as Adelaide Huntington, a widow who formerly occupied the cottage, and had a passion for sweeping. She had died a few months before by a fall down the cellar steps.[335]

Trivial though it is, this is a very significant case. Unlike those revenant cases in which the apparition has a specific task to perform, and does it more or less intelligently, Adelaide seems to be acting as a robot. There can be no sensible reason why a dead person should return to sweep the floor of the house she formerly lived in, so we can conclude either that her surviving self has lost its wits and is carrying out automatic actions like a living obses-sive, or alternatively, that Pat and her son are given a vision of Adelaide as she behaved when she was still alive.

We have to face the fact that Trudy's boy on the hillside, and Pat's sweeping housewife, are two different kinds of haunter. While the first may be the dead boy's extended self, somehow aware and interacting, the second behaves like a zombie, and something less than the extended self seems to be involved.

Occultists have proposed many degrees of secondary self, of

which the aware, intelligent extended self is only one. So perhaps the sweeping housewife is a less sophisticated model. Or the whole process may be different: perhaps there is a kind of haunter which displays no awareness because it does not emanate directly from the apparent, but is created by the percipient, using her super-psi to visualize the former occupant of the house? If so, Pat could have picked it up from the cottage's 'psi field', another approach which in various forms has been proposed by several researchers, most notably William Roll:

> Because the 'telepathic charge' of a haunted house is similar to the magnetic, gravitational, and other fields that surround physical objects, I have used the concept of psi field to describe psi phenomena that seem to depend on such objects. We can think of the psi field of an object, whether animate or inanimate, as a pattern of associations . . . In the same way as a magnet may magnetize another piece of metal and then be destroyed without affecting the new magnet, so may the images, ideas, and so on of a person continue to exist as part of the psi fields of objects with which he was once in contact, after he has gone. The image of a person seen in an apparition, whether this image was produced by him or someone else, may survive his death without being inhabited by his consciousness.[336]

It is attractive to suppose that the subconscious of some percipients – those that are, as it were, on the same wavelength as the psi field – may pick up a message from the psi field and externalize it as an apparition. That saves us having to explain why haunters go on behaving so mindlessly. However, it is difficult to apply this to Adelaide the Sweeping Housewife: can we really suppose that Pat and her son, walking through the door, both instantly connect to the psi field and see the same apparition, where they have never seen it before and will never see it again? Surely some additional factor causes it to appear then, and then only. Are we to think of the psi field as latent, but that something activates it on this one occasion, causing the widow to put on a for-one-night-only performance?

Haunters: the bottom line. By far the most plausible explanation, for those haunters which seem to display awareness and even interact with percipients, is that the extended self of the dead

person is for some reason continuing to frequent a former home
or site. When a haunter shows no signs of intelligence or awareness, this could be because something less than his whole self – a
kind of rudimentary being – is performing. As for the percipient,
her role is certainly important, if passive: her subconscious could
be collaborating with that of the apparent to arrange the visualization. It may also sometimes be that the subconscious of the
percipient is picking up on some undefined memory trace, psi
field or whatever, and converting it into an apparition. Haunters
are not all of a kind, and the different kinds may involve different processes.

The physical substance of ghosts

What is the ghost composed of? For a large number of ghosts, the
answer is: nothing. They have no substance, they are nothing but
hallucinated images, and their only existence is as impulses
within the mind of the percipient.

Nevertheless there is a strong case that some ghosts are more
than this; that some do possess substance of a sort. Carington,
who suggests that apparitions are the result of associative links
between percipient and agent, has this to say:

> My own view – tentative enough in all conscience – is that appari-
> tions are 'externalized' – i.e. 'seen' as if located outside the percip-
> ient as an ordinary object is – only by those who are capable of
> what is known as 'eidetic imagery'. This is a sort of imagery, not
> uncommon in children though rare in adults, in which the image
> is described as being literally *seen* as if it were outside the subject
> and in many respects just like a real object. It seems to me that it
> would be perverse to insist on looking further, unless we are
> obliged to do so, for the externalizing mechanism of apparitions
> and ghosts.[337]

Well, perverse or not, it seems to me we *are* obliged to look
further, even if only to leave no stone unturned. If we are willing
to opt for the super-psi-and-visualization scenario, where there
are no limits to what the subconscious can do, anything is possible. Using eidetic imaging or whatever, we can visualize a ghost

as solid or otherwise, as reflecting in mirrors or not, as casting shadows or not. So all the types of behaviour we listed in Chapter 3 as requiring to be explained can be seen as subjective, created by the mind of the percipient utilizing information it has acquired by psi or super-psi.

But what if some ghosts are – as there is good reason to think many are – projections by the apparent? Surely the extended self, by definition, has no substance? Yet the percipient sees it, and so we have a choice of options:

- the extended self does possess material substance of a sort, though unknown to our physics; or
- it possesses sufficient substance to be seen by the normal senses of the percipient; or
- it possesses no substance of its own, but manifests as a hallucination created as a co-operative venture with the subconscious of the percipient.

Are there any additional factors which would make one of these options more likely than the others? Generally, what is felt when a percipient touches a ghost is nothing, and her hand can pass through the ghost. Evidently such reality as it possesses is not our everyday, consensus reality. On those occasions where the ghost is felt, like the 'flimsy drapery' of no. 92 or the handshake of no. 134, this could be illusion created either by the percipient's subconscious as part of the visualization process, or by the apparent's extended self by way of reinforcing its believability. But we cannot altogether rule out the possibility that something more than illusion may be involved: that the apparition may be a short-lived entity brought into being by the agent, which possesses tactile as well as visual properties.

Suggestions have been made that a stuff may exist – it has been labelled 'psi-substance' – which is the raw material from which ghosts are made. Price, in his 1939 Presidential Address, invited his audience to conceive 'an ether of images [which] would be something intermediate between mind and matter as we ordinarily conceive of them . . . we could either call it mental or call it material, as we liked'. [338] There is no more evidence for this quasi-material substance than there is for Roll's psi field, but 'such a concept seems to be required', writes researcher John Vyvyan, 'it

252

makes sense in the context of the actual experiences that people have reported'.[339] Like astronomers' black holes, we infer the existence of psi-substance from its effect on its environment.

But even if we allow ghosts to have sufficient substance to be seen, to reflect, to cast shadows and sometimes to be touched, that is a long way from attributing to them the ability to actually *do* anything apart from walking around the room or making the occasional gesture like the beckoning signal in no. 61. Physical actions ostensibly performed by ghosts are very rare, but it would be wrong to pretend they don't happen at all. Almost always the action is trivial – moving a small article from one place to another, for example. Only occasionally do they involve something as sophisticated as eating or drinking or even writing a letter. The evidence for these more complicated actions is not very strong, but if we choose to give those who report them the benefit of the doubt, we may suppose that the simple actions are performed by the same kind of mental force which performs poltergeist actions – dropping crockery or throwing stones – or that which is exerted in psychokinesis, where small objects seem to be moved by some kind of force exerted by the mind, or in street-lamp interference.

When it comes to explaining why only some of those present see an apparition, it is reasonable to suppose that there exists a subconscious link between the percipient and the agent, which the non-perceivers lack. This could be psychological, psychic, spiritual, even chemical, and could operate autonomously. If you visit a haunted house, and have the appropriate qualifications, you see the haunter; if you haven't, you don't. In the churchwarden case (no. 1) the apparition is seen by three separate people, but apparently not by the rest of those present (or did they just not notice, their minds on higher things?). We could suppose that the apparent initiates the process, manifesting on a see-me-if-you-can basis. This is easier to accept than that the percipients are specified in the way the sender of an email message specifies his recipients: A, B and C shall see it, X, Y and Z won't.

The computer analogy also supports the view that the default condition is *not* to see the ghost, and that only those perceive it who have received the appropriate password. Such a ghost experience implies collaboration between the agent and the percipient. Tyrrell proposes:

> The apparitional drama is quite clearly in most cases a joint effort in which the subconscious producers of both agent and percipient take part. We know this because not only are there items in the apparition which the agent cannot have known; there are also often items which the percipient cannot have known, such as a wound in a particular part of the body.[340]

To be pedantic, one could argue that super-psi could explain this transfer of inaccessible knowledge, but Tyrrell's scenario avoids the difficulty which arises with the super-psi explanation of why the percipient should initiate those ghost experiences where the motivation seems all on the apparent's side. It seems more realistic to conclude that, in some cases at least, it takes two to make a ghost.

Chapter 9

THE IMPLICATIONS OF THE GHOST EXPERIENCE

For those who have a ghost experience, it is an end in itself. They get the message, they feel the comfort, they heed the warning. But if we can find our way beyond the immediate performance, back-stage to where the special effects are contrived and the script pre-pared, the experience has much to teach us about ourselves and the universe we inhabit.

The ultimate materialist position on the ghost experience is that it is a fantasy generated by a disturbed or deceived mind. Since we have no mind beyond the functioning of our physical brains, there is nothing to survive; so when we die, that is the end of us. What purport to be revenants returning from the dead can only be false illusions, wish-fulfilling fantasies generated by our imaginations. What purport to be projections or out-of-body experiences are also illusions, for there is nothing to project: nothing of us can leave our body. Any information ostensibly obtained in the course of ghost encounters or OBEs, or by psi, is due to coincidence, cryptomnesia (hidden memory) or mere chance.

Supporting this position is the fact that there is no hard scien-tific evidence for the mind, for psi, for the extended self; still less for survival after death or super-psi.

Challenging this position there is only a body of psi experi-ments where the odds against chance are remarkably high, the obtaining of information known to no living person where the odds against coincidence are remarkably high, and an enormous quantity of human testimony, with all that this entails in terms of forgetting or falsely remembering, confabulating or confusing, or downright lying.

The choice, which of these two positions we take, can only be a subjective one. Our understanding of the universe we inhabit is based on our experience, and experience tells us it is easy to be deceived or mistaken. But experience also tells us that if we insist on absolute certainty – will this washing machine never go wrong, is it 100 per cent sure that my flight to Stockholm will not crash or that this accused woman in the dock did what she is charged with doing – life becomes impossible. So we settle for less than 100 per cent; for probabilities, not certainties.

At this stage of our inquiry we see that there is a strong case for the proposition that some ghost experiences, at least, are something more than illusion; and a strong probability that something like the extended self, and something like super-psi, are involved. Not that the evidence for either is good, for what there is, is largely circumstantial; but because they offer the best way of accounting for events for which the evidence is very strong indeed.

At the same time, it is likely that many ghost experiences are not what they seem to be. The creative capabilities of the mind remain unplumbed, but the witchcraft and alien abduction manias, and countless psychological cases where individuals undergo delusions of demon possession, messianic mission, otherworldly lives, multiple personalities, false satanic abuse memories and more, testify to the fragility of our mental balance. Compared with these, encounters with ghosts are benign and often positively life-enhancing. Nevertheless, we must accept the possibility that they are equally imaginary.

So it is tentatively, and with one eye on these provisos, that we must consider the implications of the ghost experience.

Ghosts and the evidence for a non-physical self

The belief in a second, non-physical self is a part of almost every belief-system of mankind. This does not make it true, of course: but it requires us to take it seriously. The nearest we have to hard evidence for the notion is from experimental projections, of which a substantial number have been well documented, with the projector being witnessed at the location to which he claimed to project, and which he is able to describe despite never having physically been there. The ghost experience offers strong support for this, not because it provides direct evidence, but because the concept of an extended self is frequently the most reasonable explanation. Living ghosts ostensibly presenting bi-location are particularly persuasive (nos. 31 and 182).

Projection of the extended self seems the most plausible way of explaining crisis apparitions, where the only viable alternative, super-psi on the part of the percipient, requires us to suppose that it is the percipient, not the apparent, who not only creates the apparition but becomes aware of the crisis situation in the first place. This does not necessarily imply survival after death: the crisis apparition could be no more than a last, despairing effort on the part of the living apparent to communicate.

The moment we open the door to the extended self, many other claimants may try to crowd in, some of them rather dubious characters which we might prefer to exclude: Kirlian and spirit photography, thought-forms, astral bodies and occult entities from a diversity of belief-systems. The ancient Egyptians, for example, believed that each of us has a *ka* which is an exact duplicate of the physical self, but immaterial. This might seem to be the equivalent of our extended self, except that they also supposed another self, the *ba*, which is more truly the soul. At death the *ba* travels on to the next world while the *ka* remains in the tomb and is provided with nourishment to discourage it from emerging and harassing the living.

Apart from occult and religious teachings, similar ideas have been explored by many psychical researchers. Thus we find Adolphe D'Assier, an eminent French researcher, insisting in 1887 that there is nothing supernatural or mystical about ghosts: they are quite simply the next stage of being, and can be studied as scientifically as we who are still in the earthly stage. He distinguishes between the 'living spectre' and the 'post-sepulchral spectre' – living ghosts and ghosts of the dead – agrees that there are differences, but insists that they have much in common. Of the post-sepulchral spectre he writes:

257

It is the phantasmal replica of all the organs of the human body. It has been seen, in fact, to move, speak, take nourishment, accomplish, in a word, the different functions of animal life. The molecules which constitute it are evidently borrowed from the organism which gave it birth. It may then be defined as a gaseous tissue offering a certain resistance . . .[341]

In short, he proposes a material ghost – not as obviously material as ourselves, granted, but nevertheless having substance.

Even psychical researchers, sympathetic to the difficulties, shrink from embracing the suggestion that consciousness can exist independent of the brain. Tyrrell asks us to remember that 'behaving *as if* aware is not the same as *being* aware' and suggests that the ghost need not be housing the consciousness of the apparent, even though it moves about the room and responds to the percipients as though it is there, and intelligently there. 'The facts

The Soul leaves the Body at the moment of death, as depicted by William Blake: the notion of a separable self is found in many belief-systems, and is an important key to understanding the ghost experience

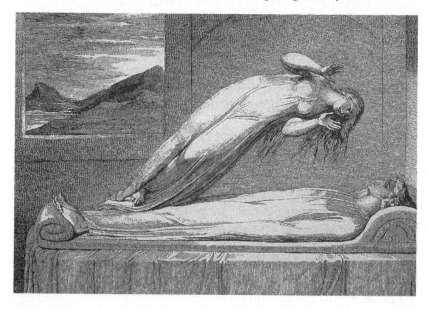

reveal the apparition to be a piece of stage-machinery . . . a psychological marionette'. He compares it to actors in a film-play: today he might compare it to a remotely controlled robot.[342]

This negative view is challenged by Thouless who says there is no reason to think that *any* consciousness, whether of living persons or of ghosts, is located in space, and suggests that it is legitimate to ask, 'Is a ghost's consciousness there in the same sense as I am inclined to say that my consciousness is here?'[343]

Price, writing as a Professor of Logic, adds: 'There are two criteria which we might use: (1) A self is in place P if P is the point of view from which that self is perceiving at the moment. (2) It is in a place P if it is *acting upon* objects which are in the immediate neighbourhood of P.'[344] By those criteria, if an individual projects her extended self to a distant place, where it moves intelligently, where it perceives its surroundings, and where it is seen by people at that location, then her conscious, aware, intelligent self can be said to be there.

In short, we should be prepared to accept that consciousness is not necessarily linked to the physical living body. Richet gives as one of his strongest arguments against the possibility of survival that 'I cannot believe that memory can exist without the anatomical and physiological integrity of the brain.'[345] Well, I think this is something we are all going to have to learn to believe, Nobel prizewinners or not. When a projector visits a remote location in her extended self, she is likely to remember afterwards and describe where she went, what she did there, and how the persons there responded: when she finds a friend there, how can she recognize him without using her memory?[346] In short, the projector's memory and her awareness are both part of her baggage. Yes, of course we can avoid this by some kind of super-psi: the subconscious of the sleeping or entranced individual would send a robot-like image of itself to the chosen location, visible to anyone who happens to be there, monitoring its behaviour, steering it round furniture, recording what it does and sees and says for future recall. But that in turn involves some kind of 'travelling clairvoyance', associated with the projection if not part of it. Whatever model we construct, we shall have to incorporate an item from science's list of prohibited articles: the notion of an extended self, equipped with awareness, intelligence and memory, is surely the least offensive, the most plausible option.

And if that is true of the extended self of a living person pro-jecting herself or appearing as a living ghost, it is hard to argue that it is any less true, or that an entirely different process is taking place, if the apparition is the extended self of a dead person. What is true of the living may also be true of the dead.

Broad, in his 1958 Presidential Address to the SPR, said, in respect of collective hallucinations:

> Undoubtedly each kind of case severally could be accounted for without postulating an 'astral double'; and with enough ingenuity and elaboration, this could probably be done for all of them taken collectively. I feel that an explanation in terms of nothing but 'telepathy' and 'clairvoyance' would tend to become extremely complex and artificial, and would moreover have to stretch the meaning and application of those terms far beyond anything for which we have independent evidence. I think we might be com-pelled to take some form of the hypothesis of an 'astral double' to the normal human body as much the simplest working hypothe-sis.[347]

Our inquiry – both the cases we have studied and our comments on the challenge those cases present – drive us to precisely that conclusion: that consciousness, awareness and memory – all that constitutes the essential 'ourself' – can exist and function inde-pendently of the physical body.

Ghosts and the evidence for survival after death

Here is a tantalizing case:

192. F. Reed Brown. Baltimore, Maryland, 1942
'One cold dawn in 1942 when I was eight, I awakened to see someone moving alongside the large double bed I shared with my brother. I thought it was my mother at first. Dressed in a white flowing gown she was looking into the mirror and combing her hair. Then I realized that this woman's hair was auburn and my mother's was completely grey. My brother Whelker, now also aroused by our visitor, sat up and

we watched her walk to the foot of the bed, look down at us, smile and then simply dematerialize. At breakfast we told Mother and we concluded that our visitor must have been the spirit of our great-grandmother. About seven years later Mother and I went to the Temple of Wisdom Spiritual Science Church. The medium came to my mother and said, "I want to speak to you for your sister." Mother said she had no sister in the spirit world. The medium insisted, "Lady, you may say you do not have a sister but she is here. She looks like you except she may be perhaps ten years younger and her hair is auburn. She tells me she materialized several years ago for your sons and that she was mistaken for a grandmother. She says she grew up in the spirit world having lived only a short time on the earth plane. She stresses that she did live and advises you to ask your mother to verify this message". After the service we went directly to Grandmother's house. She told my mother, "When you were about ten I gave birth to a premature baby girl. She lived just long enough to be baptized – about 40 minutes – and then died".'[348]

Fantasy? If so, on whose part? Super-psi? On Grandmother's part? We have looked at a number of cases where, though alternative explanations *can* be found, they seem far-fetched compared with the notion that the dead person has in some degree survived, and is responsible for the manifestation.

193. Mr T. A. 1880
'I saw a darkish vapour leave my father's head when he died, and it formed into a figure, full-sized, and for seven consecutive nights I saw it in my own room and saw it go each night into the next room, in which he died. It became more distinct each night and brighter each night, till it was quite brilliant, even dazzling, by the seventh night. It lasted, say, 1½ minutes. It was dark when the phantom used to appear. I was quite awake, going to bed.'[349]

Since Mr A. does not suggest that the figure bears any resemblance to his father, we must suppose that it doesn't, that it is simply an ill-defined human shape. Nevertheless the inference is strong that the figure is in some respect his father's ghost – an extended self or some such. Does it stay around the home during the day, or go away somewhere else and come back each night? Either way, it echoes folklore accounts of what happens to the spirits of the dead at death. While we certainly can't take this case as strong evidence for survival, it is hard to account for it on any other basis – unless, of course, we are ready to suppose that the episode is hallucinated by the percipient seven nights in a row.

On rare occasions the implication is explicit:

194. *Mr P. 17 January 1867*
'Our third child, a boy, lived only 16 days: from the first it was evident that his life would be a short one. Just before the boy died I was lying on a sofa when I saw, a few feet above my head, a blue flame. It was about 3 centimetres long, and surrounded by a slight haze or halo. It hovered above me for a few seconds, then took an irregular diagonal course towards the farthest corner of the room, finally seeming to pass through the ceiling. As it vanished a voice from nearly the opposite side of the room said, "That's his soul." A few minutes later the child died.'[350]

Many of the SPR-Group were motivated by the desire to establish whether or not survival after death is a fact. Although we may feel confident that they did not allow their interest to distort their presentation of the facts, they concluded:

Death forms a central point about which the hallucinations cluster, diminishing in number on each side of it; and this certainly suggests that there is no discontinuity at the moment of death, – no sudden transition from a state in which communication is possible to a state to which it is not . . . We have found that the distribution of recognized apparitions before, at, and after the death of the person seen affords some argument for the continuity of psychical life and the possibility of communication from the dead. We have found further that the Census affords some remarkable cases which *prima facie* are not purely subjective, and which suggest the action of the dead. The amount of evidence, however, does not appear to us to constitute anything like a conclusive case for post-mortem agency.[351]

That's right. Ghosts do not, of themselves, offer conclusive evidence for survival, because we can always refer them to fantasy on the part of the percipient, or, if hard pushed, invoke super-psi. On the other hand, a great many of our cases are most simply explained on the basis that the extended self of someone once living but now dead is manifesting as an apparition.

It is interesting that the testimony which comes to us from the ghost experience, favouring post-mortem existence, seems utterly different from the other great body of testimony, alleged spirit communication. Ghosts look entirely different from the materialized spirits of the seance room, and they behave entirely differently: they do not offer the same kind of messages, they do not perform party tricks like banging tambourines or apporting flowers. In short, they appear to be an entirely distinct phenomenon. Nor does the ghost experience figure prominently in the spiritualists' accounts of the dying process and of existence in the world to come, as we might reasonably expect. In any case, these accounts vary so much that there is every reason to think they reflect the subjective expectations of the individuals concerned, rather than a reliable objective picture of conditions.[352,353,354]

Nor does the ghost experience seem any more closely related to occult teachings. True, the notion of the extended self invariably forms a part of such esoteric belief-systems, but it is quite a different thing to derive a notion from a revelation allegedly handed down from illuminati to illuminati as part of some body of 'ancient wisdom', than to infer it from specific instances of individual experience.

It cannot be said that the ghost experience lends much support to any specific scenario of the afterlife. No ghost gives us an account of where he comes from, how he got here from there, what he is made of, what he plans to do for the rest of the day, let alone leaving an address where he may be contacted. In other words, if he exists at all, he is either bound by a vow of silence from revealing the conditions of his existence, or it is an existence so different from ours that any attempt to communicate would be doomed to failure. The eighteenth-century philosopher Immanuel Kant suggested that 'the other world is not another place, but only another view. The other world remains the same as regards objects, it does not differ in substance; only it is viewed spiritually'.[355] Well, maybe.

Two kinds of ghost appear to support the idea that after this life we move to a further phase of existence on a different plane of reality. Revenants, by definition, are apparitions of the dead, returning to the Earthly plane. Haunters, ostensibly, are apparitions of the dead who never left the Earthly plane. In both cases, the physical bodies are now burned, buried, eaten by vultures or otherwise recycled, so what we are seeing is a simulacrum of some kind, created either by some remote agent or by the living percipient using sophisticated super-psi powers, or it is the extended self which accompanied the individual during his lifetime and now continues to exist, independently. We would of course like to know what these creatures are made of, whether they are guided or free to go where they like and do as they will, the extent of their life-span, and so on. The ghost experience has offered us some clues, but such questions demand investigation of a kind they have not hitherto received.

Particularly tantalizing is the Frondorf case (no. 97), where a girl is visited by her two grandfathers on three occasions, well separated in time. This case has all the trappings of a recurring dream and it is tempting to see it as entirely subjective. But Margaret's accurate description of her grandfathers, one of whom she never met, suggests otherwise. If the ghosts are indeed their spirits, the case is rich in puzzles and implications. What are we to make of this stuff about what they are allowed to do and not do? Says who? And what are the implications for a future life? They know what's planned for her, they are able to arrange for her to avoid it if she comes with them; when she insists on remaining in this vale of tears, they let her stay on with some rather vague advice which, however, may enable her to survive where without it she might have succumbed. Does this mean the future is only provisional, and susceptible of redirection?

Paradoxically, a persuasive argument for survival is provided by haunters. The very fact that a tiny minority of people are 'left behind' on Earth implies that everyone else has gone. Gone on? or simply done with, finished with, terminated? It is easier to believe that haunters are travellers who have missed their connecting flight than that they have somehow learnt the trick of surviving – after a fashion – when the rest of us are no more, in this world or any other.

But there is one final thought which underlies all the rest: does not the very fact that we can consider the *possibility* of survival support the *probability* of survival? If existence terminates with

The implications of the ghost experience

death, where did we get the idea that there could be an alternative? Why are we able to ask if revenants and haunters exist, unless they do?

Ghosts and the nature of time

A Swiss folk-tale tells of a farmhand who wanders into an ancient monastery. An abbot asks him what time it is, and he replies 'Half-past four', at which the building and the abbot vanish. If he had not answered the question, he would have heard wonderful things and perhaps made his fortune.[356] The tale reflects an intuition that paranormal matters are outside the time dimension.

In the Giacobbe case (no. 108) a former resident is indignant when her house is demolished: it is fifteen years since she lived there, and she has been dead all this time. Has her ghost been latent from then till now, unseen by the neighbours? Or has she come back from the next world to make her protest? Or is the time lapse irrelevant in the ghost world? Several of our cases involve a lapse of time which seems meaningless: for example in no. 60 the percipient sees the ghost of her father who died five years earlier. There's a similar passage of time in the scratched face case (no. 77). Why wait so long?

There are many indications that ghosts and spirits of the next world are now living outside time. The dead seem almost always to be free when summoned to attend terrestrial seances: we are never told they are in conference, or sick, or on vacation. But surely they don't just wait around on the off-chance that we will summon them to come and be interrogated by a group of inquisitive seancers?

When they revisit Earth, however, they must enter our time dimension if there is to be any kind of interaction. Their visits occupy time – even the act of materialization takes time – and if they speak, to get from the beginning of a sentence to the end is a process requiring time.

But if time is mutable for ghosts of the dead, it is hardly less so for living ghosts. Thus in two doppelgänger cases the apparition manifests wearing clothes other than those the percipient is wearing at the time:

195. Sarah Jane Hall. Sibberton, Northamptonshire, England, autumn 1863

'One night, when we were having supper, an apparition stood at the end of the sideboard. We four sat at the dining-table: and yet, with great inconsistency, I stood as this ghostly visitor again, in a spotted light muslin summer dress. We all four saw it, my husband saying, "It is Sarah". None of us felt any fear, it seemed too natural and familiar.' (The dress was unlike anything she had at the time, though two years later she had one which was similar.) [357]

In another case the witness sees herself wearing a dress discarded some time before (no. 26). Why should one ghost manifest in a dress already discarded, another in a dress yet to be acquired? There seems no meaning in this. In the following case the meaning is evident enough, but just what is happening is puzzling:

196. Elizabeth Denton. Joliet, Illinois, summer 1861

'We were compelled to wait a weary time for the train which was to convey us. Our children had exhausted the novelties of the station, consisting of railroad charts and a few dusty seats, and now began to watch earnestly for the coming of the iron horse. At length, his unearthly scream gave warning of his approach, and he came thundering past, as if resolved to visit utter ruin on those who would chain his spirit to the sluggish will of man. "Twenty minutes for dinner!" sang out the brakeman, after announcing the name of the place, while a general rush of the passengers, some to the eating-room, others to other destinations, gave me my choice of a seat in any one of the vacant cars. Taking the children each by the hand, while my husband gave orders in reference to baggage, I selected a car and walked leisurely in, very naturally expecting myself and children to be, for a few minutes at least, its only occupants. Judge of my surprise, on glancing round as I entered the car, to find it already crowded with passengers! Many of them were sitting perfectly composed, as if, for them, little interest were attached to the station; while others were already in motion as if preparing to leave. I thought this somewhat strange, and was about-turning to find a vacant seat in another car, when a second glance around showed me that the passengers who had appeared so indifferent to the arrival of the train at Joliet, were rapidly losing their apparent entity, and in a moment more they were to me invisible. I had had sufficient time to note the features, dress, and personal appearance of several, and taking a seat, I awaited the return of the passengers, thinking it more than probable I might find in them the prototypes of the faces and forms I had a moment before so singularly beheld; nor was I disappointed. A number of those who returned to the car I recognized as being in every particular the counterparts of their late but transient representatives. But the question arises, how could these individuals be seen in the car, when, in fact, they were not in the car at all, but in the dining-room of the station? . . . That the persons or images seen were indeed the individuals who at the moment were in the station, I do not believe. That the persons who had so lately been sitting in the car, some of them, doubtless, for several hours, had radiated to the surrounding atmosphere that ethereal fluid which stamps upon it these images, it being in a condition to receive, to retain, and to render them visible in open day, I regard as a simple, safe and natural conclusion.'[358]

Elizabeth Denton was an outstanding psychometrist: when she speaks of the figures being 'rendered visible in open day', she blurs over the fact that they are visible only to someone with her rare gift. But her interesting explanation fails to explain what strikes us most forcibly about her experience – that it involves a time shift. She does not simply see the passengers as trace-images, as she suggests, she sees them at a particular moment in time, as they prepare for arrival at Joliet. We could legitimately describe this as a ghost experience, in that the people she sees are not in fact physically present, but it seems more a displacement in time. Or rather, her experience makes the point that while ghost experiences are undoubtedly set in time, they are not *firmly* set in time. Ghosts can wander from one time-frame to another just as they can wander from one level of reality to another.

Of all paranormal phenomena, those which involve precognition seem to be supported best by the evidence, for the simple reason that they are the easiest to establish. If something is predicted, and does in fact occur, then we must attribute it either to chance or hunch or to true 'seeing into the future'. The number of cases on record render chance so astronomically unlikely that we can rule it out; time and again ghosts warn that a death or an accident is about to happen and prove correct. At the very least, we have to say that someone – be it the percipient's subconscious, be it the kindly ghost from beyond the grave – is employing precognition.

Which is the more likely? We have seen that the evidence for some kind of access to information not possessed by anyone living is overwhelming. This applies particularly to precognitive information, of course: the implication is that access can be had not only to events distant in space, but also in time; and not only time present and time past, but also time future.

So who possesses this access? It is tempting to think that, when we get to the next world, one of our new privileges will be an access card which we can use to obtain unrestricted and unlim-ited information about any subject in the universe. We wondered earlier whether super-psi may be the normal mode of awareness of the extended self. But of course it may not be like that at all: the dead may be hardly less restricted than we are.

So, attractive as it may be to suppose that our dead are watch-ing over us, and come back to warn us when they see something nasty looming ahead on our life-path, super-psi on the part of the living remains a possibility, and perhaps a preferred one. Our subconscious, we may suppose, somehow picks up a titbit of information to the effect that the plane we are thinking of taking is destined to crash, and presents this information to our con-scious mind. It may do so simply as a hunch; it may give it greater clout by sending it via automatic writing; or, when it feels that a guarantor is required to give it more impact, it may provide an apparition of someone whose authority we will respect.

Two of our cases trigger another train of thought. In both the Beckleman (no. 56) and Benoist (no. 95) cases, the apparition is younger than when the person was last seen. In the first, the mother is seen as she was when the percipient was a small girl, and perhaps we may credit 18-year-old Maria with originating her experience; but it is surely very odd indeed that Marie Benoist should picture her friend as younger than she personally had *ever* known her? Hester herself, on the other hand, might well choose to appear at a younger age. To wonder what age we and our loved ones will be in the next world, if there is one, is as fruitless as wondering what we shall do if we win the lottery: we like to think we shall be at our best, with our full complement of health and good looks, rather than decrepit and sickly with old age. If so, perhaps this is expressed in the way revenants manifest.

The question of time comes up with particular force in the matter of haunters, who are not bound by time like you and me. At the same time their actions are subject to time: even if all they do is to march solemnly from one end of the castle battlements to the other, that takes time. So they have not escaped time altogether. But can we say the same of the apparents in time-shift cases such as Buterbaugh (no. 42) or Versailles (no. 41)? Here it is the percipient who feels himself 'carried back in time' (or even, as in the Goddard case (no. 34), carried forward), and so perhaps super-psi seems the mechanism of choice. Can it be that the ghosts they see are out of time altogether, and that the percipients, too, have briefly quit the time dimension? No, because time continues to exist for them. Moberly and Jourdain (no. 41) pursue their stroll through the gardens of Versailles, so time has not stopped for them even if they are in a different segment of it. It seems that neither we nor our ghosts can side-step time. Even the phrase 'the next world' implies a displacement in time, not an escape from it.

Ghosts and the nature of reality

Underlying our entire inquiry has been the question: are ghosts real? Clearly, those who see them are undergoing a real experience, as monitoring their brains would establish. But would it also establish that they were seeing something that was as real as themselves?

We have seen that there are some aspects of the ghost experience which point towards a physical, material or at least quasi-material object: one which can appear in a certain place, to be seen by several independent witnesses; and one which can be seen simultaneously by more than one person, sometimes with the added factor of perspective, reflections, shadows, etc., implying that the apparition is positioned in space so that we standing over here see it differently from those others standing over there.

We have already seen that while this could be achieved by super-psi – if necessary, *collective* super-psi – the extended-self hypothesis is often a preferable option. But we have then to ask what degree of reality the extended self possesses. And the answer is that, in order to satisfy some cases, it would be necessary for the extended self to be embodied in a figure which is not only visible but tangible. In other words, an apparition possessing – if only temporarily – a degree of substance.

We are not obliged to accept this possibility: there are alternatives. If a percipient can shake hands with his father-in-law's ghost (no. 134), this may simply be part of the illusion. But an illusion that can give the impression of substance is hardly less hypothetical than an extended self which actually possesses substance.

This substance would, of course, be different from anything we know in our material world, and we might think that sufficient reason for rejecting it out of hand. But there is evidence that there are physical forces beyond those we know, and there could well be substances outside our physics and chemistry.

One thought-provoking viewpoint has been put forward by James Crenshaw, a psychical researcher from Los Angeles.[359] Like us, he starts from the position that 'a considerable body of evidence now supports the view that haunts do have an objective substantiality,' citing some first-hand cases by way of example. Drawing on the work of Dr Gustaf Stromberg, he postulates fields of force as the basic building blocks of the universe: the particles which make up reality as we know it are merely 'evanescent indicators' of the emergence of these fields of force into our physical world of space and time.

It is these fields which control the kind of growth and development exemplified by, say, the directive process of cell division, and – I suppose – the whole forward-progressing course of evolution. Crenshaw suggests that similar processes may result in apparitions and materializations: 'the apparition appears to be made up of the same kind of transitory, emerging matter. It appears and disappears, can sometimes be seen and felt before disappearing, occasionally moves objects and leaves material traces. It behaves like ordinary matter but still has no permanent existence in the framework of our conception of space and time. After its transitory manifestation, it seems to be absorbed back into another dimension.'

He observes that this bears out the statements of supposed spirits communicating from the next world, to the effect that

> the transcendent spheres and planes of their world have percepti-ble aspects of substance and form. Simply because they are not per-ceptible to our ordinary senses does not warrant our regarding them as any less real . . . They say they have bodies, buildings, arti-cles with many forms, substantial environments and tangible being in a series of dimensions or degrees which we cannot per-ceive with our ordinary apparatus or sensitivity.
>
> The sensitivity of the residents of the so-called higher dimen-sions, it is said, is tuned to a more attenuated kind of matter, yet which is thoroughly substantial in its own right . . . Aside from the considerations of pure spirit, the same kind of vibrating energy, the same kind of dancing wave patterns that we encounter here are to be found there. Only the wave lengths, the incredibly rapid rate of vibration – frequencies of high orders unimagined in our world – appear to be different.

He suggests that the residents of the next world are able – in circumstances yet to be explained and explored – to take on a lower frequency, allowing them to manifest in our space and time. He compares it to a different radio or TV frequency, to which you need to be attuned if you are to receive the signal.

What happens when a ghost is seen? 'The atoms which moti-vate the materialization are already there. In some way, asso-ciated with particular persons or environments, their vibrations temporarily condense; their constituent wave bundles somehow, for the moment, draw to themselves earthly shells, and their pre-existing forms break through.'

I am not qualified to say whether this is gobbledegook or viable speculation, but we must applaud Crenshaw for facing up to the challenge of ghostly reality and offering us a line of approach even if it is neither clearly drawn nor certain of its direction. Most importantly, he encourages us to stop thinking of the ghost in Earthly terms, whose attributes are drawn solely from the world we know, and to see it as a temporary manifestation of a non-Earthly kind, momentarily intruding into our dimension.

Crenshaw does not mention the intelligent actions and responses of ghosts. I suppose this is because he is concerned only with the physical means which may be available to the resident of that other dimension who, for whatever reason, wishes to manifest in our dimension. Perhaps it is up to the agent to prescribe the content and the manner of the manifestation.

If that is so, then a formulation such as a force-field of energy, taking on the appearance chosen by the agent and equipped with whatever attributes of intelligent behaviour and response the agent can manage, is at least a useful working model which we can refine as our growing knowledge and experience enable us to do. The fact that some ghosts are more intelligent and responsive than others may be the result of choice, or simply greater skill on the agent's part. The fact that some ghosts are lifelike, others partially formed, or faceless, or folklorish (those cowled monks again!) may be attributed to choice on the agent's part, or to cultural influences bearing on the subconscious, whether of the apparent or the percipient.

Our inquiry has not resolved the problem of the ghost experience, but, by building on what people are experiencing, has given us some idea of what is required to bring those experiences about. Let us set them out as formal propositions:

- Because we know that the subconscious, for example in compliance with a hypnotist's suggestion, can visualize a hallucination, we may accept this as the process whereby an apparition is perceived, the suggestion either originating in the individual's own subconscious, or suggested to it by an external agent.
- Because we know no limits to the creativity of the human mind, we may accept the possibility that many ghosts, particularly of the revenant type, are visualizations, exteriorized by the percipient's own subconscious and accepted as real by his conscious mind.
- Because we know that the mind is occasionally capable of remote viewing we know that psi exists, and because the mind can be capable of precognition, we know that super-psi exists; and because we know no limits to super-psi, we may conceive it possible that the mind can obtain unlimited access to information of every kind.

- Because we know that projection takes place, we know that the extended self, or something like it, must exist. If so, it is a likely candidate for many types of apparition, notably living ghosts and those which seem to involve bi-location.
- Because the extended self, in the course of projections, displays memory, awareness and other indications of intelligence – perhaps even including the ability to conduct a rational conversation – we may accept that these faculties can exist apart from the physical body.
- Because the extended self, possessing awareness, intelligence and memory, can seemingly exist apart from the physical body, we may further conceive that it could survive the death of the physical body, and even continue to display signs of individual personality.
- Because we know that ghosts sometimes communicate information known to no living person, and utter veridical warnings, we know that whatever causes them enjoys seemingly unlimited access to knowledge; this could be the percipient's own subconscious, or the extended self of the surviving dead, using super-psi.
- Because there are cases in which more than one person sees the same ghost in natural perspective, we may conceive that the subconscious, or the extended self, or the two in collaboration, can create a short-lived apparition which has some degree of material substance.

The short answer to the question, 'Do ghosts exist?' must be, Yes.

Some ghosts are likely to be artefacts of the human subconscious, which employs psi, or super-psi if necessary, to acquire the necessary information, and employs visualization to create a hallucination which is perceived by the conscious mind as an apparition. Perhaps, though this seems very improbable, *all* ghosts may be so.

Other ghosts are likely to be projections of the extended self of the apparent, living or dead, perceived by the conscious mind of the percipient, either directly via the senses, or indirectly via the subconscious which, triggered by suggestion, employs visualization to create an apparition.

Notes

1. F. W. H. Myers, *Human Personality*, London, Longmans, Green & Co., 1903, vol. 2, p. 19
2. Letter to Andrew MacKenzie in Andrew MacKenzie, *Hauntings and Apparitions*, London, Heinemann, 1968, p. 215.
3. Ibid., p. xiii.
4. Andrew Lang, *Dreams and Ghosts*, London, Longmans, Green, 1899, p. 29
5. Le Loyer *Discours des spectres*, summarized by Thurston in *Ghosts and Poltergeists*, London, Burns Oates, 1953, p. 80.
6. William Oliver Stevens, *Unbidden Guests*, London, Allen & Unwin, 1949, p. 294, from the *JASPR*, 1928.
7. *JSPR*, 27, Oct. 1932, p. 297.
8. *PSPR*, 33, p. 156.
9. Ernesto Bozzano, *Phénomènes de bilocation*, Paris, Leymarie, p. 96.
10. *PSPR*, 10, p. 117.
11. *Fate*, 9(5), May 1956, p. 62.
12. Hilary Evans, *From Other Worlds*, London, Carlton, 1999.
13. *Fate*, 8(12), Dec. 1955, p. 107.
14. *Fate*, 10(7), July 1957, p. 106
15. John G. Fuller, *The Ghost of Flight 401*, New York, Berkley, 1976.
16. Minot Savage, *Can Telepathy Explain?* New York, Putnam, 1902, p. 42.
17. Notably in Sir William Barrett, *Deathbed Visions*, London, Methuen, 1926.
18. *Fate*, 42(3), March 1989, p.95.
19. Aniela Jaffé, *Apparitions and Precognition*, New Hyde Park, NY, University Books, 1963, p. 25.
20. Plato, *Phaedo* trans. Benjamin Jowett (many editions).
21. Carl Wickland, *Thirty Years Among the Dead*, London, Spiritualist Press, 1924.
22. Terry and Natalia O'Sullivan, *Soul Rescuers*, London, Thorsons, 2000.

Notes

23. *JSPR*, 24: 444 (April 1928), p. 229.

24. Andrew MacKenzie, *The Unexplained*, London, Arthur Barker, 1966; *Apparitions and Ghosts*, Barker, 1971; *Hauntings and Apparitions*; update with additional information in *Fate* magazine, Sept. 1988; B. Abdy Collins, *The Cheltenham Ghost*, London, Psychic Press, 1948.

25. *PSPR*, 10, p. 85.

26. *Fate*, 9(10), Oct. 1956, p. 111.

27. *Fate*, 28(8), Aug. 1975, p. 118.

28. Cyril Scott, *The Boy Who Saw True*, London, Spearman, 1953, p. 98.

29. *PSPR*, 3, April 1885, p. 104.

30. *Fate*, 16(8), Aug. 1963, p. 96.

31. *PSPR*, 10, 1894, p. 10.

32. Edmund Gurney, F.W.H. Myers and Frank Podmore, *Phantasms of the Living*, London, Society for Psychical Research, vol. 1, p. 26.

33. For a first-person account of just such a process see Barbara O'Brien, *Operators and Things*, Cranbury, NJ, Arlington Books, A. S. Barnes & Co. 1958, reissued London, Thomas Yoseloff, 1975.

34. John Ferriar, *Theory of Apparitions*, London, Cadell and Davies, 1813, p. 58, quoting Drummond's *Heads of Conversation*.

35. *PSPR*, 10, p. 214.

36. *Fate*, 22(7), July 1969, p. 7.

37. *PSPR*, 10, p. 260.

38. Ibid., p. 263.

39. *JASPR*, 1910, p. 277, quoted in Bozzano, *Phénomènes de hantise*, Paris, Leymarie [1920s?], p. 107.

40. Sir Ernest Bennett, *Apparitions and Haunted Houses*, London, Faber & Faber, 1939, p. 1.

41. *JSPR*, 8, Dec. 1898, p. 321.

42. Richard Baxter, *Certainty of a World of Spirits* (1691), reprinted in Robert Dale Owen, *Footfalls on the Boundary of Another World*, Philadelphia, Lippincott, 1860, p. 187.

43. Celia Green and Charles McCreery, *Apparitions*, London, Hamish Hamilton, 1975.

44. Ibid., p. 75.

45. *PSPR*, 10, p. 199.

46. *British Medical Journal*, 185(6), p. 808, reported by Paul Chambers in *Fortean Times*, 133, April 2000, p. 16.

47. *Fate*, 6(9), Sept. 1953, p. 67.

48. *PSPR*, 10, p. 74.

49. Gabriel Delanne, *Apparitions des vivants*, Paris, Leymarie, 1909, p. 388.
50. Montague Summers, *The Physical Phenomena of Mysticism*, London, Rider, 1960, p. 61.
51. T. D. Kendrick, *Mary of Agreda*, London, Routledge & Kegan Paul, 1967.
52. Owen. *Footfalls on the Boundary of Another World*, p. 378.
53. *Fate*, 26(4), April 1973, p. 62.
54. *PSPR*, 10, p. 332.
55. Victor Goddard, *Flight towards Reality*. London, Turnstone, 1975.
56. Mark Chorvinsky, 'Encounters with the Grim Reaper', *Strange*, 18, (summer 1997).
57. *Fate*, 26(11), Nov. 1973, p. 64.
58. *Fate*, 11(5), May 1958, p. 55.
59. *Fate*, 7(9), Sept. 1954, p. 89.
60. Max Beerbohm, *Zuleika Dobson*, London, Heinemann, 1911, p. 217.
61. Julian Franklyn, *A Survey of the Occult*, London, Barker, 1935, p. 103.
62. *Fate*, 14(8), Aug. 1961, p. 69.
63. *JASPR*, 61(1), Jan. 1962, p. 37.
64. [Annie Moberly and Eleanor Jourdain] (first published anonymously) *An Adventure,* London, Macmillan, 1911.
65. Notably by Michael H. Coleman in *The Ghosts of the Trianon*, Wellingborough, Aquarian, 1988.
66. Andrew MacKenzie, *Adventures in Time*, London, Athlone, 1997.
67. Gardner Murphy and Herbert L. Klemme, 'Unfinished Business', *JASPR*, 60 (4), p. 306.
68. John H. Ingram, *Haunted Homes and Family Traditions*. London, Gibbings, 1897; Antony B. Hippisley Coxe, *Haunted Britain*, London, Hutchinson, 1973.
69. *Fortean Times,* 82 (Aug–Sept. 1995) and 100 (July 1997).
70. *Fate*, 17(8), Aug. 1964, p. 61.
71. Harry Price, *The Most Haunted House in England*, London, Longmans, Green, 1940.
72. Peter Underwood, *A Host of Hauntings*, London, Leslie Frewin, 1973.
73. D. Scott Rogo, *An Experience of Phantoms*, New York, Taplinger, 1974, p. 119.
74. Raymond Duplantier, 'La Famille hantée d'Yzeures', in *L'Initiation*, autumn, 1897.
75. *JSPR*, 5 Dec. 1892, p. 331.
76. *PSPR*, 14, p. 283.
77. *PSPR*, 10, p. 305.

78. *JSPR*, 46: Sept. 1972, p. 112.
79. *PSPR*, 10, p. 227.
80. Ibid., 1894, pp. 113–14.
81. *PSPR*, 33, p. 170.
82. Gurney et al. *Phantasms*, case 264, vol. 2, p. 97.
83. *Fate*, 17(7), July 1964, p. 91.
84. Jaffé, *Apparitions and Precognition*, p. 58.
85. Gurney et al. *Phantasms*, case 210 , vol. 1 p. 556.
86. *PSPR*, 10, p. 192.
87. *Fate*, 23(7), July 1970, p. 102.
88. A. D. Cornell, 'The Seen and Unseen Ghost', *International Journal of Parapsychology*, 11(1), 2000, p. 143.
89. G. N. M. Tyrrell, *Apparitions*, London, Duckworth, 1953, p. 102.
90. *PSPR*, 10, p. 115.
91. Ibid.
92. *Fate*, 19(5), May 1966, p. 95.
93. Jaffe, *Apparitions and Precognition*, p. 164.
94. *Fate*, 16(2), Feb. 1963, p. 53.
95. *PSPR*, 10, p. 116.
96. *Fate*, 21(9), Sept. 1966, p. 99.
97. *PSPR*, 3, p. 133.
98. *Fate*, 12(8), Aug. 1959, p. 55.
99. *Fate*, 16(8), Aug. 1963, p. 62.
100. *PSPR*, 10, p. 122.
101. W. G. Roll, *The Poltergeist*, Metuchen, NJ, Scarecrow, 1976, p. 98.
102. *PSPR*, 10, p. 122.
103. Vincent Gaddis, *Invisible Horizons*, Philadelphia, Chilton Books, 1965, p. 79.
104. *PSPR*, 10, p. 218.
105. *PSPR*, 6, p. 17.
106. *PSPR*, 10, p. 189.
107. *JSPR*, 5, March 1892, p. 223.
108. *PSPR*, 10, p. 186.
109. *JSPR*, 10, Dec. 1902, p. 308.
110. *Fate*, 15(9), Sept. 1962, p. 98.
111. *PSPR*, 6, p. 27.
112. *PSPR*, 10, pp. 187–8.
113. Ibid., p. 194.
114. *PSPR*, 3, p. 133.
115. Jaffé, *Apparitions and Precognition*, p. 57.
116. *PSPR*, 10, p. 79.
117. Ibid., p. 80.

118. Gurney et al., *Phantasms*, case 312, vol. 2, p. 178.
119. *JSPR*, 4, July 1890, p. 286.
120. *PSPR*, 3, p. 122.
121. W. T. Stead (ed.) *Review of Reviews*, Christmas number 1892, London, p. 71.
122. *JSPR*, 6(103), Oct. 1893, p. 135.
123. Roll, *Poltergeist*, p. 98.
124. Jaffé, *Apparitions and Precognition*, p. 164.
125. *Fate*, 10(9), Sept. 1957, p. 108.
126. Ibid., p. 103.
127. *Fate*, 19(7), July 1966, p. 97.
128. Jaffé, *Apparitions and Precognition*, p. 165.
129. *PSPR*, 10, p. 115.
130. *Fate*, 3(2), March 1950, p. 88.
131. Rose Henniker Heaton, *The Perfect Guest*, London, Methuen, 1931.
132. *Fate*, 26(1), Jan. 1973, p. 112.
133. *Fate*, 1(3), Fall 1948, p. 108.
134. Gurney et al., *Phantasms*, vol. 2, p. 216.
135. *PSPR*, 10, p. 416.
136. Collins, *Cheltenham Ghost*.
137. *PSPR*, 10, p. 198.
138. Ibid., p. 199.
139. Hornell and Ella B. Hart, 'Visions and Apparitions Collectively and Reciprocally Perceived', PSPR, 41, 1932, pp. 205–49.
140. Jaffé, *Apparitions and Precognition*, p. 129.
141. *Fate*, 37(8), Aug. 1984, p. 55.
142. *Fate*, 11(9), Sept. 1958, p. 97.
143. Matthew Manning, *The Strangers*, London, W. H. Allen, 1978.
144. Ian Stevenson, *Reincarnation and Biology*, Westport, Conn., Praeger, 1997, pp. 2100, 2094.
145. Daniel Defoe, writing as Andrew Moreton, *The Secrets of the Invisible World Disclos'd; or, an Universal History of Apparitions*, 2nd edition, printed for J. Watts and sold by Thomas Worral, 1735, p. 101.
146. Ibid., p. 133.
147. Aurelio Augustine, *De cura pro mortuis gerenda*, cited by Jean-Claude Schmitt, in *Les Revenants*, Paris, Gallimard, 1994.
148. *PSPR*, 26, p. 517.
149. *JSPR*, 45(746), Dec. 1970, p. 388.
150. *PSPR*, 6, p. 27.
151. *Fate*, 18(9), Sept. 1965, p. 94.
152. Joshua Slocum, *Sailing Alone around the World*, London, Sampson Low, *c*. 1900.

153. *PSPR*, 10, p. 382.
154. Private communication to the author.
155. *Fate*, 3(4), July 1950, p. 78.
156. *Fate*, 9(7), July 1956, p. 107.
157. *Fate*, 1(3), Fall 1948, p. 105.
158. *Fate*, 15(1), Jan. 1962, p. 86.
159. *Fate*, 18(2), March 1965, p. 95.
160. *PSPR*, 10, p. 193.
161. Ibid., p. 380.
162. Robert Dale Owen, *The Debatable Land*, London, Trübner, 1871, p. 319.
163. *Fate*, 19(4), April 1966, p. 95.
164. *Fate*, 34(11), Nov. 1981, p. 66.
165. *Fate*, 12(1), Jan. 1958, p. 97.
166. *Fate*, 14(5), May 1961, p. 95.
167. *PSPR*, 11, p. 483.
168. Jaffé, *Apparitions and Precognition*, p. 30.
169. *Fate*, 9(8), Aug. 1956, p. 108.
170. *PSPR*, 10, p. 385.
171. Ibid., p. 224.
172. *Fate*, 18(7), July 1965, p. 102.
173. *Fate*, 10(11), Nov. 1957, p. 55.
174. *Fate*, 7(7), July 1954, p. 88.
175. *Fate*, 25(9), Sept. 1972, p. 69.
176. Owen. *Footfalls on the Boundary of Another World*, pp. 333–41.
177. *PSPR*, 10, p. 72.
178. [Mrs] F. E. Leaning, 'An Introductory Study of Hypnagogic Phenomena', *PSPR*, 35, 1935.
179. Robert Macnish, *The Philosophy of Sleep*, New York, Appleton, 1834.
180. Aurelio Augustine, *The Letters of Saint Augustine*, trans. J. G. Cunningham, Edinburgh, T. & T. Clark, 1875, vol. 2, p. 274.
181. Owen, *Footfalls on the Boundary of Another World*, reprinted from the *Gentleman's Magazine* 1800, p. 1216.
182. Lang, *Dreams and Ghosts*, p. 12.
183. *PSPR*, 10, 1894, p. 30.
184. Henri Ey, *Traité des hallucinations*, Paris, Masson, 1973.
185. A. Brierre de Boismont, *Des Hallucinations*, Paris, Germer Baillière, 1852, p. 49.
186. Griffith Pugh, cited in 'I See by the Papers', in *Fate*, 24(8), Aug. 1971, p. 25.
187. *Fate*, 20(3), March 1967, p. 56.
188. Alexandra David-Neel, *Mystiques et magiciens du Thibet*, Paris, Plon, 1929.

189. Nathan L. Comer, Leo Madow and James J. Dixon, 'Observations of Sensory Deprivation in a Life-threatening Situation', *American Journal of Psychiatry*, 124(2), Aug. 1967.

190. N. J. White, 'Complex Visual Hallucinations in Partial Blindness due to Eye Disease', *British Journal of Psychiatry*, 136, 1980, pp. 284–6.

191. Charles Bowen, *UFO Report*, 5(1) Nov. 1977, p. 48.

192. J. Kroll and B. Bachrach, 'Visions and Psychopathology in the Middle Ages', *Journal of Nervous and Mental Disease*, 170(1), 1982, pp. 41–9.

193. *PSPR*, 18, part 47, p. 308: Honeyman, 'On Certain Unusual Psychological Phenomena' (1904).

194. *PSPR*, 10, p. 73.

195. Ibid., p. 76.

196. Ibid.

197. Hellmuth Hoffmann, 'Filming Hallucinations', *Fate*, 35(11), Nov. 1982, p. 68.

198. *Fate*, 26(4). April 1973, p. 98.

199. See, for example, René Laurentin, *Lourdes, documents authentiques*, and *Lourdes, histoire authentique*, Paris, Lethielleux, 1957, 1961.

200. Frère Michel de la Sainte Trinité, *Toute la vérité sur Fatima*, Saint-Parres-les-Vaudes, Renaissance Catholique, 1983.

201. Laurentin, *Lourdes, documents authentiques*, vol. 7, Paris, Lethielleux, 1965.

202. Fina D'Armada, *Fatima, o que se passou em 1917*, Amadora, Portugal, Livraria Bertrand, 1980.

203. *Fate*, 18(1), Jan. 1965, p. 69.

204. *Le Pelèrin*, 30, 29 April 1923.

205. B. Dupi, 'La Dame Blanche ou quand l'auto-stoppeuse se volatalise', *Lumières dans la nuit*, March–April 1982, pp. 20–2.

206. Michael Goss, *The Evidence for Phantom Hitch-hikers*, Wellingborough, Aquarian, 1984; Sean Tudor, *Fortean Times*, 73 (Feb.–March 1994) and 104 (Nov. 1997).

207. *Fate*, 14(12), Dec. 1961, p. 52.

208. Joy Snell, *The Ministry of Angels*, London, The Greater World Association, 1950.

209. Carl Gustav Jung, *The Archetypes and the Collective Unconscious*, London, Routledge & Kegan Paul, 1959 (first published in German from 1933 onwards).

210. Jaffé, *Apparitions and Precognition*, p. 85ff.

211. *PSPR*, 10, p. 283

212. *Fate*, 41(11), Nov. 1988, p. 97.
213. For example, Bernard-Marie Maréchaux. *La Réalité des apparitions démoniaques*, Paris, Douniol, 1899.
214. Joachim Bouflet, *Medjugorje, ou la fabrication du surnaturel*, Paris, Salvator, 1990.
215. Jenny Randles, *The Truth behind Men in Black*, London, St Martins Press, 1997.
216. *PSPR*, 10, p. 310.
217. *Fate*, 29(8), Aug. 1976, p. 92.
218. Jaffé, *Apparitions and Precognition*, p. 104.
219. David Hufford, *The Terror That Comes in the Night*, Philadelphia, University of Pennsylvania Press, 1982.
220. Whitley Strieber. *Communion*, New York, Morrow, 1987.
221. Hilary Evans, 'From Fait Divers to Folklore and Back Again', *The Anomalist*, 2 , Jefferson Valley/San Antonio, 1995.
222. David Jacobs, *Secret Life*, New York, Simon & Schuster, 1992.
223. Patrick Huyghe, *A Field Guide to Extraterrestrials*, New York, Avon 1997.
224. Desmond Leslie and George Adamski, *Flying Saucers Have Landed*, New York, The British Book Centre, 1953.
225. Elizabeth Klarer, *Beyond the Light Barrier*, Cape Town, Howard Timmins, 1980.
226. Hilary Evans, *Gods, Spirits, Cosmic Guardians*, Wellingborough, Aquarian, 1987.
227. William Crookes, *Researches in the Phenomena of Spiritualism*, London, J. Burns, 1874.
228. Nicholas Mamontoff, 'Can Thoughts Have Forms?' *Fate* 16(6), June 1960, p. 41.
229. W. J. Crawford, *The Psychic Structures at the Goligher Circle*, London, Watkins, 1921.
230. Charles Richet, *Traité de la métapsychique*, Paris, Alcan, 1922, p. 645.
231. *PSPR*, 10, p. 378.
232. *Fate*, 38(7), July 1985, p. 55.
233. Shirley Jackson Case, *Experience with the Supernatural in Early Christian Times*, New York, Century, 1929, p. 34.
234. G. L. Domeny De-Rienzi, *Océanie*, cited by César Baudi De Vesme, *Spiritualisme experimental*, Paris, Meyer, 1928, p. 99.
235. Homer, *The Odyssey*, Book 11, line 555.
236. T. W. Doane, *Bible Myths*, New York, Commonwealth, 1882, Chapter 22.
237. De Vesme, *Spiritualisme*, p. 333.
238. Plato, *Phaedo*.

239. Plutarch, *Life of Dion*, trans. Dryden. Modern Library edition, New York, *c.* 1950, p. 1156.

240. Louis Lavater, *Of Ghostes and Spirites Walking by Nyght* (1572), Oxford, the Shakespeare Association, University Press, 1929.

241. Pierre LeLoyer, *Discours des spectres*, Paris, 1608 edition.

242. Jean-Claude Schmitt, *Les Revenants: les vivants et les morts dans la société médiévale,* Paris, Gallimard, 1994.

243. Thurston, *Ghosts and Poltergeists*, p. 56.

244. Balthasar Becker, *Le Monde enchanté*, Amsterdam, Pierre Rotterdam, 1694.

245. Joseph Glanvil, *Saducismus triumphatus*, London, Tuckyr, 1700.

246. J. Tregortha, *News from the Invisible World*, Burslem, England, Tregortha, 1808.

247. Samuel Hibbert, *Sketches of the Philosophy of Apparitions,* Edinburgh, Oliver & Boyd, 1825, p. 45.

248. Ibid., p. 61.

249. Catherine Crowe, *The Night Side of Nature*, London, Newby, 1848.

250. Ibid., p. 17.

251. Adolphe d'Assier, *Revenants et fantômes*, trans. H. S. Olcott as *Posthumous Humanity*, London, Redway, 1887.

252. *Report on Spiritualism of the Committee of the London Dialectical Society*, London, Longmans, Green, Reader and Dyer, 1871.

253. Gurney, et al., *Phantasms.*

254. *PSPR*, 10, 1894, p. 25ff.

255. Ibid., p. 212.

256. Andrew Lang, *The Book of Dreams and Ghosts*, 2nd edition, London, Longmans, Green, 1899, pp. vi–vii.

257. William James, *The Principles of Psychology*, London, Macmillan, 1890, vol. 2, p. 130.

258. Gurney et al., *Phantasms*, p. xxxv.

259. *PSPR*, 10, p. 301.

260. Andrew MacKenzie, *The Seen and the Unseen*, London, Weidenfeld and Nicolson, 1987; *Adventures in Time*, Athlone, 1997.

261. Robert W. Pelton, *Confrontations with the Devil*, South Brunswick, A. S. Barnes, 1979, p. 34.

262. O'Sullivan, *Soul Rescuers*, p. 133.

263. Robin Furman and Moira Martingale, *Ghostbusters UK*, London, Robert Hale, 1991, p. 22.

264. Rick Darby, 'US Television Looks at "Real Ghosthunters"', *Paranormal Review*, 14, April 2000.

265. Ibid.

266. Vincent London and H. Gaddis, 'Electrical Ghosts', *Fate*, 4(3), April 1951, p. 22.
267. Brad Steiger, *Mysteries of Time and Space*, New York, Prentice-Hall, 1974.
268. T. Peter Park, *Fate*, 15(7), July 1962, p. 107.
269. Michaeleen C. Maher and George P. Hansen, 'Quantitative Investigation of a Reported Haunting', in *JASPR*, 86(4), Oct. 1982, p. 357, and 'Quantitative Investigation of a "Haunted Castle" in New Jersey', *JASPR*, 89(1), Jan. 1995, p. 19.
270. Emily Peach, *Things That Go Bump in the Night*, London, Aquarian, 1991, p. 108.
271. Jaffé, *Apparitions and Precognition*, p. 77.
272. *PSPR*, 10, 1894, p. 25ff.
273. *PSPR*, 3, 1885, p. 145.
274. *JSPR*, 6 (Nov. 1893) 146, and 9 (Oct. 1900), p. 298.
275. Gurney et al., *Phantasms*, case 242, vol 2, p. 61.
276. Sylvia Hart Wright, 'Paranormal Contact with the Dying', *JSPR*, 63(857), Oct. 1999, p. 258.
277. Jaffé, *Apparitions and Precognition*, p. 151.
278. *Fate*, 53(8), 3 Aug. 2000.
279. Whately Carington, *Telepathy*, London, Methuen, 1945, p. 76.
280. *Fate*, 6(10), Oct. 1953, p. 70.
281. Kenneth Ring, *The Omega Project: Near-Death Experiences, UFO Encounters, and Mind at Large*, New York, Morrow, 1992.
282. Fund for UFO Research, *Final Report on the Psychological Testing of UFO 'Abductees'*, Mount Rainier, Fund for UFO Research, 1985.
283. Robert E. Bartholomew, Keith Basterfield and George S. Howard, 'UFO Abductees and Contactees: Psychopathology or Fantasy Proneness?' *Professional Psychology: Research and Practice*, 22(3), 1991, pp. 215–22.
284. James Houran, Rense Lange, et al., Various papers in *Perceptual and Motor Skills*, 1996ff.
285. Peach, *Things That Go Bump in the Night*, p. 22.
286. *Fate*, 20(5), May 1967, p. 63.
287. Hilary Evans, *Alternate States of Consciousness*, London, Aquarian, 1989.
288. Hilary Evans, 'The Life Review Experience', *The Unknown*, March 1986, p. 25.
289. Walter N. Pahnke and William A. Richards, 'Implications of LSD and Experimental Mysticism', in Charles T. Tart, (ed.) *Altered States of Consciousness*, New York, Wiley, 1969.

290. René Laurentin, *Le 20 Janvier 1842 Marie apparait à Alphonse Ratisbonne* and *Preuves et documents sur l'apparition de Marie à Alphonse Ratisbonne*, Paris, Oeil, 1991.

291. Judith M. and Alan L. Gansberg, *Direct Encounters*, New York, Walker, 1980.

292. Johann Wier, *De praestigiis daemonum &c.* (1563) trans. as *Histoires des illusions et impostures des diables*, Paris, Progrés Médical, 1885.

293. Evans, *Alternate States*.

294. Curtis Fuller, editorial in *Fate*, 39(11), Nov. 1986.

295. Reported in *Fate*, 29(9), Sept. 1976, p. 87.

296. James Wentworth Day, *In Search of Ghosts*, London, Muller, 1969, p. 6.

297. Edith Olivier, *Without Knowing Mr Walkley*, London, Faber & Faber, 1938, pp. 226–30.

298. John Pendragon, 'Cosmic Waves and Ghosts', *Fate*, 7(7), July 1954, p. 93 reprinted from *Prediction*.

299. Michael A. Persinger, 'The UFO Experience: a Normal Correlate of Human Brain Function', in David Jacobs (ed.) *UFOs and Abductions*, Lawrence, Kansas, University Press of Kansas, 2000.

300. *PSPR*, 10, p. 136.

301. D. Scott Rogo, 'Apparitions, Hauntings and Poltergeists', in Edgar D. Mitchell, *Psychic Exploration*, New York, G. P. Putnam's Sons, 1974, p. 382. Emphasis in the original.

302. Morton Schatzman, *The Story of Ruth*, London, Duckworth, 1980.

303. Tyrrell, *Apparitions*, p. 9.

304. *PSPR*, 10, p. 295.

305. *Fate*, 24(8), Aug. 1971, p. 56.

306. Loyd Auerbach, 'Psychic Frontiers', *Fate* 53(8), Aug. 2000, p. 9.

307. Tyrrell, *Apparitions*.

308. Gurney et al., *Phantasms,* case 20, vol. 1, p. 194.

309. *Fate*, 12(3), April 1959, p. 33.

310. Carington, *Telepathy*, p. 74.

311. Hornell Hart, 'Six Theories about Apparitions' *PSPR*, 50, May 1956.

312. John Robert Colombo, *Mackenzie King's Ghost and Other Canadian Hauntings*, Willowdale, Ontario, Hounslow Press, 1991.

313. *Fate*, 34(3), March 1981, p. 69.

314. *JSPR*, 45, July 1929, p. 127.

315. Janet Lee Mitchell, 'Is Anything Out?' *Fate*, 41(5), May 1988, p. 60.

316. *Fate*, 27(2), Feb. 1974, p. 82.

317. Frank Podmore, *Apparitions and Thought-transference*, London, Walter Scott, 1894, p. 228.

318. De Vesme, *Spiritualisme*, p. 174.
319. H. H. Price, 'Haunting and the Psychic Ether Hypothesis', *PSPR*, 45, 1939, p. 338.
320. Evans, 'The Life Review Experience'.
321. Hornell Hart, *The Enigma of Survival*, London, Rider, 1959, p. 139.
322. Louisa Rhine, *The Invisible Picture*, Jefferson, NC, McFarland, 1981.
323. *Fate*, 27(8), Aug. 1974, p. 118.
324. *Fate*, 10(1), Jan. 1957, p. 117.
325. *Fate*, 11(2), Feb. 1958, p. 104.
326. *Fate*, 19(3), March 1966, p. 54.
327. Schatzman, *Story of Ruth*, p. 138.
328. Bertrand Méheust, *Somnambulisme et mediumnité*, Le Plessis-Robinson, Institut Synthélabo, 1998, vol. 1, p. 209ff.
329. *JSPR*, 16, March 1914, p. 205.
330. *Fate*, 13(11), Nov. 1960, p. 95.
331. Price, *Most Haunted House*, p. 307.
332. Lang, *Dreams and Ghosts*, p. 109.
333. Price, *Most Haunted House*, p. 337.
334. Stevenson, *Reincarnation and Biology*.
335. *Fate*, 12(9), Sept. 1959, p. 99.
336. William G. Roll, 'Survival Research: Problems and Possibilities', in Edgar G. Mitchell, *Psychic Exploration*, New York, Putnam, 1974, p. 404.
337. Carington, *Telepathy*, p. 76.
338. H. H. Price, 'Presidential Address', *PSPR*, 40, p. 320.
339. John Vyvyan, *A Case against Jones*, London, James Clarke, 1966, p. 30.
340. Tyrrell, *Apparitions*, pp. 101–2.
341. Adolphe D'Assier, *Posthumous Humanity*, London, Redway, 1887, p. 84.
342. Tyrell, *Apparitions*, pp. 47–8, 60, 101–2, 121.
343. Letter quoted in Hornell Hart, 'Six Theories about Apparitions', *PSPR*, 50, May 1956, p. 193.
344. Ibid.
345. Charles Richet in *PSPR*, 34, 1924, pp. 107–13.
346. Beard, in account of projection in Gurney et al., *Phantasms of the Living*, case 7, vol. 1, p. 93.
347. *PSPR*, 52, Feb. 1959, p. 77.
348. *Fate*, 23(3), March 1970, p. 119.
349. *PSPR*, 10, p. 117.
350. Ibid., p. 126.
351. Ibid., pp. 376, 392.

352. For example Oliver Lodge, *Raymond*, London, Methuen, 1916; Elsa Barker, *Letters from a Living Dead Man*, London, Rider, 1915; J. S. M. Ward, *A Subaltern in Spirit-land*, London, Rider, 1920.

353. For an extreme example, see *Life and Labor in the Spirit World*, Colby & Rich, Boston, 1887, communicated to Miss M. T. Shelhamer by Members of her Spirit-Band.

354. A lucid account of the spiritualists' ideas about post-mortem existence can be found in Peach, *Things That Go Bump in the Night*.

355. Jaffé, *Apparitions and Precognition*, p. 177.

356. Ibid., p. 119.

357. Gurney et al., *Phantasms*, vol. 2, p. 218.

358. William and Elizabeth Denton, *Nature's Secrets, or Psychometric Researches*, London, Houlston and Wright, 1863, p. xiii.

359. James Crenshaw, 'An Atomic Theory of Apparitions', *Fate*, 16(2), Feb. 1961, p. 59.

Further reading

(*All books are published in London unless otherwise specified, though in many cases American editions exist.*)

The literature of ghosts is enormous, and what follows can only be a personal choice of books I have found useful or thought-provoking. I have not attempted to select among the countless guide-books to ghosts in stately homes, haunted pubs and local regions: though they serve a valuable purpose in showing us the extent of the ghost phenomenon, they do not directly help us to understand it. I have listed very few books from outside Britain, for the simple reason that this is where ghosts have been most widely and most competently studied.

By far the largest category consists of collections of ghost stories, told more or less at face value with little attempt to go beneath the surface. These are useful in that they present the broad, popular idea of what a ghost is: unfortunately they tend to focus on hauntings which, as this book shows, represent a minority of ghost experiences.

In the books listed here the cases are chosen with care, and benefit from an intelligent commentary by the compiler:

Sir Ernest Bennett. *Apparitions and Haunted Houses* Faber and Faber 1939. More than 100 cases are intelligently discussed in this classic collection.

John Robert Colombo. *Ghost Stories of Canada* Toronto: Hounslow Press 2000. This is just one of Colombo's excellent collections of paranormal experiences in Canada, which consist of first-person narratives introduced by a perceptive commentary.

Andrew Mackenzie. *A Gallery of Ghosts* Arthur Barker 1972.

Unlike Mackenzie's other books listed below, this is an anthology of good cases recounted by others.

Peter Moss. *Ghosts over Britain* Book Club Associates 1977. A fine collection of modern ghosts experienced by the man and woman in the street.

The American monthly magazine *Fate* has for more than fifty years included a section in which people tell of their own experiences in their own words: many of the cases in this book come from this source. They constitute one of the largest collections in existence of 'raw' stories, undistorted by investigation or interpretation. Though they should be read with due caution, they constitute a unique and invaluable source.

A few ghost authors are also investigators, whose subject-matter consists largely of cases they have personally investigated. Though they look for explanations of these cases, they rarely attempt to analyse the phenomenon as a whole:

Anthony D. Cornell. *Investigating the Paranormal* New York: Parapsychology Foundation 2001. A first-hand account by one of Britain's most experienced investigators, this is far and away the best guide to how – and how not – to investigate a ghost.

Andrew Green and Peter Underwood are two prolific authors who have written too many books to list here. Both are serious investigators with first-hand knowledge of their subject: their books, which tend to be of the guidebook kind, can be recommended.

Andrew Mackenzie has authored a series of books over the years which I unhesitatingly consider the best of their kind: *The Unexplained* Arthur Barker 1966; *Apparitions and Ghosts* Barker 1971; *Haunting and Apparitions* Heinemann 1982; *The Seen and the Unseen* Weidenfeld and Nicolson 1987; *Adventures in Time* Athlone Press 1997. Many of the cases were personally investigated by the author.

Some worthwhile studies of individual cases:

Eric J. Dingwall & Trevor H. Hall. *Four Modern Ghosts* Gerald Duckworth 1958

[C.A.E.Moberly and E.F.Jourdain] *An Adventure* Macmillan 1911. The experience of two teachers at Versailles is probably the most discussed ghost story ever: there have been many editions, each editor adding or subtracting to create a new perspective. The most comprehensive treatment is that of Michael Coleman, *The Ghosts of the Trianon* Aquarian 1988, which includes the original text and comments intelligently both on the account and the theories offered to explain it.

The challenge of explaining the ghost phenomenon as a whole has been taken up by only a few authors. These seem to me the most successful:

Celia Green and Charles McCreery. *Apparitions* Hamish Hamilton 1975. The authors approach the subject according to the characteristics of the sighting.

Andrew Lang. *Cock Lane and Common-sense* Longmans, Green 1894; *The Book of Dreams and Ghosts* Longmans, Green 1897. This great folklorist wrote two of the best inquiries into ghosts which raise many of the problems we continue to face a hundred years later.

Emily Peach. *Things That Go Bump in the Night* Aquarian 1991. Despite its title, this is a serious, accessible and perceptive discussion ranging sensibly over facts and theories.

Ian Wilson. *In Search of Ghosts* Headline 1995. A well-informed study, illuminated by personal experience and first-hand research.

Foreign-language books about ghosts tend to draw heavily on the SPR's publications, resulting in a lot of duplication. The most comprehensive book in French is:

Gabriel Delanne. *Les apparitions materialisées des vivants & des morts* Paris, Leymarie: Tome I *Les Fantômes des vivants* 1909: Tome II *Les Apparitions des morts* 1911. Its 1,400+ pages contain an enormous bulk of case histories and intelligent discussion.

Fewer still are those authors who approach the ghost enigma in what can be loosely called a scientific manner. Nearly all are associated with the Society for Psychical Research in London or with the American Society in New York:

Edmund Gurney, Frederic W. H. Myers and Frank Podmore. *Phantasms of the Living* Trübner, 1886. This monumental work is by far the most important collection of ghost stories ever assembled, and has the advantage that every case was checked and investigated. The *Proceedings* and *Journal* of the Society for Psychical Research contain a wealth of additional cases.

Frederic W. H. Myers. *Human Personality* Longmans, Green 1903. Eighty pages of volume II are devoted to 'Phantasms of the Dead', supplementing his contribution to the preceding work.

Aniela Jaffé. *Apparitions and Precognition* New York: University Books 1963. This is 'a study from the point of view of C. G. Jung's analytical psychology', containing many interesting cases and an illuminating commentary from a psychological perspective.

Louisa E. Rhine. *Hidden Channels of the Mind* Gollancz 1961, *ESP in Life and Lab* New York: Macmillan 1967; and *The Invisible Picture* Jefferson, North Carolina: McFarland 1981. While her husband occupied himself with psi in the laboratory, Louisa Rhine focussed on psi in everyday life. Though not exclusively ghost books, these contain illuminating ghost cases and an intelligent commentary from the perspective of psychical research.

G. N. M. Tyrrell. *Apparitions* Gerald Duckworth 1943. This 170-page book is the most penetrating attempt to date to establish the ghost phenomenon on a scientific basis.

There have been valuable studies of particular aspects:

A Brierre de Boismont. *Des Hallucinations* Paris: Germer Baillière 1852. The classic work on the subject: supplemented but not outdated by later work, it remains the best general survey of hallucinations.

David J. Hufford. *The Terror That Comes in the Night* Philadelphia: University of Pennsylvania Press, 1982. A landmark study of the 'bedroom visitor' which relates the ghost experience to folklore.

Claude Lecouteux *Fantômes et revenants au Moyen Age* Paris: Imago 1996. An excellent study of the ghost experience in the Middle Ages.

Finally, the best of the reference books devoted to the subject:

Rosemary Ellen Guiley. *The Encyclopedia of Ghosts and Spirits* (second edition) New York: Facts on File 2000. A monument of research, this is a comprehensive source of information on all aspects of the phenomenon and an indispensable research tool.

Acknowledgements

All the illustrations are reproduced with the kind permission of the Mary Evans Picture Library, London and can be seen on their website: www.mepl.co.uk: p.2, Aldo Molinari in the *Domenica del Corriere*, 25 January 1931; p.8, engraving by Mirys, *c.* 1800; p.14, illustration by Florence Harrison for Christina Rossetti, *Collected Poems*, 1910; p.23, drawing by an unnamed artist in Abdy Collins, *The Cheltenham Ghost*; p.30, illustration by Warwick Goble in the *Strand* magazine, December 1908; p.49, engraving by an unnamed artist in Grunbeck, *Eine neue Auszlegung der seltzamen Wunderzachen*; p.52, reproduced by courtesy of Peter Underwood; p.61, Warwick Goble in the *Strand*, December 1908; p.69, Warwick Goble in the *Strand*, December 1908; p.72, H. C. Bevan-Petman, illustration to Elliott O'Donnell, *Twenty years a Ghost-hunter*; p.75, photograph reproduced in Vincent Gaddis, *Invisible Horizons*; p.103, engravings by an unnamed artist in *Secrets of the Invisible World*; p.108, illustration by Thomas Fogarty, in the *Century*, September 1899; p.115, H. C. Bevan-Petman, illustration to Elliott O'Donnell, *Twenty years a Ghost-hunter*; p.122, Ma-No-Yuki, from a sketch by R. Gordon-Smith, in *Ancient Tales and Folklore of Japan*; p.124, H. C. Bevan-Petman, illustration to Elliott O'Donnell, *Twenty years a Ghost-hunter*; p.126, illustration by J. Copland to J. Maxwell Wood, *Witchcraft in south-western Scotland*; p.135, illustration by W. D. Stevens in *Harper's Magazine*, March 1906; p.147, illustration by Gignoux in *Le Pelerin*, 29 April 1923; p.151, E. Docker jr. late nineteenth century; p.154, drawing by Albert K. Bender in his book, *Flying Saucers and the Three Men*; p.161, Gerloff, *Phantome von Kopenhagen*; p.167, engraving by Henry Fuseli to illustrate Homer's *Iliad*; p.186, photo by Julie and Mark Hunt, for ASSAP; p.202, lithograph by an unnamed artist in *Las Supersticiones de la Humanidad*, 1891; p.238, Warwick Goble in the *Strand*, December 1908; p.258, William Blake, engraved by Schiavonetti, illustrating Robert Blair's 1743 poem *The Grave*.

Index

Index